'Anagrams of desire'

MANCHESTER
UNIVERSITY PRESS

You never saw such a wild thing as my mother, her hat seized by the winds and blown out to sea so that her hair was her white mane, her black lisle legs exposed to the thigh, her skirts tucked round her waist, one hand on the reins of the rearing horse while the other clasped my father's service revolver and, behind her, the breakers of the savage, indifferent sea, like the witness of a furious justice.

(Angela Carter, *The Bloody Chamber*)

# 'Anagrams of desire'

## Angela Carter's writing for radio, film and television

**CHARLOTTE CROFTS**

Manchester University Press

MANCHESTER AND NEW YORK

distributed exclusively in the USA by Palgrave

*Published by* Manchester University Press
Oxford Road, Manchester M13 9NR, UK
*and* Room 400, 175 Fifth Avenue, New York, NY 10010, USA
http://www.manchesteruniversitypress.co.uk

*Distributed exclusively in the USA by*
Palgrave, 175 Fifth Avenue, New York, NY 10010, USA

*Distributed exclusively in Canada by*
UBC Press, University of British Columbia, 2029 West Mall,
Vancouver, BC, Canada V6T 1Z2

*British Library Cataloguing-in-Publication Data*
A catalogue record for this book is available from the British Library

*Library of Congress Cataloging-in-Publication Data applied for*

ISBN 0 7190 5723 x *hardback*
     0 7190 5724 8 *paperback*

First published 2003

10   09   08   07   06   05   04   03        10   9   8   7   6   5   4   3   2   1

Typeset in Scala with Meta display
by Koinonia, Manchester
Printed in Great Britain
by Biddles Ltd, Guildford and King's Lynn

# Contents

# Figures and tables

## Figures

## Table

# Acknowledgements

Acknowledgement is due to Patricia Allderidge, the Richard Dadd archivist, Royal Bethlem Hospital Archives and Museum; Guido Almansi, for his correspondence about Carter's radio drama; Mark Bell, editor of Carter's dramatic writings, for generous access to proofs and archive material; Glyn Dearman, BBC Radio Drama, for clarifying the transmission dates of Carter's plays; producer John Ellis for allowing me extended access to archives at Large Door Productions Ltd and giving permission to include excerpts from the script and storyboard of *The Holy Family Album*; Kim Evans, BBC Head of Music and Arts, for her interview and allowing me access to the post-production script of *Angela Carter's Curious Room*; Elaine Jordan for her interest and support in getting this book published; director Jo Ann Kaplan for giving such an insightful and illuminating interview on *The Holy Family Album*; the late Lorna Sage for being instrumental in securing funding for this book; illustrator Corinna Sargood; Brian Stableford for his comments and encouragement; Jenny Uglow at Chatto & Windus for giving me astute advice and employment; David Wheatley for his rosemary, time and generosity in facilitating my research, as well his permission to use photographs of the production of *The Magic Toyshop*; Anne White at the University of Bradford for constructive feedback; and Mark Wolstonecroft at the Media Support Unit at Manchester University.

Special thanks go to Rachel Connor, both for her perceptive editorial help and the 'working lunches' which inform the theoretical foundation of my research; I am also very grateful to Joy Anderson, Elizabeth Hammond and Alison Metcalfe. Finally, love and thanks to all my family and Paul.

# Introduction: 'Anagrams of desire': Angela Carter's writing for radio, film and television

Angela Carter is best known for her novels, short fiction and journalism, but she also produced a large body of writing for media other than the printed page. Despite the current academic interest in her work, these dramatic writings have largely been ignored. This book redresses this lack of critical attention by examining her writings for radio, film and television and giving them a more central position in the Carter canon.

The book specifically examines those of Carter's dramatic writings which were actually realised and publicly transmitted in the medium for which they were intended, and with which she had a collaborative involvement, comprising five radio plays, two films, and two television documentaries. Primary emphasis is on these mediated texts, although extensive reference is also made to source texts and written scripts. Carter wrote a number of texts for stage and screen which are not fully discussed here, including two screenplays, 'Gun for the Devil' and 'The Christchurch Murder', an operatic libretto 'Orlando: The Enigma of the Sexes' and a stage play 'Lulu' (Carter, 1996). While I touch on them in the Envoi, these works do not form part of the major thrust of this book because they do not constitute mediated texts, either because they were never produced or, if they were realised, because Carter was not involved in their production.[1] However, they do illustrate Carter's ongoing experimentation with both modern mass media and traditional dramatic forms, such as theatre and opera, reinforcing the case for an examination of her dramatic writings.

The book is divided into three sections, each examining a particular medium. This structure is largely chronological, mapping the development in Carter's writing for media from her initial work in radio (1976–84, Chapters 1–3), through her adaptations for film (1984, 1986, Chapters 4–6) and then on to television (1991, Chapters 7–8). Each section is introduced with a chapter exploring the specific properties of the medium. Each of the sections has a different emphasis according to the extent of Carter's engagement with that particular medium, the range of criticism and the utility of the theoretical approaches available. For example, the section on film is the most explicitly theorised because of the considerable amount of film theory with which it has been necessary to engage and because of Carter's extensive interrogation of cinema in her journalism and fiction. Conversely, the section on television is more descriptive and functional because of the amount of technical material garnered from interviews with producers and directors.

The first section focuses on Carter's five radio plays. Chapter 1, 'Aural hallucinations', draws on Carter's preface to her play anthology, *Come Unto These Yellow Sands: Four Radio Plays* (1985), examining her attraction to the medium, and discussing its formal and technical properties. In Chapter 2, 'Voices in the dark', I discuss the role of the various voices in *Vampirella, The Company of Wolves* and, to a lesser extent, *Puss in Boots*, linking radio to the oral tradition and Carter's feminist reworkings of traditional fairy tale in *The Bloody Chamber*.[2] In Chapter 3, 'Artificial biography', I explore *Come Unto These Yellow Sands*, Carter's play about Victorian painter Richard Dadd, and *A Self-Made Man* on Ronald Firbank, examining how she uses the possibilities of radio as a medium to deconstruct biography as a genre and to challenge the concept of unified identity.

The film section addresses current debates in film theory in relation to gender, spectatorship and the gaze and examines Carter's two screen adaptations. Chapter 4, 'Anything that flickers', examines Carter's fiction and non-fiction writings about cinema which reveal an intelligent engagement with the concerns of contemporary feminist film theory, including a discussion of her little-known poem, *Unicorn*. While the emphasis in Chapters 5 and 6 is on the filmic texts, extensive reference is made to the short stories and novel on which these two adaptations are based. Chapter 5, '(Re)animating the body of the text', theorises adaptation through a discussion of the figure of the werewolf, yoking discourses around textual transformation, reanimation and abjection to offer a feminist re-reading of the film, *The Company of Wolves*. Chapter 6, 'Looking askance', posits a dual feminist strategy of looking in the film, *The Magic Toyshop*, investigating Carter's deployment of an active female gaze and exploring her use of life-like puppets and self-activating toys to unsettle the epistemological field of vision. The final section addresses Carter's work in television. Chapter 7, 'The box does furnish a room', examines her writings about television, outlining her equivocal relationship with the medium. In Chapter 8, 'Acting up on the small screen', I discuss her own involvement in an irreverent documentary on representations of Christ in Western art, *The Holy Family Album* and look at how Carter herself was represented in a BBC Omnibus documentary, *Angela Carter's Curious Room*.

The book draws extensively on exclusive interviews and correspondence with producers and directors with whom Carter collaborated, David
Wheatley (director of *The Magic Toyshop*), John Ellis and Jo Ann Kaplan
(producer and director of *The Holy Family Album*) and Kim Evans
(director of *Angela Carter's Curious Room*) (transcribed in Crofts, 1998b).[3]
These interviews offer a unique insight into the technologies of media
production and processes of collaboration and adaptation, which may
have eluded traditional research methods. Dealing with adaptations has
presented a particular challenge. For example, in dealing with the film
*The Company of Wolves* in Chapter 5 it has also been necessary to refer to
the screenplay, the radio play in performance, the radio play script and the
original short stories on which they are based. These multiple texts and
the degree of collaboration involved in realising them raises complex
questions of authorial control and responsibility, making it difficult to
identify and describe the relationship between author and text.

If these questions seem outdated in this era of 'the death of the author',
they nevertheless need to be addressed. As Lorna Sage (1994) observes,
Carter 'had a position on the politics of textuality. She went in for the
proliferation, rather than the death, of the author'. Carter's mediated texts
perform this 'proliferation' both in terms of the multiple adaptations of
texts and the collaborative relationships between Carter as original
author/ scriptwriter and the various directors with whom she worked. My
interviews with directors and producers help to clarify these processes of
collaboration and emphasise Carter's intellectual generosity within the
collaborative relationship. Not precious about her own work, she was
prepared to share her material, whether collaboratively adapting a novel
or writing directly for the medium, acknowledging the director's expertise
(see Wheatley, 1996, and Kaplan, 1995, in particular). The interviews also
reveal Carter's informed grasp of the various media for which she wrote.
Aware of the complex processes involved in transforming a text from one
medium to another, Carter understood the need to take both the aesthetic
and the technologies of the new medium into account when adapting her
own work. Those texts which were written directly for the medium
illustrate Carter's media-literacy and her growing confidence in working
directly with the language of communications media.

The challenge of dealing with mediated texts has encouraged me to
embrace a multiplicity of theoretical perspectives rather than employing
any single theoretical framework. This follows Douglas Kellner's 'multiperspectival approach' (1995: 98) which 'draws on a wide range of textual
and critical strategies to interpret, criticize, and deconstruct the artifact
under scrutiny'. Kellner favours 'a pragmatic contextualised approach to
theory' and argues that 'the more perspectives that one brings to bear on a

phenomenon, the better one's potential grasp or understanding of it could be' (1995: 26).

While I utilise an overwhelmingly feminist frame, this is not incompatible with a multiperspectival approach. In fact, current feminist theory is becoming increasingly multiperspectival in its growing recognition of a number of previously disregarded theoretical axes, such as sexuality, race and class, and in its tendency to combine Marxist, psychoanalytical, poststructural and postcolonial paradigms. The usefulness of a multiperspectival approach for contemporary feminism is obvious. It offers a critical arsenal with which to interrogate grand theoretical narratives which have traditionally either essentialised 'Woman', such as psychoanalysis, or have tended to ignore gender as a political axis, such as Marxism. This is not to suggest that these theoretical approaches cannot be illuminating in their own right, but that an informed awareness of the complex interactions between a range of theories is likely to be more illuminating. As Kellner suggests, 'combining powerful approaches like Marxism, feminism, post-structuralism and other contemporary theoretical optics might yield more insightful and useful analyses than those produced by one perspective alone' (1995: 26).

It is worth acknowledging the potential pitfalls of such a multiperspectival approach, which, as Kellner argues, might end in an '"anything goes" liberal pluralism' if not securely grounded in an awareness of historical contexts (1995: 100). Furthermore, it is important to confront the fact that, however multiperspectival I attempt to be, I am ultimately limited by my own partial perspective.[4] But this partiality need not be antithetical to theory if read in the context of an anti-essentialist feminist strategy which recognises personal experience as an alternative to the universalising tendencies of ahistorical master narratives. In employing a multiperspectival stance in this book, I have attempted to bring an awareness of both historical and personal contexts, as well as utilising a range of theoretical axes.

I also embrace Kellner's related notion of a 'transdisciplinary' approach, crossing the borders of literary, film, media and cultural studies (1995: 27). Researching Carter's work in media, it has been necessary to engage with a range of theory outside the usual scope of literary study. In particular, feminist film theory has proved very productive not only in the discussion of Carter's two film adaptations, but also in theorising her work in radio and her fictional exploration of spectacle. I have also found media, communications and cultural theory useful in thinking anew about audiences and contexts, as I go on to discuss below. Such a multiperspectival, interdisciplinary stance is particularly productive when discussing Carter's mediated texts, not only because of the imperatives of discussing a wide range of media, but also because Carter's writing practice and feminist strategy are similarly polyvalent.

The rest of this Introduction will concern itself with a number of overlapping issues which cross-fertilise to generate a multiplicity of meanings around gender and representation: feminism's engagement with the mainstream, the intricacies of Carter's demythologising feminist project, the problematics of appropriation and the relationship between cultural production and consumption. It has been necessary, for the purposes of linear argument, to tease out the strands of this complicated web into some semblance of order, but I want to stress the interconnectedness and complexity of the arguments and acknowledge that the following is only one way of drawing the various threads of the argument together. This interweaving of ideas is indicative of both my own multiperspectival approach and Carter's oscillating, 'paradoxical' feminist strategy of writing, which I will come to discuss at the end of this Introduction.

## Carter, media and the academy

Carter is becoming an increasingly popular subject for academic research, postgraduate and undergraduate teaching, and at A-Level. In 1994, more students applied for funding for doctoral theses on Angela Carter than on the entire eighteenth-century literary offering (Sanders, 1994: 6).[5] Yet her work in media still remains on the periphery of the Carter canon. Three book-length studies on Carter which have appeared since her death in 1992 either ignore her mediated texts entirely, or mention them in passing. In *Angela Carter: The Rational Glass*, Aidan Day acknowledges Carter's versatility as a writer, 'she wrote children's stories, radio plays, film scripts, poetry, journalism and criticism of various kinds', but decides 'she is principally a writer of fiction', and consequently limits his discussion primarily to her novels (1998: 1).[6] While Linden Peach recognises Carter as 'more than a novelist', in *Angela Carter*, he similarly neglects her mediated texts, concentrating, instead, on 'Carter's contribution to the development of the novel' (1998: 2–3). In *Angela Carter: Writing from the Front Line* (1997), Sarah Gamble cites the radio and film adaptations of 'The Company of Wolves' and the screen version *The Magic Toyshop*, but does not offer any sustained analysis.

Another recent publication, *The Infernal Desires of Angela Carter*, a collection of essays edited by Joseph Bristow and Trev Lynn Broughton, also marginalises Carter's writing for media. Bristow and Broughton acknowledge that while 'the work of evaluating and historicizing Carter's achievement has now begun ... many aspects of Carter's work remain to be broached in a systematic way', but do not list her work in media among them (1997: 19). While some of the contributors mention Carter's work in film or radio, once again it does not form the main focus of discussion.[7] Elaine Jordan's 'Afterword' to the collection points out its emphasis on 'political argument' at the expense of 'formal and generic' analysis (Bristow and Broughton (eds), 1997: 217). I do not think Jordan was specifically referring to Carter's media, here, but nevertheless she points to a gap in the current 'canonisation' of Carter.[8] This book proposes to address this gap, both in terms of its discussion of the formal properties of the range of media for which Carter wrote in addition to the printed page, and in terms of how such an analysis must inform any discussion of her writing practice. The majority of research which does engage directly with Carter's mediated texts can be found in isolated articles, most of which have focused on her film adaptations.[9] Guido Almansi (1994) has been alone in writing on Carter's work in radio. There has been little, or no academic study of Carter's work for television.

There is therefore clearly a need for a full-length study which addresses these texts as a body of work worthy of critical attention in its own right. Moreover, there is a specific need for a feminist analysis of the interrelationship between Carter's self-declared feminism and her work in media. Of course, Carter's feminist politics should not be taken as read and it is necessary to delineate her feminist strategies and their critical reception before assessing their translation to the mainstream.

## The reception of Carter's feminist strategies

While Carter's fiction has received an extensive feminist critique, the diversity of which indicates a healthy dialogue within the feminist sisterhood, her work in media has received a limited feminist explication. In 'Pleasure and Interpretation', for example, Catherine Neale discusses Carter's work in film, asserting that Carter generally receives 'sympathetic explication, commentary and contextualisation' from the feminist sisterhood, but remains frustratingly vague about exactly what has been written (claiming that there are 'a limited range of articles and chapters, and it is fairly easy to gain a sense of their general drift'): 'what her work does not receive, it seems, is that element of critique that might examine the implications and potential contradictions of her projects, or place her work within a framework that is not dictated by Carter herself' (Neale, 1996: 99).[10] Having dismissed the feminist critique of Carter's work as either limited, hagiographic, or bamboozled by Carter's critical persona, Neale neglects to address feminism in 'the shift from writing to image' in her own critique of Carter's two film adaptations which, she argues, 'emerge as curiously downbeat hybrids' (1996: 101).

While Neale outlines 'the struggle that feminist criticism in particular has to identify a methodology' (1996: 99), Christina Britzolakis identifies a hegemony of 'gender-performance' criticism in response to Carter's work in her article 'Angela Carter's Fetishism' (1995). She proposes that Carter's writing lends itself to this type of analysis because of its densely theatrical quality:

> If there is a single theme that appears central to criticism of Carter's writing, that theme must surely be theatricality. This is not surprising, since dramatic performance in all its varieties – masquerade, carnival, burlesque, travesty, cross-dressing, drag – leaps out at the reader from the pages of Carter's texts as both style and subject. (1995: 459)

Britzolakis claims that there is too straightforward an elision between these dominant notions of performativity, Carter's fictional theatricality and her 'self-proclaimed "demythologising" project' and questions whether 'the staging of femininity as spectacle [can] indeed be linked with a liberatory feminist project' (1995: 459–60). Certainly, performativity has become common currency within contemporary feminist theory, developing from Joan Riviere's seminal essay, 'Womanliness as a Masquerade' ([1929] 1986), through Irigarayan concepts of mimicry and Judith Butler's theories of 'gender performance' (1990, 1993). But, while much of the feminist criticism of Carter's work takes theatricality as its point of inspiration, this does not mean, as Britzolakis seems to suggest, either that theories of gender-performance are deployed uncritically, or that Carter's feminism is held up as inherently liberatory.[11] But if these complex, interconnected issues around gender, theatricality, performance, spectacle, audience, fetishism and objectification are already fraught, how then, do they relate to Carter's mediated texts?

## Carter's demythologising practice

It is necessary to address Carter's self-defined demythologising project before we can evaluate its translation to the mainstream. In 'Notes From the Front Line', she claims 'I believe that all myths are products of the human mind and reflect only aspects of material human practice. I'm in the demythologising business' (1983d: 71). Seeing the act of writing as the 'investigation of the social fictions that regulate our lives', Carter maintains that her appropriation of hegemonic structures is part of 'the slow process of decolonialising our language and our basic habits of thought'

(1983d: 71, 75). The act of reappropriating language to express experience outside the dominant culture is also pertinent to postcolonialist literary theory. In fact, Carter sees herself as linked to such postcolonial writers as Gabriel García Márquez and the black South African writer, Bessie Head, 'who are transforming actual fictional forms to both reflect and to precipitate changes in the way people feel about themselves' (1983d: 76). Supporting the argument that a 'reactionary' form can indeed be rewritten, Makinen cites the postcolonial appropriation of the novel as an example of successful decolonialisation: 'when the form is used to critique the inscribed ideology ... then the form is subtly adapted to inscribe a new set of assumptions' (1992: 4–5).

In interview with John Haffenden, Carter puts forward an argument for a type of 'moral curiosity', a kind of cultural investigation which exposes social constructs and opens up new areas of discourse: 'I would see it as a moral compunction to explicate and to find out about things. I suppose I would regard curiosity as a moral function' (1985: 96). Carter sees writing as a 'moral function', not in the didactic sense, but as a process of challenging cultural assumptions, raising questions, exploring experience and making room for the expression of things traditionally silenced or unheard by society:

> it has nothing at all to do with being a 'legislator of mankind' or anything like that; it is to do with the creation of a means of expression for an infinitely greater variety of experience than has been possible heretofore, to say things for which no language previously existed. (1983d: 75)

In an interview with Anna Katsavos, she further defines her demythologising project as the job of 'trying to find out what certain configurations of imagery in our society, in our culture, really stand for, what they mean, underneath the kind of semireligious coating that makes people not particularly want to interfere with them', defining myth both in 'a sort of conventional sense; also in the sense that Roland Barthes uses it in *Mythologies* – ideas, images, stories that we tend to take on trust without thinking what they really mean' (1994: 11–12). For Carter, then, this is a defamiliarising process. As Lorna Sage observes in an interview for the BBC Omnibus documentary, *Angela Carter's Curious Room*:

> She took apart the pictures we have of ourselves with a very sceptical eye. We live nowadays surrounded by images of ourselves – blow ups of our-selves, representations of ourselves, shadows of ourselves through the media, through film and of course through books – a much older medium. But a lot of the time our art ignores this fact, but she took it on and her books introduce people, if you like, to their images, introduce people to their shadows, introduce them to their other selves. (Evans and Carter, 1992: 11)

## The problematics of a feminist politics of cultural appropriation

Some feminist critics, however, have questioned the success of Carter's self-proclaimed demythologising feminist project. Indeed, the issue of whether feminism can reappropriate patriarchal forms has been a major concern of much recent feminist theory. Naomi Schor, for example, describes mimesis as 'a parodic mode of discourse designed to decon-struct the discourse of misogyny through effects of amplification and rearticulation' (1994: 67, see also Irigaray, 1985: 220 and Vice (ed.), 1996: 176).[12] This is descriptive of the way in which Carter attempts to reappropriate supposedly misogynistic genres, such as pornography and fairy tale, and put them in the service of women. But, mimicking patriarchal structures in order to subvert them, there is always the danger that mimesis might be mistaken for endorsement. Similarly, irony as a subversive narrative practice can easily be inverted for reactionary ends. But, as Schor argues, 'mimesis signifies not a deluded masquerade but a canny mimicry ... a joyful reappropriation of the attributes of the other that is not in any way to be confused with a mere reversal of the existing phallocentric distribution of power' (1994: 67). Indeed, Anne Fernihough emphasises 'how politically complex the issues of mimicry and masquer-ade really are, and how they cannot be understood as straightforwardly radical *or* reactionary' (1997: 100, all emphasis in the original unless stated otherwise). Paulina Palmer astutely pinpoints the problematics of a feminist politics of appropriation: 'how does one distinguish between a text which constitutes a serious consideration of the topic and one that is an exercise in pornography? The question is complicated by the fact that ... the meaning of a visual image or fictional episode is frequently ambiguous' (1987: 189).

This is a point which Clare Whatling takes up in her consideration of 'the appropriateness of appropriation' (1997: 13), arguing that, while holding an obvious attraction for a lesbian/feminist politics, 'appropria-tion remains a strategy whose potential for subversion is always under contention':

> On the one hand, appropriative reading seems a valid strategy of wilful misreading. On the other hand, there is a danger that appropriative reading merely sustains, as it were by default, the reproduction of the status quo. (1997: 22)

Similarly, Fernihough acknowledges that Carter's reappropriation of male-constructed images of women, such as Fevvers' impersonation of the Winged Victory in *Nights at the Circus*, is a risky strategy because it is open to misreading:

> The fetishistic responses of the Grand Dukes and other eccentric admirers of dubious intent show how vulnerable the transgressive sign is, and how crucial the notion of 'right' and 'wrong' reading is to the semiotics of the body. (1997: 99)

As Fernihough argues, 'the transgressive body, the body that subverts cultural stereotypes, creating its own paradigm, is always at risk of being read as freakish. Performance implies an audience, and to some extent that audience is beyond the performer's control' (1997: 99). Britzolakis (1995) similarly questions a feminist politics of gender as performance when she suggests that, because spectacle requires an audience, it therefore fails to escape the very voyeuristic structures of looking which Carter claims to demythologise.

But, as Fernihough argues, while 'there will always be the fetishistic Grand Dukes who read on their own terms. Carter is alert to these complexities' (1997: 101). Audiences, it seems, are becoming increasingly important. This is never more explicit than in the critical reception of Carter's engagement with pornography, one of the most mediated of discourses, in her fiction and non-fiction.[13] Pornography, like adaptation, foregrounds the theoretical rift between modernist and postmodern figurations of media culture, but also, importantly, highlights the fact that gender is central to these debates around representation. Endeavours to differentiate between pornography and erotica often lead to futile attempts to pin down the meaning of artistic representation itself. Carter caricatures this modernist tendency to hierarchise between erotic art and pornography: 'bad dirty books never did anyone any harm, except make their teeth rot or give them hairy palms. But *good* dirty books do the real damage ... And it isn't the dirt that does it. It's the art' (1977: 9). As Jennifer Wicke argues (1993: 63), 'pornography is a secret sharer in the canon debate, and a hidden partner of the high art/mass culture conflict that rages beyond the perimeters of the canon':

> I'm not proposing anything utopian about this transfigured pornographic consumption, nor making the familiar claim that sexuality is always and everywhere transgressive and consequently liberatory. Rather I want to direct attention to what is usually left out of the equation in discussing consumption, let alone pornographic consumption, which is the work of consumption. (1993: 70)

Furthermore, as Makinen argues, anti-pornographic readings of *The Bloody Chamber* ignore 'the notion of consent within the sado-masochistic transaction' (1992: 12). As Makinen goes on to suggest, it is precisely these 'debates around the marginalized and pathologized "perversities" that are breaking up the phallocentric construction of sexuality' and while

'These new representations may not fit into comfortable notions of sisterhood ... they may well prove liberating all the same' (1992: 13–14). Similarly, while acknowledging the problematics of appropriative reading, Whatling argues 'for its radical impact as a politics of reversal and recontextualisation' (1997: 4).

## Writing on the edge of paradox

I do not aim to defend Carter hagiographically, or posit hers as an *inherently* radical feminist politics, but to strongly register my disagreement with those readings which construe Carter's 'simultaneous deconstruction and celebration' (Neale, 1996: 102) as somehow cancelling each other out. These two projects are not necessarily mutually exclusive, and it is this oscillation between celebration and deconstruction which is the key to Carter's multiperspectival feminist strategy of writing: a strategy which combines a 'semiological conception of culture' (Britzolakis, 1995: 460) (seeing culture as a system of signs and surfaces to be read and interpreted) with a committed materialism (seeing these signs as the 'real' products of our cultural imagination). Magali Cornier Michael identifies Carter's feminism as incorporating 'more than one strand of feminism, an engaged Marxist feminism and a subversive utopian feminism', creating 'not a tension but rather a space where possibilities for change can be explored' (1994: 492). As Anne Fernihough similarly argues, the 'two perspectives, post-structuralist and materialist, are, of course, not incompatible' (1997: 102). Fernihough notes an uncomfortable oscillation between various theoretical perspectives at play in Carter's fiction: 'it is often the interplay, or "balancing", of post-structuralist and materialist perspectives that accounts for the curious mixture of the utopian and the brutally realistic in Carter's later work' (1997: 102).

Carter's ambivalent relationship with both feminism and socialism can be seen as part of a conscious refusal to be integrated 'into the mainstream of these movements' (Gamble, 1997: 4). As Sarah Gamble asserts, Carter deliberately occupies a borderline position which is 'primarily concerned with maintaining a sceptical, interrogatory position on the periphery of dominant cultural attitudes and conventions' (1997: 3). While potentially empowering, this position on the margins also has its risks. But, as Gamble points out, 'Carter was also not unaware of the dangers inherent in the cultivation of a marginalised position or perspective. The trouble is, of course, that existing on the peripheries of anything involves performing an extremely delicate balancing act' (1997: 5). Significantly, both Gamble and Fernihough use the language of the tightrope artiste. However, while acknowledging the difficulty of this balancing act, Fernihough argues that it is Carter's 'deliberate insistence on irony and parody that differentiates' (1997: 103). As Jordan concurs, 'Carter's mode is characteristically, though not always, ironic', noting a 'failure to negotiate "echoic irony"' in some of the essays in the Bristow collection which, she argues, leads to a 'confusion between what a character is saying, and what Carter's argument might be claiming' (Bristow and Broughton (eds), 1997: 218). Jordan theorises irony 'as an echo, a quotation of what some person might say or think, which an alert listener would recognize as something for them to consider critically' (Bristow and Broughton (eds), 1997: 218). Irony is therefore indicative of an open-ended writing strategy which, as I argue in Chapters 1 and 2, Carter deliberately deploys.

It is clearly important to acknowledge the dangers of such a risky strategy. However, as Jordan suggests, the dangers, difficulties and risks of Carter's writing practice are also their strengths:

> The disease, diagnosis and cure, in Carter's new myths of modernity and its dreams, are a hair's-breadth apart – except that her fictionality and whole way of writing insist that we must know that a space must be kept for uncertainty and recreation. (1994: 214)

As Michael (1994) and Fernihough (1997) have also argued, these dual perspectives do not cancel each other out – they exist simultaneously, on the edge of paradox. Carter's feminism, then, is paradoxical both on the level of ironic appropriation and in her oscillation between various feminist, theoretical and political perspectives: joint aspects of a feminist practice of writing which recognises ongoing textual negotiations and refuses to come to rest in a single, definitive position. The real political potential of Carter's feminist politics of cultural appropriation lies in awareness of the ambiguities of ironic appropriation. Furthermore, this paradoxical feminist strategy points up the weaknesses of all-encompassing political or theoretical frameworks, such as the totalising grand narratives of psychoanalysis, Marxism and liberal humanism. Her conscious oscillation between various theoretical perspectives is not, as Britzolakis suggests, a political failure, but an awareness of the complexity of the existing situation and a refusal to offer any simplistic solutions – hence the need for a multiperspectival approach in any discussion of her work. Carter's is an empowering feminist strategy of writing which invites the reader to generate her own meanings. The aim of this book is to illustrate that this radical feminism is maintained and sustained in her work in media.

## Media, feminism and the mainstream

In order to examine the transition of Carter's feminist strategy of writing from the literary arena to mainstream media it is necessary to engage with a number of key questions around what Cartmell *et al.* (1996) have coined as the 'literature/media divide'. Adaptation is therefore a major concern throughout the book. The adaptation of literary texts has always been a prominent source of narrative for radio, television and cinema. As Mark Lawson (1995) maintains, modern media is heavily book-dependent, with around 80 per cent of cinema releases based on books, and television and radio also relying extensively on dramatisations of books. Although playing a significant role in media culture, adaptation remains under-theorised. Yet it is a privileged site for the examination of a number of current theoretical debates surrounding art, authorship and audience which are of particular interest to us here. Very briefly these debates can be seen to centre around a paradigm shift from modernist to post-structuralist and/or postmodern conceptions of culture which is currently taking place across a number of academic fields.[14]

In its transgression of genre and discipline, and in its erosion of the boundaries between high art and popular culture, adaptation challenges notions of authenticity and 'hierarchisation'(Thompson, 1996: 12) which have been the cornerstones of traditional canon formation. Media adaptation unsettles modernist concepts of individual creativity and artistic integrity by its very nature as collaborative, mass-produced, mass-disseminated and mass-consumed. Discourse analysis of modernist discussions of media adaptation betrays an implicitly gendered vocabulary in which the (active/masculine) adaptation is seen to somehow exploit or defile the (passive/feminised) literary original (see Shaughnessy's 1996: 43–4, reading of Woolf's essay on 'The Cinema', 1994: 350). But, if the very act of adapting a literary text is already figured as some sort of (sexual) assault, what then are the implications for the adaptation of feminist writing for mass media?

It is useful to turn to feminist cultural studies and the notion of textual 'negotiation' as an alternative to this modernist double bind in which feminism cannot engage with the mainstream without somehow being violated. In such work, as Sue Thornham suggests, 'the text ceases to exercise a determining power and identities, though constructed within representation, are the result of processes of negotiation and contestation, constantly in flux' (1997: 91). These theoretical developments reveal a growing acknowledgement of audience reception as the site of meaning-production. As Jennifer Wicke argues in her discussion of academic interventions in pornography, this signals a shift from 'an unexamined attitude toward the complexity of mass-cultural formations' (1993: 54) to a recognition that 'people transform the mass-cultural objects that come before them in a variety of ways' (1993: 79). A similar shift in emphasis can be identified in media and communications theory where, as Gill Branston suggests, the main focus is no longer 'the study of the texts as site of meaning and effect, the puzzle to be solved, but the active production of meaning on *both* sides of the text' (Branston and Stafford, 1991: 114–15). Rather than adhering to an unexamined modernist conception of popular culture as inherently exploitative of women and passively consumed by mass (masculinised) audiences, current theoretical discourses which acknowledge the complexities of cultural production, spectatorship and identification and the agency of the consumer are more useful for feminism. This is not to propose that the material and economic interstices of popular cultural production should be ignored, or to set up a utopian free-for-all in which meaning is completely ungrounded in the text, but to suggest that feminism needs to embrace alternative paradigms with which to engage with the mainstream if it is to continue to have any significant impact. Carter simultaneously understood, interrogated and celebrated this in her fiction and in her work in media.

Carter was fascinated by the distinction between 'high art' and 'popular culture': 'it's a very crude distinction, and I'm not the first person to have made it, but ... there is this distinction, this enormous distinction between *fat* culture and *thin* culture' (Bailey, 1992). In an American interview, she maintains that her last novel, *Wise Children*, is 'very broadly about class, about our two distinct cultures in Britain' (Bradfield, 1994: 91):

> The absolute fissure between bourgeois culture and non-bourgeois culture. The absolute division between people who go to the National Theater, say, and the sort who frequented the old time music halls. You've got this one class in Britain which pretends to be so proper and respectable, but all the time they're completely repressed. This *other* culture they're trying so hard to distance themselves from – the live sex shows, the louts, the hooligans – is *their* culture, too. They just don't know it yet.[15]

But Carter is more interested in the connection between the two than in perpetuating their binary opposition: 'what I find fascinating is not that there are two sides to British culture – but that the English pretend that such an absolute division exists between them' (Bradfield, 1994: 93). In her own writing practice Carter rejects this modernist dichotomy and the consequent privileging of literary texts over other cultural forms. Popular culture filters into Angela Carter's work for the written page. Her writing in general is highly allusive and eclectic, borrowing from both high culture and 'trash-art' (Bradfield, 1994: 91): 'I feel free to loot and rummage in an official past, specifically a literary past, but I like paintings and sculptures and the movies and folklore and heresies, too' (Carter, 1983d: 74).[16] This practice gives a new authority to popular culture and at the same time undermines the authority of an official literary past. Her ongoing engagement with the oral tradition springs from this reluctance to privilege the official culture: 'ours is a highly individualized culture, with a great faith in the work of art as a unique one-off, and the artist as an original, a godlike and inspired creator of unique one-offs. But fairy tales are not like that, nor are their makers' (Carter (ed.), 1990: x).[17] In her introduction to *Expletives Deleted*, Carter explains that she sees narrative as not being tied to the written word, but harking back to the oral tradition and linking forward to future technologies:

> I can contemplate with equanimity the science-fiction future world that every day approaches more closely, in which information and narrative pleasure are transmitted electronically and books are a quaint antiquarian, minority taste. (Carter, 1992: 2)

But while admitting to a 'fetishistic attitude to books', she continues, 'a book is simply the container of an idea – like a bottle', returning to a favourite metaphor (Carter, 1992: 2).[18] The fact that Carter chose to adapt her own work, together with her ongoing preoccupation with the inter-relationship between high art and low culture in her fiction and journalism, demonstrates the degree of her engagement with these debates.

I particularly take issue, therefore, with Britzolakis' contention that Carter's later work fails to confront the implications of contemporary media culture:

> It is worth noting that both of the last novels find their inspiration and point of reference in pre-electronic forms of entertainment – the circus, the music-hall – a celebration which in some ways sidesteps the more troubling implications of the way in which subjectivity might be inflected by spectacle in a culture of consumption. (1995: 472)

Music-hall and circus are patently not outside a 'culture of consumption', nor does Carter suggest that they are. Britzolakis makes an odd distinction between traditional and electronic entertainment which betrays an elitist distrust of mass media as more ideologically suspect than earlier cultural formations.[19]

Furthermore, while it may be true of *Nights at the Circus* which, set at the turn of the century, indeed examines pre-electronic entertainment, I wholly disagree with the suggestion that Carter's last novel, *Wise Children*, ignores the ramifications of today's electronic, post-industrial, consumer society. Although music-hall is central, electronic media also forms an important point of reference throughout the novel. Cinema features heavily, from the girls' 'first matinée' (1991a: 54) to their starring role in the Hollywood film adaptation of *A Midsummer Night's Dream* (1991a: 120–61). As ever, Carter's celebration of the magic of Hollywood is grounded in the material. Here she revels in *The Dream* as the last word in Hollywood kitsch, while at the same time offering a pointed critique of the interrelationship between the sexual commodification of women and the exploitative production values at work within the film industry:

> The love of Mammon lay behind it all. We worked like slaves. Take after take after take. The same routine, the same song, the same line – over and over and over. We were both product *and* process, simultaneously, and it very near broke us. And what did all our hard work add up to? Just another Saturday night at the pictures! Your one shilling and ninepenn'orth. Your helping of dark. What an equation. Our sweated labour = your bit of fun. 'Like tarts,' said Nora, with prim distaste. (1991a: 142)

The girls prostitute themselves in the name of a night at the movies. Later, they receive mail from 'some kid in New Jersey wanting to interview us for his Ph.D., Film Studies, bloody *Midsummer Night's Dream*, again' (1991a: 8). Hollywood kitsch becomes high art, further eroding the boundaries between elite and popular culture. As old ladies, they watch their younger selves on the silver screen, their youth preserved like celluloid jam (1991a: 10–11, 125).

More recent forms of electronic entertainment are also well represented, such as Tristram Hazard's 'Lashings of Lolly', the popular television game-show with an S&M twist (1991a: 10–11, 40). Dora writes her memoirs on a word processor, bringing the novel right into the computer age (1991a: 3) and the Chance sisters are at home with the latest video technology, manipulating the medium for their own viewing pleasure: 'we got the VCR to catch up with those Busby Berkeley musicals they put out Saturday afternoons. We tape them, watch them over and over, freeze-frame our favourite bits' (1991a: 10). Electronic culture even plays a formal role in the novel's structure with a thirty-page digression signalled via the language of the video remote-control: 'Freeze-frame' (1991a: 11) and 'press the button for "Play"' (1991a: 40). Nora and Dora's viewing practices confound any straightforward theorisation of spectatorship, illustrating what Thornham has identified as the 'decentred screen' of contemporary 'mass media apparatuses'(1997: 160), in which the relation between viewer and filmic text has been democratised: 'I may segment it, replay it, interrupt it with other segments from different media, overlay it with other media texts, use it as a primer for dance routines, clothing, body image, "permitted" behaviours and identities, and so on' (1997: 161).

Carter's extensive interrogation of media culture in *Wise Children* demonstrates that she was alert to the complex relationship between reader and text, the 'work of consumption' and the agency of the consumer in cultural transactions (Wicke, 1993: 70). Rather than sidestepping these issues, the novel thoroughly engages with the *material* as well as the *semiotic* implications of spectacle in both traditional, popular and electronic culture. It is Britzolakis, on the contrary, who sidesteps the implications of Carter's exploration of electronic entertainment. By choosing to devalue Carter's engagement with the mainstream, both her writing for media and her extensive critique of popular culture in her fiction and journalism, Britzolakis misses the valuable opportunity to extend her arguments about gender and commodity fetishism.

Furthermore, in her eagerness to foreground Carter's 'fetishism of the signifier', Britzolakis overlooks Carter's committed material investigation of these cultural formations (1995: 464). Citing Robert Clark (1987) and John Bayley (1992) in a footnote, she argues that:

> For a certain purist tradition of Marxism, as much as for liberal humanist criticism, Carter is a deeply embarrassing figure, adopting as she does a postmodern aesthetic which, it has been argued, privileges style over substance, eroticizes the fragment and parasitically colludes with consumer capitalism. (1995: 460)

Britzolakis goes on to rely heavily on Clark and Bayley without explicitly acknowledging her allegiances, mirroring Bayley's emphasis on a close reading of *Love* at the expense of later work and taking Clark's 'postmodern aesthetics' as read.[20] But, as Nanette Altevers argues, 'there is no evidence in Carter's work that her "primary allegiance is to a postmodern aesthetics," whatever that may mean' (1994: 19). Lorna Sage also resists this definition of Carter as a postmodern writer, reluctant to use the term because 'it seems to me to convey a kind of terminal reflexiveness, a notion of fiction as a vacated fun-house, a spatialized model for narrative, which I don't think fits exactly' (1994: 58). Other critics, however, offer a convincing case for the term as descriptive of Carter's subversive writing practice.[21]

Britzolakis' article is blinkered by an underlying Marxist–humanist distrust of feminism's engagement with poststructuralist theory and postmodernism. This is symptomatic of a traditional mistrust of the mainstream from within the feminist sisterhood which stems from an amalgamation of modernist fears of dilution and massification, a Marxist suspicion of media culture as inherently hegemonic and an undigested deployment of the terminology of early feminist film theory.[22] Wicke identifies this phenomenon at work in feminist academic interventions in pornography:

> the meshing of an ahistoricist apolitical American feminist criticism with certain discrete and selectively chosen pieces of (psycho-analytic and Althusserian) feminist film theory, giving it enough theory to posit an 'objectifying gaze', in collision with the deep social conservatism of so-called 'radical' feminism. (Wicke, 1993: 64)

Radical feminism, Wicke argues, has co-opted the language of feminist film theory for ultimately conservative ends, ironically reinscribing the binary opposition in which woman is figured as the passive object of a masculine gaze. However, this reliance on early feminist film theory is misplaced because it ignores the historical contexts from which theories of the gaze developed, emerging in the early 1970s and becoming the dominant discourse of feminist film theory by the 1980s. It is important to remember that this terminology arose out of theoretical discourses around specific Hollywood film genres of the 1930s and 1940s, such as melodrama and the 'weepie'. Laura Mulvey's seminal theory of 'woman as image, man as bearer of the look' was productive in exposing the structure of looks at play in classical narrative cinema ([1975] 1989: 14–26). To apply it blindly to the whole of media culture is neither appropriate nor particularly productive for feminist politics.

Feminist film theory has had particular problems in attempting to theorise the female spectator. In particular, there has been much debate around the issue of whether the gaze is inherently male, or whether a female gaze can be effectively utilised. Thornham identifies a 'troubling triangular relationship between the feminist, the textually inscribed female spectator, and the woman in the audience' (1997: 166). The notion of any one female subject position, whether textually inscribed or available outside the text, is becoming increasingly problematic in the context of current developments in film theory and the 'gender scepticism' of recent research into media consumption, which posits that gender is only one of a complex network of identifications at work in the viewing process (Thornham, 1997: 165). I am particularly thinking here of developments which move beyond theories of Mulvey's objectifying 'male gaze' to figurations of the voice (Doane, [1978] 1980, [1980] 1986), fantasy (Clover, 1992; Creed, 1993), female subjectivity and desire (Williams, 1984; Doane, 1987). As Whatling also suggests, 'more recent feminist film criticism has testified to the role that audiences or individual viewers have in altering the focus and interpretation of a given film' (Whatling, 1997: 13; see also hooks, 1996; Tasker, 1993; Williams, 1990).

These developments in contemporary feminist theory, across a number of disciplines, offer productive ways with which to approach both Carter's mediated texts and her multiperspectival, appropriative feminist strategies of writing. Wicke's notion of the work of consumption and Whatling's theorising of a lesbian/feminist politics of cultural appropriation situate meaning-production with the audience and recognise the diversity of audience constituencies. Rather than seeing popular cultural forms as having a single, dominant, fixed meaning which is passively consumed by a mass (masculinised) audience, this recent research posits more complex cultural interactions at play in the consumption of such mainstream genres as pornography and classical narrative cinema.

As I have established, the diversity of feminist responses to Carter's fiction demonstrates the healthy heterogeneity of the feminist sisterhood. Rather than the 'gaps and silences' which Neale (1996) identifies, or Britzolakis' (1995) hegemonic 'gender-performance' discourse, an examination of the existing literature reveals a lively and productive dialogue among a community of feminist critics who expand and qualify each other's work. Carter's work in media, however, has not yet received this type of extended analysis and current Carter criticism fails to take on board the scope and variety of her mediated texts. While individual texts and groups of texts receive some critical attention, this usually occurs in a vacuum and there is a general absence of the study of Carter's mediated texts as a body of work in its own right. Hence the need for this book. As her literary executor, Susannah Clapp, asserts, Carter's writings for media 'enlarge the scope and alter the contours of a rich body of work' (Carter, 1996: ix). As I demonstrate in the following chapters, an examination of Carter's mediated texts is not simply rewarding, it is essential, in illuminating her fiction and reinvigorating the critical reception of her work.

## Notes

1  A production of Carter's 'Lulu' is not addressed here because it was staged after her death. Neither is 'The Kitchen Child' (Perino (dir.), 1990), a television adaptation of Carter's short story, because, according to director Joy Perino, Carter played no part in either its adaptation or production (in personal conversation) and, as producer John Ellis maintains, 'those *Short and Curlies* are fundamentally the director's creation' (1995: 257).
2  See Table 1.1 (p. 28) for full transmission details of the radio plays, provided by BBC Radio director, Glyn Dearman.
3  Unfortunately neither Neil Jordan nor Stephen Woolley (director and producer of *The Company of Wolves*, respectively) responded to my correspondence, so I was unable to interview them.
4  It therefore might be worth situating myself at this juncture as a single-parented, middle-

class, university-educated, white, British woman, while acknowledging that these self-definitions are in themselves partial.

5 This article is indicative of the academy's moral panic at the developing popularity of twentieth-century fiction and literary theory.

6 However, Day is one of the few critics to mention *The Holy Family Album* (1998: 27–8).

7 Lucie Armitt ends her essay, 'The Fragile Frames of *The Bloody Chamber*', with a reference to the film, *The Company of Wolves* (Bristow and Broughton (eds), 1997: 97–8) and Gina Wisker mentions *Vampirella* in 'Revenge of the Living Doll: Angela Carter's Horror Writing' (Bristow and Broughton (eds), 1997: 128–9), but unfortunately, gets the date wrong.

8 However, elsewhere Jordan (1994: 211) acknowledges both Carter's fictional engagement with mass media and her active involvement in radio, film and opera: 'Her sensitive, exuberant, enlivening skill in effects of writing also celebrates – not uncritically – the projections of fantasies on the silver screen, whose various forms and transmissions cross the difference between public and private (she became equally interested in the auditory imagination and effects of radio; and how good it would have been to have had her libretto of Virginia Woolf's *Orlando* realised at Glyndebourne).'

9 See in particular Maggie Anwell's reading of *The Company of Wolves* (1988). Flora Alexander (1989) straightforwardly agrees with Anwell's reading of the film, as does Merja Makinen (1992); see also John Collick (1991) and Paul Sutton and Anne White (1997). For a discussion of *The Magic Toyshop* see Robyn Ferrell (1991). For discussions of both films see Laura Mulvey (1994) and Catherine Neale (1996).

10 Although acknowledging Carter's treatment of sexual violence as a point of contention for at least one critic, Neale seems unaware of a substantial body of criticism which problematises Carter's work from a variety of other theoretical perspectives. Neale only cites Patricia Duncker (1984) in this connection. See Chapter 2 for further discussion of this anti-pornography criticism. I engage further with Neale's criticisms in Crofts (1998a).

11 In particular Anne Fernihough (1997), writing about the most theatrical of Carter's novels, *Nights at the Circus*, qualifies and desimplifies these debates in an intelligent analysis of Carter's writing practice.

12 Irigaray's concept of 'mimicry' aims to expose the cultural production of femininity by exaggerating patriarchal ideologies: 'to play with mimesis is thus, for a woman, to try to recover the place of her exploitation by discourse, without allowing herself to be simply reduced by it. It means to resubmit herself inasmuch as she is on the side of the "perceptible," of "matter" – to "ideas," in particular to ideas about herself, that are elaborated in/by a masculine logic, but so as to make "visible" by an effect of playful repetition, what was supposed to remain invisible: the cover-up of a possible operation of the feminine in language' (Irigaray, 1985: 76).

13 It is particularly apposite to a discussion of Carter's mediated texts that some feminists have found her exploration of the pornographic imagination so controversial. See Kappeler (1986); Robert Clark (1987: 147–61) and Lewallen (1988: 144–58). This 'anti-pornography lobby' have had most difficulty with Carter's explorations of the mysteries of sado-masochistic desire in *The Bloody Chamber* and her polemical essay *The Sadeian Woman* – about which Carter comments '*moral pornographer* was a phrase that got me into a lot of trouble with the sisters' (Katsavos, 1994: 16). See McNair (1996) for a discussion of the mediation of pornography. See Chapters 2 and 5 for a more detailed discussion of these issues in the context of radio and film versions of *The Company of Wolves*.

14 This tension between modernism and postmodernism has also been noted in relation to the remake, see Thompson (1996: 11–28) and Trahair (1991: 183–208) whose work is discussed in more detail in Chapter 5.

15 This is an interesting comment in the light of her own ambivalent relationship with the National Theatre after they ditched her 'Lulu' project, as discussed in the Envoi.

16 The mention of 'heresies' here is particularly resonant in terms of the blasphemous erosion of boundaries between classical and pop art in Carter's iconoclastic documentary, *The Holy Family Album* (see Chapter 8).

17 As discussed in Chapter 2, Carter enjoyed recreating the voice of fairy tale for radio.

18 She used the bottle metaphor to describe her writing in terms of 'new readings of old texts' in 'Notes From the Front Line' (1983d: 69): 'I am all for putting new wine in old bottles, especially if the pressure of the new wine makes the old bottles explode', using it later in the same essay to describe the transformation of 'actual fictional forms to both reflect and to precipitate changes in the way people feel about themselves – putting new wine in old bottles and, in some cases, old wine in new bottles' (1993d: 76). Carter's writing for media is clearly part of this transformative project.

19 Carter acknowledged that literature, too, was part of that culture of consumption. She saw herself as being in the entertainment business as well as the 'demythologising business': 'I've tried to keep an entertaining surface to the novels, so that you don't have to read them as a system of signification if you don't want to' (Haffenden, 1985: 87).

20 Clark and Bayley's critique of Carter has prompted a fierce response from feminist critics. On Clark see Altevers (1994: 18–23); Jordan (1990: 19–40, 1992: 119–31). On Bayley see Jordan (1994: 189–215); Lee (1994); Sage (ed.) (1994: 1–23).

21 See in particular Wilson (1989: 96–114), and Michael (1994: 492–521). As an analytical and descriptive term 'postmodernism' remains fraught with ambiguities. I align myself with Wilson's figuration of the postmodern which occupies the interstices between a Marxist critique of postmodernism as politically bankrupt in its collusion with post-industrial, consumer culture (see Jameson, 1984: 53–93; Britzolakis, 1995; Bayley, 1992) and the poststructuralist celebration of the postmodern as the anarchic free-play of the text (see McHale, 1987; Hutcheon, 1989).

22 As I demonstrate in Chapter 5, Maggie Anwell's critique of *The Company of Wolves*, in 'Lolita Meets the Werewolf' (1988: 76–85), is contingent upon just such an amalgamation.

# 'Aural hallucinations': radio drama

Angela Carter's relationship with radio began with an accidental sound effect – the 'metallic, almost musical rattle' of pencil on radiator, 'the noise that a long, pointed fingernail might make if it were run along the bars of a birdcage' – which inspired her to create the 'lovely lady vampire' in *Vampirella* ([1976] 1992). She was instantly 'hooked' on radio (1985: 10). She went on to write two documentary-dramas directly for the medium, *Come Unto These Yellow Sands* ([1979] 1992a), on the Victorian painter Richard Dadd and *A Self-Made Man* (1984a), on Edwardian novelist Ronald Firbank, in addition to reformulating two short stories for radio, *The Company of Wolves* ([1980] 1992) and *Puss in Boots* ([1982] 1992).[1] This chapter situates the radio plays and explores Carter's attraction to the medium, examining radio's formal properties and how these relate to her demythologising practice. I also discuss why this substantial body of work remains on the margins of critical studies of Carter's writing, arguing for its inclusion in a more prominent position in the Carter canon.

## Aural hallucinations

A child of the 'radio age', as a writer Carter was fully conversant with radio's extensive technical possibilities. In the preface to her play anthology, *Come Unto These Yellow Sands: Four Radio Plays* (1985), she celebrates the elasticity of the medium: 'in a radio drama studio, the producer, the actors, the technical staff, create an illusion, literally, out of the air ... The resources are insubstantial but infinite' (1985: 8).[2] For Carter, radio's technological resources amplify and extend the power of the written word, blurring the 'linearity' of traditional story-telling, 'so that a great number of things can happen at the same time' (1985: 7). These technologies share the fluidity of film editing whereby, as John Drakakis suggests, 'sound-effects could be regarded as aural transformations of the film's camera angle and focus' (Drakakis (ed.), 1981: 4–7). But, as Carter points out, radio's 'extraordinary collage and montage effects' are also 'beyond the means of any film-maker' precisely because they are not fixed to the visual image: 'as with all forms of story-telling that are composed in words, not in visual images, radio leaves that magical and enigmatic margin, that space of the invisible, which must be filled in by the imagination of the listener' (1985: 7).

If 'writing for radio involves a kind of three-dimensional story-telling' (Carter, 1985: 7), then radio's third dimension is clearly more than just the sum of its technological parts: it is the particular way in which radio invokes 'the presence of the margin of the listener's imagination' (1985: 11) that most attracts Carter as a writer:

> It is the necessary open-endedness of the medium, the way the listener is invited into the narrative to contribute to it his or her own way of 'seeing' the voices and the sounds, the invisible beings and events, that gives radio story-telling its real third dimension, which is the space that, above all, interests and enchants me. (Carter, 1985: 7)

Radio's 'open-endedness' mirrors the elliptical structure of many short stories which, as Clare Hanson has argued, stirs the imagination of the reader in a particular way:

> Ellisions [*sic*] and gaps within a text offer a special space for the workings of the reader's imagination, offer a space for the work of the image-making faculty which would otherwise lie dormant: the reader's desire is thus allowed, or rather invited, to enter the text. (Hanson (ed.), 1989: 23)

It is productive to take this formal comparison between the radio play and the short story further. Both forms paradoxically contain more imaginative space precisely because of their 'lack'. The 'blindness' of radio, the absence of visual stimuli, necessitates the stimulation of the listener's imagination (in Hanson's terms, activating the 'image-making faculty'), creating space for their active involvement in the process of meaning production (inviting the listener's 'desire' into the text).[3] The lack of narrative space in short fiction contributes to its open-endedness as a medium, demanding a similarly active readership. That short fiction appealed to Carter as a form is evidenced by her numerous short story collections.[4] Writing in the 'Afterword' (1974) to her first short story collection, *Fireworks*, Carter comments that 'the limited trajectory of the short narrative concentrates its meaning'. Carter's attraction to both the short story and the radio play correlates with what Merja Makinen has described as her insistence that her texts were 'open-ended, written with a space for the reader's activity in mind' (1992: 6).

Furthermore, both the short story and the radio play are formally suited to dealing with those elements normally excluded from, or marginalised within, the dominant realist mode. As Hanson (Hanson (ed.), 1989: 6) argues, 'the formal properties of the short story – disjunction, inconclusiveness, obliquity – connect with its ideological marginality and with the fact that the form may be used to express something suppressed/repressed in mainstream literature'.[5] Sharing the short story's position on the edges of literary discourse, radio similarly lends itself to the portrayal of those elements which have been marginalised by mainstream culture. As Carter asserts, 'it is *par excellence*, the medium for the depiction of madness; for the exploration of the private worlds of the old, the alienated, the lonely' (1985: 8).[6] The technologies of radio also make it particularly adept at portraying the fantastic. As Carter argues, 'because of the absence of the visual image, radio drama need not be confined to the representation of things as they are' (1985: 8). John Drakakis suggests that 'fantasy and the supernatural presented the radio play with special opportunities' (Drakakis (ed.), 1981: 24). It is helpful, here, to turn to Rosemary Jackson's formative work on the fantastic. Jackson suggests that the fantastic expresses 'a desire for something excluded from cultural order – more specifically, for all that is in opposition to the capitalist and patriarchal order which has been dominant in Western society over the last two centuries' (1981: 176).

Jackson argues, convincingly, that fantasy as a literary practice is revolutionary because it attempts to disrupt the unities which uphold the dominant order:

> fantasies image the possibility of radical cultural transformation through attempting to dissolve or shatter the boundary lines between the imaginary and the symbolic. They refuse the latter's categories of the 'real' and its unities. (1981: 176)

The unities she refers to are the literary and philosophical unities of time, place and character which work to uphold the construction of a stable universe, which in turn supports the ideology of the coherent subject in conventional rationalistic texts.[7] By challenging these unities, Jackson argues, the modern fantastic aims at the 'dissolution of an order experienced as oppressive and insufficient' (1981: 180). The fantastic can therefore be seen to be sympathetic to a feminist strategy of writing. But it is important to note Jackson's speculative language here. Fantasies only 'image the possibility' of cultural change. She does not advocate fantasy as an *inherently* radical writing strategy, but posits that it nevertheless always holds the *potential* to disrupt the dominant ideology.[8]

Carter's writing for radio attempts to rupture and interrogate these unities. She states that she preferred to use radio 'not for creating dramas on a theatrical model so much as to create complex, many-layered narratives that play tricks with time ... and also with place, for radio can move from location to location with effortless speed, using aural hallucinations to invoke sea-coast, a pub, a blasted heath' (1985: 7). This project is facilitated by radio's technical resources. According to Drakakis, the invention of the 'dramatic control panel' in 1928 enabled 'radio drama to dissolve both temporal and implied spatial boundaries' and the introduction of stereophonic sound allowed movement across an imagined 'sound screen' (Drakakis (ed.), 1981: 4). Maximising radio's temporal and spatial agility, Carter choreographs the feline acrobatics in *Puss in Boots* and realises the metamorphosis of man into beast in *The Company of Wolves*. She uses acoustic images and spot-effects to conjure up the Gothic *mise-en-scène* in *Vampirella*. The 'screech of a bat', the 'hoot of an owl', the 'clink of spade upon coffin' and Count Dracula's 'dreadful, posthumous chuckle' situate the play firmly in the land of the vampires (1985: 84–6, 116). Mrs Beane, the Countess' pragmatic governess, heads a lively supporting cast, including the terrible Scottish cannibal, Sawney Beane, indicated by the 'skirl of bagpipes. Jaunty. Proud' (1985: 95), Elizabeth Ba'athory, the 'Sanguinary Countess' and the infamous Parisian necrophile, Henri Blot.

Radio is 'an ideal medium for the "world of myth, dream and fairy-tale"' that so fascinated Carter (Dearman, 1992). The crucial function of the voice in radio, 'the principal means of sustaining the radio drama illusion', enabled Carter to recontextualise fairy tale in the oral tradition, imitating the role of 'the most antique tellers of tales' (1985: 8, 13). At the same time, radio's technical capabilities facilitated her deconstructive approach to the original tales, extending the demythologising project of *The Bloody Chamber*. In *The Company of Wolves*, Granny's old wives' tales are qualified and revised by Red Riding Hood. This interactive storytelling process is discussed further in Chapter 2, in the context of an extensive analysis of the complex interrelationship between radio and the voice of fairy tale.

The 'invisible' medium of radio is also effective at tampering with the concept of the unified subject. Character need not be limited to naturalistic representation. As Drakakis suggests:

> what the medium could do best was to represent the psychological processes of the human mind, as evidenced in stream-of-consciousness technique, along with those elements of metaphysical 'reality' which could only be imperfectly realised in visual terms. (Drakakis (ed.), 1981: 24)

Embracing radio's capacity to portray shifting, polymorphous identity, Carter challenges the concept of the 'self' as fixed and whole, offering alternative paths in the construction of identity. This is especially true of her two documentary-dramas *Come Unto These Yellow Sands* and *A Self-Made Man*. Testing out her hypothesis that 'radio is the most visual of mediums because you cannot see it', she brings a whole picture gallery to life on radio in *Come Unto These Yellow Sands*, in which the bizarre characters in Dadd's paintings are given a voice (1985: 11).[9] Oberon lectures on the pastoral exotic to an unruly rabble of creatures from the stereophonic id; we hear 'footsteps trooping into the lecture theatre; squeaks, gibbers, honking'. This is 'not a *normal* crowd' (Carter, 1985: 22). The play shifts dexterously between the 'real' Middle Eastern setting of Dadd's 'grand tour' to the minutiae of the fairy kingdom he imagined in his paintings. Fantastic episodes are interwoven with biographical sketches of the events that led up to Dadd's madness, patricide and incarceration in Bethlem Hospital. A similar collage technique is used to map Firbank's self-creation as a literary aesthete in *A Self-Made Man*. Cross-cutting between the fashionable Eiffel Tower Restaurant and the 'exotic elsewhere' of Firbank's imagination, the play explores the conflicting 'legends' which have grown up around his fragile persona. Carter's experimentation with the documentary format in these two plays radically challenges the concept of the unified self and these 'artificial' biographies form the focus of Chapter 3.

## Loud silence

For Carter, 'radio remains a challenging medium, because so much is possible in it. I write for radio by choice, as an extension and an amplification of writing for the printed page' (1985: 12–13).[10] However, despite her evident enthusiasm for the medium, her radio plays have received surprisingly little critical explication. If Carter's writing for media has generally been neglected, there is a particularly loud silence regarding her work in radio. One of the major barriers to the academic study of Carter's radio drama is the relative inaccessibility of the radio plays. Originally broadcast on Radios 3 and 4 during the mid- 1970s to the early 1980s, four of the plays were re-transmitted after her death in 1992.[11] Unless you are lucky enough to have taped these transmissions, they are virtually unavailable for further consumption.[12] According to David Wade (1981: 224): 'most radio plays are broadcast once; some twice; a few, a very few, three or more and after that, if not destroyed, the recordings end up in the limbo of the Tape Library. Few find their way into print.'[13] It is clearly difficult to evaluate the radio plays effectively without access to them in performance. While we are privileged to have access to the written scripts, the experience of reading a text is very different from that of listening to a radio play. It is crucial to make this distinction between text and performance. Radio drama is the union of words and sounds and the written text cannot do justice to the rich textures woven by these two elements.

The fact that Carter's radio plays have received so little critical analysis is indicative of the ambivalent position radio drama occupies within the academy. Uncomfortably straddling the intellectual ground between Literary and Media Studies, radio drama is not fully claimed by either discipline: not quite popular culture, but too implicated in mass communications to be literature either. What attention the plays have received within literary studies has generally been in the context of a discussion of *The Bloody Chamber*, in which they are used to expand upon analyses of the short stories (see Makinen, 1992: 3; Gamble, 1997: 131, 136–7). This privileging of the original short stories stems from a combination of a modernist mistrust of the copy and a hierarchisation of traditional forms over electronic media. As we have seen in the Introduction, media adaptation often foregrounds this hierarchical construction of the high art/ low culture binary. The marginalisation of Carter's radio plays as adaptations betrays a lack of understanding of the extent and importance of Carter's working relationship with radio. The two adaptations *Puss in Boots* and *The Company of Wolves* deserve to be studied in their own right, not least because of the skill with which Carter 'reformulates' the original material, successfully taking the new medium into account.[14]

But to dismiss Carter's radio drama as adaptations is also misinformed, for while *The Company of Wolves* and *Puss in Boots* were adapted from existing short stories in *The Bloody Chamber*, the other plays were written directly for the medium. Nevertheless, the ambiguous textual status of *Vampirella* has caused problems for some critics (see Almansi, 1994: 335, n. 16; Gamble, 1997: 131; Wisker, 1997: 128) who mistakenly discuss it as an adaptation of the short story 'The Lady of the House of Love' which later appeared in *The Bloody Chamber* (Carter, [1979] 1981). Gina Wisker claims that 'Carter reworked the story for a radio play, *Vampirella*, first broadcast on BBC Radio 3 in 1978' (1997: 128), incidentally getting the transmission date wrong (see Table 1.1 for full transmission details). In fact the radio play came first, as Carter confirms: 'I never thought of any other medium but radio all the time I was writing the script ... It *came* to me as radio, with all its images ready formed, in terms of words and sounds' (1985: 10), explaining that she later 'took the script of *Vampirella* as the raw material' for the short story, 'The Lady of the House of Love'. Robert Coover (1994: 9) corroborates this, stating that 'she converted the radio play *Vampirella* into the brilliant tale of "The Lady

**Table 1.1**   Radio play transmission information

| TITLE | ORIGINAL BROADCAST | REPEAT BROADCAST | MEMORIAL BROADCAST |
|---|---|---|---|
| *Vampirella* | 20 July 1976, Radio 4 | 29 May 1977, Radio 3 | 15 November 1992, Radio 4 |
| *Come Unto These Yellow Sands* | 28 March 1979, Radio 3 | 1 July 1979, Radio 3* | 7 April 1992, Radio 3 |
| *The Company of Wolves* | 1 May 1980, Radio 3 | | 19 November 1992, Radio 4 |
| *Puss in Boots* | 20 December 1982, Radio 4 | | 16 November 1992, Radio 4 |
| *A Self-Made Man* | 4 May 1984, Radio 3 | | |

\* Sony Award winner

This information was kindly provided by Glyn Dearman, BBC Radio Drama, director of all five of Carter's radio plays.

of the House of Love" for the *Iowa Review* (Summer/Autumn, 1975). While *Vampirella* was not broadcast until 1976, its creation precedes the short story and this chronology demonstrates that Carter's work in radio has a more direct relationship with her reworking of fairy tale in *The Bloody Chamber* than has hitherto been acknowledged, as I go on to argue in Chapter 2.

In the transposition Vampirella's bloodthirsty ancestors are replaced with a series of anonymous family portraits and the forthright Mrs Beane is replaced by a dumb crone. Neither, Carter argues, did the narrative line of the short story 'have sufficient space to discuss the nature, real and imagined, of vampirism' (1985: 10). This is not to privilege the radio play over the short story (which would be a reenactment of the very modernist hierarchisation of the original discussed above). In Carter's own words 'one is neither better nor worse than the other. Only, each is quite different' (1985: 10).

Carter's two 'artificial' biographies *Come Unto These Yellow Sands* and *A Self-Made Man* were also written directly for the medium. As Carter asserts, 'I don't see how it would have been possible for me to discuss Dadd in the way I wanted in any other medium than radio':

> with its ability to cross-cut from subjective to objective reality, from the inner, personal voice to the conflicting voices of those bearing witness to the diverse manifestations of that inner voice. From the apparently real to

the patently imagined. From a Victorian mad-doctor discussing Dadd's case-notes to Oberon, King of the Fairies, discussing the marginalisation of folklore in the bourgeois period. (1985: 12)

The play forms a bridge between Carter's fascination with fairy tale in the earlier plays and her formal experimentation with documentary-drama, which culminates with her last play, *A Self-Made Man*. Generic hybrids, combining elements of cultural criticism, drama and fantasy, both plays extend the voice of Carter's fiction and journalism and as such deserve further examination.[15]

Guido Almansi's celebratory essay, 'In the Alchemist's Cave', offers the most extensive engagement with Carter's work in radio to date. Almansi captures her enthusiasm for the medium, arguing that 'in the alchemist's cave her imagination makes of a radio studio, with all the possibilities offered by a repertoire of sound-effects, Angela Carter seems delirious with joy' (1994: 222). But, while Almansi effectively conveys Carter's enjoyment and astute awareness of radio's formal properties, he is unable to offer a detailed analysis of the plays in performance because he has not heard all of them.[16] He consequently fails to appreciate the way in which Carter's complex structuring of words and sounds acts on the listener's imagination in *Come Unto These Yellow Sands*: 'I doubt whether a listener, without previous knowledge of Dadd's paintings and of his unhappy life, would make head or tail of these uncanny sounds ... (the other plays are easier to understand)' (Almansi, 1994: 228). While *Come Unto These Yellow Sands* is indeed experimental, pushing the medium to its limits (winning the Sony Award for Best Drama Documentary in 1979, Carter, 1996: 503), Almansi underestimates the intelligence of the highly aurally literate radio audience who recognise 'sound-signs' with ease.[17] Whereas Almansi has little faith in the audience's ability to conjure up mental images and juggle with multiple strands of sounds and meaning, for Carter, the listener's imagination is one of radio's most important resources.

## Acoustic images

In order to examine the pivotal role of the listener's imagination in radio drama, I conducted an experiment in which I played a recording of the following extract from *Come Unto These Yellow Sands* to a group of students and asked them to draw what they heard:[18]

> MALE NARRATOR. [...] Oil on canvas, twenty three and a quarter inches by twenty three and a quarter inches. Puck ...
> *Brisk plucking notes into brisker fairy music*

PUCK. (*Leaping up from nowhere.*) ... whom he painted as a plump, white, juicy child seated on a toadstool of a botanically imprecise description with, directly above my head, a bindweed blossom looking not unlike a particularly vulgar satin lampshade, because it dangles a fringe of pendant dewdrops for all the world like glass beads. Around my little pedestal, which looks far too frail to support my Bacchic corpulence, dance dozen[s] of those tiny nudes, dozens of them.
*Fairy music speeds up behind following:*
Dozens of them, jigg[er]ing[19] about with positively frenetic abandon, whirling like dervishes, dervishes ...

And I am bathed in the coolest, purest light, the light of another world. (1985: 21–2)

First, it is important to reiterate the differences between the script and the recorded text.[20] Arguably, a similar response could have been elicited from an examination of the written extract, but the performance includes a number of non-verbal cues which contribute to the image-making

**1–8** Student sketches of Puck describing himself in extract from *Come Unto These Yellow Sands*

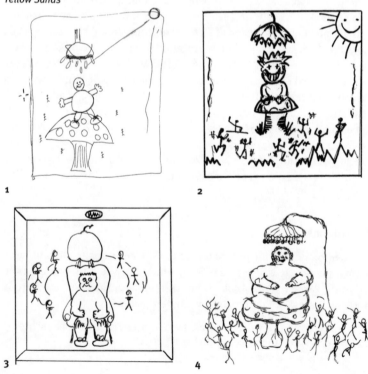

1

2

3

4

process, particularly the use of music and voice. A sense of movement is created by the fairy music which is artificially speeded up as the sound cuts back and forth between Puck's monologue and the background acoustic, creating an uncanny, distorting effect. The authoritative voice of the male narrator, with its received pronunciation and knowledgeable tone, contrasts with the high-pitched, nasal voice and regional accent of Puck, whose intonation and vocabulary could be described as 'camp'.[21] There is also an uncomfortable disjuncture between Puck's adult voice and his description of his depiction as a 'plump, white, juicy child' in the painting, reinforcing the play's message about the pastoral exotic and the Victorian eroticism of both fairies and children. As you can see from the student drawings (Figures 1–8), the results of the experiment were varied!

Differences in artistic ability aside, these drawings not only demonstrate that radio directly stimulates the 'image-making faculty', but also reveal that there is room for individual interpretation within that imaginative process. For example, some students choose to include the

5

6

7

8

square frame, the measurements for which are provided by the narrator (see Figures 1–3). Others attempt to indicate the movement of the fairies, 'whirling like dervishes' (the action lines in Figures 2 and 3 ), or focus on their nudity (the tiny breasts in Figures 3 and 4). Many of the drawings emphasise Puck's 'Bacchic corpulence' and his size in relation to his 'little pedestal' (particularly Figures 4, 5 and 6). The resemblance of the bindweed to a 'vulgar satin lampshade' captures the imagination of a number of students (indeed, Figure 4 depicts a standard lamp and Puck wears the lampshade in Figures 6 and 7). One student gets so carried away with the lampshade analogy that he or she also furnishes the scene with an armchair (Figure 3). A number of students also include the source of light, 'the coolest, purest light, the light of another world' (see Figures 1, 2, 5 and 7).

But what these drawings also illustrate is the fact that, while contributing to meaning-production, the listener's desire is also always, to a certain extent, already culturally situated. Information not included in the extract, nor in the original painting, forms a common theme across drawings by both groups of students. For example, a significant number of drawings depict spots on the toadstool (Figures 1, 2, 4, 5 and 6), although there are none mentioned in the extract, and indeed none appear in the original painting (*Puck*, 1841).[22] This suggests that there is an 'ur-toadstool' of the cultural imagination, the toadstool we remember from the fairy stories of childhood, demonstrating that radio's 'third-dimension' is not an unlimited space outside of the symbolic order giving free-rein to the listener's imagination, but is always still influenced by cultural and social factors outside the text.

## Blindspot

Considering the rapid and ongoing development of Cultural and Media Studies within British universities, and the increasingly interdisciplinary nature of academic study across the humanities, it is curious that radio has been so thoroughly neglected. Moreover, an examination of recent Media Studies texts reveals a marked lack of attention to radio drama as a specific genre.[23] Of the three indexed entries for radio in *The Media Studies Book*, none mentions radio drama, simply listing broadcast radio as one example of the increasing 'range of alternative and overlapping sources of information and entertainment, instruction and art' (Lusted (ed.) 1991: 3). The more recent *Media Student's Handbook* has a more extensive entry on radio, but again omits to mention radio drama, concentrating instead on talk radio, music, news and sports broadcasting (Branston and Stafford, 1996).

One of the factors contributing to radio's low status within contemporary Media Studies is its reputation as a bourgeois medium. While early radio criticism applauded radio's educative function (see Styan, 1960, and Drakakis (ed.), 1981: 17, who describes BBC Radio Drama as the 'National Theatre of the Air'), its implicit dissemination of bourgeois ideology has been criticised in more recent analyses. David Buckingham, for example, argues that John Reith's vision of centralised broadcasting at the expense of local 'narrowcast', or community-based radio, led to the blanket spread of 'middle-class culture and moral values' (1991: 28), not allowing for regional and social differences.[24]

Another reason why radio drama is ignored is because Media Studies tends towards a semiological approach, which is necessarily less interested in genre. This is revealed in Gill Branston and Roy Stafford's examination of the cultural codes at play in broadcast radio (1996). Just as in the analysis of the visual image, they argue, the sound image is made up of cultural and technical codes which can be interpreted. Radio is no more neutral or natural than film and is equally constructed via technological processes such as microphone technique, signal compressing, and background acoustics (1996: 21–5). Branston and Stafford's semiotics of sound is a useful starting point, but these cultural codes are of limited use in discussing the intricate interweaving of voice, music and sound-effects at work in radio drama. Furthermore, their potentially fascinating analysis of the sound image does not go far enough.[25] In particular, they do not offer any specific analysis of how the sound image stimulates the imagination of the listener, and how this might be different from the visual image.[26]

The limitations of this semiological approach emphasises the need for a cross-disciplinary approach. While a great deal of critical analysis has been devoted to the visual image, the semiotics of radio remains a relatively underdeveloped science. Attempting to find a language for the analysis of radio, Branston and Stafford argue that 'it is difficult to discuss what we hear in the same way as what we see. After decades of analysis the visual image is more readily recognised as "made-up", and there exists more detailed terminology with which to discuss it than there does for the sound image' (1996: 21). Demonstrating the difficulty of escaping the language of the visible, their analysis of radio takes the form of a comparison with visual media: 'Radio is *coded* and it signifies in ways as complex as a photographic image' (Branston and Stafford, 1996: 21).

This difficulty in describing radio without recourse to visual comparisons does not just reflect the predominance of the visual arts within Media Studies, it is also symptomatic of a wider cultural privileging of the visible.[27] Luce Irigaray (1985) has identified a hierarchy of the senses in which the visible is privileged in Western culture.[28] As Philippa Berry argues, Irigaray's rereading of Western philosophers, from Plato to Freud, reveals the 'visual or "oculocentric" bias ... implicit in patriarchal models of knowledge' (1994: 231).[29] Indeed, the language of the visible is deeply ingrained within theoretical discourse, where clarity of thought has parity with clarity of vision. As Berry maintains, 'a scopic bias was in fact fundamental to the project of Western philosophy from its inception, since the Greek word *theorein* whence we derive our term *theory*, actually means to contemplate' (Berry, 1994: 231). Jane Gallop also foregrounds this ancient connection between theory and the specular, pointing out that the Greek *theoria* stems from *theoros*, 'spectator' and *thea*, 'viewing' (Gallop, 1982: 58). It becomes clear, then, that Carter's writings for radio have been 'overlooked' because they do not fit comfortably within dominant cultural and theoretical figurations which privilege the visible and that the lack of theoretical discourse surrounding radio reveals a gap or blindspot in this specular economy. The invisible medium of radio disrupts the hegemony of the visible which underpins Western thought, by refusing to be contained within the language of vision.

Although an examination of film theory may seem a little incongruous here, and may even appear to be a repetition of this privileging of the visible, it is useful to examine the treatment of sound within cinematic discourse in the context of this debate. Jean-Louis Comolli identifies 'an almost total lack of theoretical work on the sound track' in film theory, 'a lack which can only be explained by the dominance of the visible at the heart of both cinematic practice and reflection' (1980: 126–7). Both within cinematic discourse and the film industry itself, the camera lens has come to stand metonymically for the entire cinematic apparatus, effacing its constituent technologies, including those of sound (Comolli, 1980: 126). This privileging of the camera lens and the consequent marginalisation of film sound is a magnification and intensification of what Comolli identifies as a wider cultural 'hegemony of the eye' (Comolli, 1980: 127).

As Mary Ann Doane suggests, the lack of attention to the sound track in film 'indicates the efficacy of a particular ideological operation which is masked, to some extent, by the emphasis placed on the "ideology of the visible"' ([1978] 1980: 47). The 'ideological operation' Doane refers to is the way in which sound seamlessly supports the image in order to uphold the dominant ideology of the unified self in dominant narrative cinema. Since the advent of the 'talkie' film sound has been dominated by the imperative of synchronisation. The convention of synchronising the body and the voice aims to guarantee the concept of the 'self' as unified and whole, making the viewer feel safe in the knowledge of his or her coherence as a subject (Doane, [1980] 1986: 335–48, 236–7).[30] Doane's argument, here, is reminiscent of Jackson's figuration of the 'unities' which uphold the dominant order in rationalistic texts. Just as the realist text conceals its art in order to create the illusion of a coherent reality, the practice of synchronicity works to conceal its own 'highly specialised and fragmented process' (with the associated technological apparatus of sound recording, mixing, and 'lip-sync' dubbing), thus denying the 'material heterogeneity' of the medium (Doane, [1978] 1980: 51–2).

While the sound-track functions to reinforce the ideology of the unified self within classic narrative cinema, it is also the site of a potential slippage in the dominant ideology (see Crofts, 2001: 19–29). As Doane suggests, figuring a different relationship between sound and image 'has the potential to provoke a fundamental rent in the ideology of the visible' ([1978] 1980: 49). She refers specifically to those cinematic conventions, such as voice-off and mood music, in which the imperative of synchronisation is sacrificed to the creation of an illusion of a different kind of reality:

> If the ideology of the visible demands that the spectator understand the image as a truthful representation of reality, the ideology of the audible demands that there exist simultaneously a different truth and another order of reality for the subject to grasp. (Doane, [1978] 1980: 49)

The 'ineffable, intangible quality of sound', Doane suggests, brings about an emotional excess which threatens to overspill the visual economy ([1978] 1980: 47–9). Thus, even within classical narrative cinema, sound represents 'a leakage, an excess' of meaning which cannot entirely be subsumed (Doane, [1978] 1980: 52).

If, as Doane proposes, the crucial difference between radio and film is 'the image which anchors the sound in a given space' ([1978] 1980: 54), what happens when sound is divorced from the image, as is the case in radio? While it is tempting to champion radio as inherently more disruptive of the specular ideology than film, the absence of the visual image by no means *guarantees* radio's subversive status as a liberatory alternative to the image. The technological apparatus of radio can function just as much to sustain the dominant ideology as the cinematic apparatus. The same imperative demands that the imagination of the listener construct a body on which to hinge the voice.[31] However, radio still offers a potentially radical space from within which to disrupt the dominant ideology of the visible because, as argued above, the formal properties of the medium allow it to disrupt the unities of character, time and place. Radio therefore remains an ideal site for the exploration of alternative theoretical paradigms such as the pleasure of hearing and a politics of the voice.[32]

As an aural medium, radio provided Carter with an alternative discursive space within which to play out her concerns with gendered and sexual identities. The technological versatility of the medium, its capacity for experimenting with language and identity, lent itself to her decon-structive writing practice. As argued above, this is patently not to suggest that radio is inherently subversive. Nor is it to lay claim to some utopian liberatory space for radio outside the dominant ideology of the visible. It is to suggest, however, that Carter was attracted to radio because of its potential for subverting the dominant visual economy, a potential which she exploits to the full in the radio plays discussed in Chapters 2 and 3.

Radio enabled Carter to fulfil her joint roles as demythologiser and entertainer. She liked to use the medium to 'explore ideas, although for me, that is the same thing as telling stories, since, for me, a narrative is an argument stated in fictional terms' (1985: 7). But the plays remain enter-taining as well as challenging, with their quality of performance, variety of tone, pace and, above all, humour – with Mrs Beane, Vampirella's grimly jocular governess; the furiously copulating Puss and Tabs in *Puss in Boots;* the Middle Eastern shopkeeper's lecture on Orientalism in *Come Unto These Yellow Sands* and the prancing, laughing Firbank in *A Self-Made Man.* Carter's engagement with radio informs, and is informed by, the same subversive writing strategy at play in her fiction and, as such, it is crucial that her radio drama be given greater recognition within the Carter canon. The fact that she chose to write for radio challenges the boundaries between high art and popular entertainment, between mass media and literary culture, emphasising the need for an interdisciplinary approach to her work.

## Notes

1  Please see Table 1.1 for full details of transmission dates, which were kindly provided by Glyn Dearman, BBC Radio Drama, who directed all five of Carter's radio plays. *Come Unto These Yellow Sands, The Company of Wolves, Vampirella* and *Puss in Boots* were originally collected in the play anthology *Come Unto These Yellow Sands: Four Radio Plays* (1985). *A Self-Made Man* was first published, along with the other four plays in *The Curious Room: Collected Dramatic Works* (1996). All further references are to the first publication of the plays.

2  This is one of the most illuminating pieces of writing on radio that I have come across in my own research. Glyn Dearman says 'I don't think there is much I can add to Carter's Foreword to *Come Unto These Yellow Sands*' (in personal correspondence). Carter retained a great respect and admiration for his 'style, sensitivity and enthusiasm' which she argues 'would irradiate dramatised readings of the London telephone directory' (1985: 10). As previously observed, it is important to acknowledge the collaborative nature of Carter's work in radio, not only the contribution of Dearman, but also those of the actors, sound technicians and editors.

3  It is worth again mentioning Jennifer Wicke's theory of 'the work of consumption' (1993:

62–80), as outlined in the Introduction, in which she emphasises the consumer's involvement in meaning production.

4 In the 'Afterword' to her first collection she states, 'I started to write short pieces when I was living in a room too small to write a novel in. So the size of my room modified what I did inside it and it was the same with the pieces themselves' (1974: 121). She went on to publish *The Bloody Chamber* ([1979] 1981) and *Black Venus* ([1985] 1986). *American Ghosts and Old World Wonders* (1993) and *Burning Your Boats* (1995) were published post-humously.

5 Indeed, Carter's self-acknowledged attraction to the short story as a form has much to do with its long association with the fantastic. She preferred 'Gothic tales, cruel tales, tales of wonder, tales of terror, fabulous narratives that deal directly with the unconscious' (1974: 121).

6 Just as Hanson identifies the short story as subordinate to the dominant form of the novel within literary discourse, the 'blind' medium of radio occupies a similarly marginal position in relation to the dominant ideology of the visible, as I go on to explore below.

7 Although Jackson is not explicit about this, these unities relate to Aristotle's 'dramatic unities', as outlined in *Poetics*, part of the classical origins of the liberal humanist tradition.

8 Jackson goes on to be more explicit about the dangers of defending fantasy as necessarily transgressive, arguing that to do so 'would be a vast, over-simplifying and mistaken gesture' (1981: 175).

9 She discussed with Glyn Dearman the possibility of a play about Jackson Pollock 'that would re-invent Pollock's paintings, and his times, in the same way as we re-invented Dadd's paintings for radio' (Carter, 1985: 12).

10 Carter's writing for radio is literally an extension of her published work in the sense that it reaches a wider, more diverse audience than the literary public. Although often seen as a minority taste, radio remains a means of mass-communication with a broad listening base. As John Drakakis asserts, this 'minority of listeners may be counted in their millions' (Drakakis (ed.), 1981: 17). It seems likely, therefore, that Carter's radio plays reached listeners who may never have come into contact with her work in any other context. As Sarah Gamble concurs, Carter's work in radio brought 'her name to the attention of people who might not necessarily read her books' (1997: 131).

11 *A Self-Made Man* has not been retransmitted to date, see Table 1.1 for full transmission details.

12 I have off-air recordings of *Vampirella*, *Puss in Boots* and *Come Unto These Yellow Sands* from their retransmission in 1992 and recordings of *The Company of Wolves* and *A Self-Made Man* direct from the BBC, with thanks to Glyn Dearman (Director and Producer) and Eoin O'Callaghan (Editor, Plays and Readings) at BBC Radio Drama.

13 It is possible to access Carter's radio plays at the London Sound Archive, which is where I first heard *A Self-Made Man*. Recordings have to be requested well in advance. Strict security measures are in operation in the Listening Room. Each listening booth is furnished with a cassette deck for the temporary recording and playback of the master-recording which is piped through a pair of headphones. The cassette deck is fitted with an alarm to prevent any tampering or removal of the tape. These conditions are hardly conducive to research or listening pleasure!

14 Carter writes, 'these aren't adaptations so much as reformulations. As radio, both stories found themselves ending up much closer to specific types of genre' – specifically, horror and *commedia dell'arte* (1985: 10–11).

15 Illustrating this generic hybridity, Carter describes *Come Unto These Yellow Sands* as 'a piece of cultural criticism in the form of a documentary-based fiction' (1985: 12).

16 'I cannot comment on the difference between the written and the performed version[s], because I have never heard a performed version, except one of *Puss in Boots*, which I translated for the Italian radio one or two years ago (or perhaps even earlier before Angela died)' (personal correspondence, 6 March 1995).

17  The ubiquitous BBC seagull signifying a seaside town, the same cow on *The Archers* for twenty years, the rattle of tea cups signifying a cozy kitchen, a door closing signifying a room, 'live' and 'dead' sound signifying space and intimacy.

18  The experiment was conducted on two separate occasions with groups of third-year undergraduate students at Manchester University in May 1996 and 1997. The resulting drawings number twenty in total. The eight included here are a representative, but not random, sample from across both groups. While I am not attempting to make any empirical claims for this experiment, it has nevertheless proved to be an illuminating research tool.

19  The performance has 'jigging about'.

20  It is also important to acknowledge the fact that in asking the students to visualise and then draw what they heard, I immediately privilege the visible, whereas the imagination is not inherently visual, as the *Chambers Twentieth Century Dictionary* definition of 'image' attests: 'a picture or representation (*not necessarily visual*) in the imagination or memory' (emphasis mine).

21  Gill Branston and Roy Stafford outline the different cultural codes and language registers of the reading voice and note the privileged status of the presenter's voice in talk radio (Branston and Stafford, 1996: 21–5). I examine the role of the voice in radio in more detail in Chapter 2.

22  It is important to acknowledge the artistry and selection which has already occurred in Carter's fictionalisation of the image, yet despite being filtered through Carter's imagination, the student drawings remain very close to the spirit of the painting, while retaining their individual characteristics. Unfortunately I am unable to reproduce the painting here, but it can be found in Carter (1985: 20), or see Allderidge (1974).

23  It is important to differentiate between radio drama and other types of radio (talk radio, music and sports broadcasting), as well as other modes of fiction on radio. David Wade makes the useful distinction between radio drama – dramatic writing specifically for radio – and 'drama-by-means-of-radio', such as straight, one-voice readings and abridgements (Wade, 1981: 219).

24  Radio drama is further implicated in this class bias, being predominantly the provenance of the 'high-brow' and elitist Radios 3 and 4.

25  Their analysis is limited to a prosaic discussion of the differing social registers of Radio 1 and Radio 4 presenters' voices, and the fact that while Radio 1 has an explicitly 'branded' station identity, Radios 3 and 4 tend not to use jingles.

26  Although the experiment described above begins to address these issues, more research needs to be conducted in this area.

27  The industry itself borrows from the language of film, with terms such as 'fade-in', 'fade-out' and 'cross-fade' adopted from the film industry. Carter, too, uses the language of the visible to describe radio, '"seeing" the voices and the sounds' in 'the mind's eye', although she was well aware of the 'fruitful paradox' of radio's status as an 'invisible' medium within a predominantly visual economy (1985: 7, 11).

28  Irigaray's theories of this specular bias in theoretical discourse will be examined in more detail in Chapter 2.

29  Sue Vice also discusses Irigaray's critique of the 'prioritization of the visual' in patriarchal culture (Vice (ed.), 1996: 179).

30  Significantly, Kaja Silverman observes that the practice of 'synchronization is imposed much more strictly on the female than on the male voice within dominant cinema' (1990: 309–27).

31  This is evidenced, to a certain extent, by the student drawings of Puck (Figures 1–8), although this may be misleading because he is in effect describing himself. See also, my discussion of the voice of the Hero in *Vampirella* in Chapter 2.

32  These issues are discussed in relation to the voice in Chapter 2.

# 'Voices in the dark': *The Company of Wolves* and other radio plays

The main focus for this chapter is the interrelationship between Angela Carter's recognition of the possibilities of radio as a medium for story-telling and her interest in the subversive potential of fairy tale. I delineate Carter's extended engagement with the genre in her fiction and journalism, arguing that her writing for radio both informed her interest in the oral tradition and facilitated her stated demythologising practice. I also discuss the role of the voice in radio, developing the arguments outlined in Chapter 1 and examining whether a feminist politics of the voice can provide a viable alternative to the ideology of the visible. The chapter ends with a detailed consideration of these issues in relation to the voice and the role of story-telling in the radio play, *The Company of Wolves*.

## Word of mouth

Carter's interest in fairy tale was extensive and well informed, developing from her involvement with the folk movement in the early 1960s, to an extended scholarship which spanned the rest of her career and informed her writing practice.[1] This is evidenced in her journalism and the illuminating introductions to the numerous collections she edited and translated, which demonstrate a committed engagement with the cultural function of fairy tale as a genre, as well as its potential for magical transformations.[2] Carter's concern with the folk form has been well documented (see Rose, 1983: 209–43; Jordan, 1992: 119–31; Makinen, 1992: 2–15; Atwood, 1994: 117–35). But, while it seems fairly straight-forward to trace the development of her ideas from her translation of *The Fairy Tales of Charles Perrault* (Carter (ed. and trans.), 1977), to her fictional engagement with the genre in *The Bloody Chamber* ([1979] 1980), this trajectory is more complicated than at first appears.[3] It is difficult to untangle the precise chronology of influences that combine to inform the reworking of fairy tale in *The Bloody Chamber*, but radio has a more central role in that configuration than has previously been supposed. Yet, most critics have neglected to notice that Carter's relationship with the oral tradition is also intimately connected with her work in radio.[4] Radio's formal capacity for story-telling enabled Carter to literally recreate the voice of fairy tale. Her translation of Perrault coincides with the transmission of her first radio play, *Vampirella*, in the summer of 1976.[5] In turn, her initial work in radio informs her later fictional engagement with the genre. As I have already established, *Vampirella* was later reformulated into prose fiction as 'The Lady of the House of Love', the earliest published story of the collection. In turn, her critical writings about fairy tale inform her work in radio. 'The Better to Eat You With' (1976: 188), for example, begins by invoking 'the horrid example of Richard Dadd', the Victorian painter of fairy subjects who she later went on to explore in her second radio play, *Come Unto These Yellow Sands* (1979). The reciprocal relationship between Carter's interest in fairy tale and her work in radio is further imbricated with the reformulation of two short stories, *The Company of Wolves* (1980) and *Puss in Boots* (1982) for radio.

Radio's technological resources enabled Carter to realise the impossible worlds and metamorphoses of fairy tale, but radio was also the ideal medium for exploring fairy tale beyond these technical capabilities:

> even if stripped of all the devices of radio illusion, radio retains the atavistic lure, the atavistic power of voices in the dark and the writer who gives words to those voices retains some of the authority of the most antique tellers of tales. (Carter, 1985: 13)

Seeing the oral tradition as forming 'the most vital connection we have with the imaginations of the ordinary men and women whose labour created our world' (Carter (ed.), 1990: ix), Carter was attracted by what John Drakakis (Drakakis (ed.), 1981: 32) has identified as the 'bardic function of radio' because it enabled her to get even closer to that pre-literate source, with its reliance on the spoken word. As she argues:

> speaking is a public activity and reading is a private activity. For most of human history, 'literature', both fiction and poetry, has been narrated, not written – heard, not read. (Carter (ed.), 1990: ix)

Lorna Sage (1977: 53) notes that Carter enjoyed reading her own work aloud and 'laments that prose writers are seldom asked to' and that the 'fairytale idea enabled her to *read* in public with a new appropriateness and panache, as though she was *telling* these stories' (Sage, 1994: 40). For Carter, therefore, writing for radio was 'an extension and an amplification of writing for the printed page' (1985: 13) because it allowed her to partake in a specifically oral story-telling culture.[6] Radio also enabled Carter to explore the processes at work in the transmission of oral narratives and their audiences – the active relationship between the teller of the tale and the listener – which foregrounds the potential for renegotiating the patriarchal structures of the literary versions. As I go on to demonstrate, this both informs and extends her project in *The Bloody Chamber*.

Carter celebrates the folk tale as an 'unofficial', 'anonymous and genderless' art form, in her introduction to *The Virago Book of Fairy Tales* (Carter (ed.), 1990: x). Mapping the evolution of the genre from the oral tradition to its current literary status in 'About the Stories', a note to her translation of *Sleeping Beauty and Other Stories*, Carter argues that 'the fairy tale lost all contact with the illiterate peasantry and, indeed, with children. It became a highly developed literary form' (Carter (ed. and trans.), 1982: 127):

> When Charles Perrault first wrote down the fairy tales that have come to us under his name, they had already existed, in various forms, for centuries, part of the unwritten tradition of folk-lore handed down by word of mouth. The difference was, these stories were printed in books for children themselves to read. They had been taken out of the mouths of grannies, nannies and old wives, skilfully retold, and, once in print, became "fixed" in forms that have remained remarkably unaltered until our own day, even when they have reverted again to the oral tradition. (Carter (ed. and trans.), 1982: 125–6)

In the foreword to her translation of *The Fairy Tales of Charles Perrault*, Carter suggests that Perrault's versions have become standard, entering back into the oral tradition of most European countries 'through translation and continuous reprintings and retellings' (Carter (ed. and trans.), 1977: 13), a process to which she herself contributed in her capacity as editor and collector of the two classic fairy tale volumes for Gollancz and the two Virago collections of fairy tales.

Carter's is a complex and often contradictory relationship with fairy tale, in which she privileges the oral tradition, but also admires the artistry of the literary versions. She acknowledges the role of fairy tales in the acculturation of children to traditional gender roles, while at the same time celebrating the 'wily stratagems' of their protagonists and the possibilities of the genre for transgressive retellings (Carter (ed.), [1992] 1993: xi). She found fairy tale a productive form for her own demythologising project because its roots in the oral tradition might offer a way to circumscribe the phallogocentric, patriarchal constructions of gender which had become inscribed in the fixed literary versions.

## Feminist interventions in fairy tale

Before going on to discuss the radio plays, it is important to situate Carter's reworking of fairy tale within contemporary feminist critical and imaginative perspectives on fairy tale. There is a large body of feminist scholarship which identifies fairy tale as a site for the socialisation of women into patriarchal order.[7] In 'Shoot the Wolf', her review of Jack Zipes' extensive work on fairy tale, Carter comments on the role of traditional fairy tales as 'vehicles for bourgeois ideology' which are 'especially concerned with inculcating patriarchal socialisation into young girls' (1983e: 367). When Carter reads traditional fairy tales as 'parables of instruction' in 'About the Stories' (Carter (ed. and trans.), 1982: 125) she echoes Marcia Lieberman's identification of their function as 'training manuals for girls' serving 'to acculturate women to traditional social roles' (1986: 185, 200). Similarly, Karen Rowe argues that traditional fairy tales 'prescribe approved cultural paradigms which ease the female's assimilation into the adult community':

> The pattern of enchantment and disenchantment, the formulaic closing with nuptial rites, and the plot's comic structure seem so conventional that we do not question the implications. Yet, traditional patterns, no less than fantasy characterizations and actions, contribute to the fairy tale's potency as a purveyor of romantic archetypes and, thereby, of cultural precepts for young women. (1986: 212, 218)

But, if Carter was writing alongside a feminist critique which focuses on the damaging gender roles propagated by traditional fairy tale, she also saw the potential for 'recycling' the genre; its history of evolution. As Zipes argues, one of the primary tasks of feminist interventions in fairy tale has been:

> to discover how and why certain changes were made in the tales during the course of centuries so that women can regain a sense of their own history and possibly alter contemporary socio-political arrangements. (Zipes (ed.), 1986: 6)[8]

In her introduction to The Virago Book of Fairy Tales, Carter celebrates the adaptability of the genre: 'old wives of any sex can participate in this endless recycling process, when anyone can pick up a tale and make it over' (Carter (ed.), 1990: xi). Carter actively participates in this 'recycling process' in her recasting of the traditional tales.

It is also important to recognise that Carter is indebted to, and indeed writes from within, a feminist tradition of reappropriating the genre. As Zipes argues, 'women writers up to the present have felt compelled to confront the stereotypical fairy tale roles in some form or another to establish a sense of their own identities and voices' (Zipes (ed.), 1986: 10). Citing Carter alongside Tanith Lee, Joanna Russ, Anne Sexton and the Merseyside Fairy Tale Collective, among others, Zipes celebrates 'the great breadth and quality of experimental feminist fairy tales which seek to provoke the reader to re-examine his or her notion of sexual arrangements and the power politics of those arrangements' (Zipes (ed.), 1986: 12).

It is where Carter's preoccupations with fairy tale and pornography intersect that the most fierce criticism has arisen about her work. The stories in *The Bloody Chamber* have frequently been criticised via hostile readings of her contemporaneous, polemical non-fiction work, *The Sadeian Woman* ([1979] 1992b).[9] But if her fascination with fairy tale and her investigation of the sexual politics of sado-masochistic desire coalesce disturbingly in *The Bloody Chamber*, this is part of a deliberate engagement with the existing sado-masochistic power relations exhibited in the traditional tales.[10] Remarking on the sexual prohibitions inherent in classic fairy tales, Carter jokes, 'isn't the function of a good fairy tale to instil fear, trembling and the sickness unto death into the existential virgin, anyway?' (1976: 188). In her own versions she chose to foreground the latent sexual content of fairy tale in an attempt to address and make explicit the implicit ideologies and assumptions about sexual difference contained within the tales.

Carter's exploration of the sexual subtext of fairy tale in *The Bloody Chamber* should, therefore, be read in this light and in the context of other feminist fiction which attempts to challenge the traditional power structures of the genre. But, while Carter's project in reappropriating fairy tale is obviously a feminist one – to deconstruct myths about femininity contained within the tales – the success of this project has been questioned by some feminist critics, who have attacked the stories in *The Bloody Chamber* for failing to break the formulaic structures of fairy tale and ultimately reinscribing patriarchal power relations. Patricia Duncker, for instance, argues that Carter falls into an 'infernal trap inherent in fairy tale' which 'proves too complex and pervasive to avoid' (1984: 6). Duncker particularly takes issue with Carter's attempts to reappropriate pornography as a productive site for feminist intervention. Although she applauds Carter's 'ambition' in attempting to re-imagine these 'archetypes of imagination', Duncker suggests that 'she could go much further than she does' (1984: 3, 12).[11] Despite 'shifting the perspective from the impersonal voice to the inner confessional narrative as she does in several of the tales', Duncker argues, Carter 'merely explains, amplifies and reproduces rather than alters the original, deeply, rigidly sexist psychology of the erotic' (1984: 6). Avis Lewallen quotes at length from Duncker's essay, departing slightly from Duncker's analysis in her acknowledgment of this 'inner confessional narrative' as an ironic strategy which 'both acknowledges patriarchal structures and provides a form of critique against it' (1988: 147). However, despite her recognition of this 'ironic narrative stance', Lewallen argues, with Duncker, that the 'ideological parameters' of fairy tale remain intact and that Carter's rewritten tales remain 'ultimately politically untenable' (1988: 157).[12]

Duncker's (1984: 4) (and by extension Lewallen's) argument about the restrictive patriarchal structure of the tales relies on Andrea Dworkin's simplistic reading of traditional fairy tale as inherently sexist, and her concomitant, equally reductive, configuration of pornographic representation as necessarily exploitative.[13] But the sexual politics of the traditional tales, and their reception, are more complex and less inflexible than this 'anti-pornographic' feminist critique suggests.[14] As Zipes observes, implicit in Dworkin's analysis 'is the assumption that the tales are automatically received in fixed ways' (Zipes (ed.), 1986: 5).[15] It is this issue of the reception of the tales which most interests me. Merja Makinen sees the stories in *The Bloody Chamber* as 'an exuberant re-writing of the fairy-tales that actively engages the reader in a feminist deconstruction' (1992: 3), acknowledging the role of the reader alongside this ironic deconstructive technique.[16] Makinen argues, persuasively, for a feminist irony which 'enacts an oscillation that is itself deconstructive' (1992: 5), creating a productive space from which to critique patriarchal structures. While the reader must clearly have at least some awareness of feminist thinking to 'get' the irony of Carter's appropriative strategy, there is no reason, as Elaine Jordan has observed, 'for a feminist writer to assume naive readers, or for every reader to see all possible readings' (1994: 122).

In *The Bloody Chamber* Carter effectively challenges the formulaic structures of fairy tale from within, through a combination of this ironic narrative stance and a formal strategy which self-consciously foregrounds repetition and narrative doubling, allowing space for the interactive involvement of the reader in the interpretative act. As Jordan argues, *The Bloody Chamber* should not be seen as 'a coherent whole, but neither is it entirely heterogeneous and fragmentary. The fairy stories are played with and worked as different versions ("see what we can do with this one, then?")' (1994: 126). The various versions operate in dialogue with each other, as well as their classic precursors, and this multiplication of versions is further amplified by the mediated texts. Two versions of Beauty and the Beast interact, drawing attention to and revising the gender dynamics of the original tale. In 'The Courtship of Mr Lyon' the patriarchal bond between Beauty's father and the Beast is exaggerated and destabilised by another retelling, 'The Tiger's Bride', in which Beauty discovers her own beastliness.[17] Similarly, the intersections between the three wolf narratives, 'The Werewolf', 'The Company of Wolves' and 'Wolf-Alice', create a productive space from which to rewrite/reread the acculturating message of Perrault's Red Riding Hood.[18] Jack Zipes, in *The Trials and Tribulations of Little Red Riding Hood*, identifies the literary version of Red Riding Hood as a tale of male aggressivity against female sexuality outside the societal and cultural 'norm' – but significantly cites an earlier oral version in which Red Riding Hood outwits the wolf and escapes (Zipes, 1983: 5–6; see also Zipes (ed.), 1986: 228–9). In the literary versions, the cunning and ingenuity of the strong female folk heroine of the oral tradition is exchanged for the passive girl who gets her just deserts for straying from the path.

In *The Uses of Enchantment* (1979), Bruno Bettelheim explores the function of fairy tale in the process of socialisation. For Bettelheim, universal truths contained in the fantasy element of fairy tale, help children to explore and overcome the Oedipal stage in order to negotiate the difficult passage into adulthood and become assimilated into the symbolic order. Referring to Red Riding Hood, Bettelheim asserts:

> Deviating from the straight path in defiance of mother and superego was temporarily necessary for the young girl, to gain a higher state of personality organization ... She has learned that it is better to build father and mother, and their values, deeper and in more adult ways into one's superego, to become able to deal with life's dangers. (1979: 181)

This 'higher state of personality organization' refers to the girl's successful negotiation into the dominant ideology. Red Riding Hood learns to conform to the expectations of a patriarchal society. But while Bettelheim demonstrates the role of fairy tale in the socialisation of children to adult roles, he is unconcerned with the gender implications.[19] Carter rewrites the fairy tales in answer to Bettelheim as much as Perrault, consciously attempting to avoid fixing the tales in her own multiple versions.[20] Reversing the traditional telling of Red Riding Hood in the short story, 'The Company of Wolves', Carter foregrounds the latent sexual content of the original tale, so it becomes a tale of repression being liberated by libido, symbolised by the wolves. Rather than a rape myth, punishing female sexuality, Carter's version portrays a girl embracing the animal side of her self, asserting her sexuality, reversing the moral of the fairy tale, 'she eats the wolf, in effect' (Haffenden, 1985: 83).

As Makinen argues, the 'strengths', as well as the 'dangers' lie in the 'aggressive subversiveness' and 'active eroticism' of Carter's texts (1992: 3). If the use of an appropriative narrative strategy cannot guarantee right readings, it has never been Carter's project to write texts with fixed or restrictive meanings, feminist or otherwise; quite the opposite in fact. As we have seen, Carter's texts recognise and invite the imaginative activity of the reader.[21] Situating herself politically as a writer in 'Notes From the Front Line' she writes:

> I try, when I write fiction, to think on my feet – to present a number of propositions in a variety of different ways, and to leave the reader to construct her own fiction for herself from the elements of my fictions. (Reading is just as creative an activity as writing and most intellectual development depends upon new readings of old texts.) (1983d: 22)

One of the hazards of a formal strategy which invites the active imaginative involvement of the reader is that not all the readers will respond in the same way. There is always a danger, therefore, that the act of reappropriating patriarchal structures might be misinterpreted as actually upholding them. While recognising the risks of Carter's ironic, appropriative strategies, Jordan asserts that her writing remains 'constructive, productive and positive, for women and feminism' (1992: 120). Foregrounding 'Carter's insistence on the dialectical openness of her fictions', Jordan maintains that she 'accepts open-endedness, the possibility of different readings of her work, and she is not without contradictions' (1990: 35, 22). It is because of, not despite, these contradictions, that Carter's writing remains challenging for a feminist readership.

## The voice of fairy tale[22]

It has become almost axiomatic that women are silenced in and by patriarchal discourse. As Kaja Silverman observes, when women do speak their discourse is 'associated with unreliable, thwarted, or acquiescent speech' (1990: 309–10).[23] This silence, if not always literal, represents 'an absence of female voices and concerns from high culture' (Cameron (ed.), 1990: 4). As Deborah Cameron asserts in her introduction to *The Feminist Critique of Language*:

> If we look at a society's most prestigious linguistic registers – religious ceremonial, political rhetoric, legal discourse, science, poetry – we find women's voices for the most part silent – or rather, *silenced*, for it is not just that women do not speak: often they are explicitly *prevented* from speaking, either by social taboos, restrictions or by the more genteel tyrannies of custom and practice. (1990: 4)

Much feminist theory has been devoted to what Cameron has termed, 'the quest for the female voice in culture' (Carter (ed.), 1990: 3). Carter herself was well aware of these debates, recognising the 'patriarchal bias of the English language' in her article, 'The Language of Sisterhood' (1980b: 226–34).[24] She was equally concerned with giving expression to those elements which have been silenced by mainstream discourse in her fiction. Describing her own writing practice, she affirms 'it is so enormously important for women to write fiction *as* women – it is part of the slow process of decolonialising our language and our basic habits of thought' in order to create 'a means of expression for an infinitely greater variety of experience than has been possible heretofore, to say things for which no language previously existed' (1983d: 75).

Indeed, as Marina Warner suggests in her introduction to *The Second Virago Book of Fairy Tales*, Carter's involvement with the women's publishing house, Virago, clearly 'helped establish a woman's voice in literature as special, as *parti pris*, as a crucial instrument in the forging of an identity for post-imperial, hypocritical, fossilised Britain' (Carter (ed.), [1992] 1993: xv). These issues also find thematic expression in Carter's fiction, as Warner argues:

> The issue of women's speech, of women's noise, of their/our clamour and laughter and weeping and shouting and hooting runs through all Angela Carter's writings, and informed her love of the folk tale. (Carter (ed.), [1992] 1993: x)

When Aunt Margaret recovers her voice in *The Magic Toyshop* , she also finds her strength, 'a frail but constant courage like spun silk. Struck dumb on her wedding day, she found her old voice again the day she was freed' ([1967] 1981: 197). Carter's female characters become increasingly outspoken in her later novels. In *Nights at the Circus* Fevvers mesmerises Walser with her voice:[25]

> Her voice. It was as if Walser had become a prisoner of her voice, her cavernous, sombre voice, a voice made for shouting about the tempest, her voice of the celestial fishwife. Musical as it strangely was, yet not a voice for singing with; it comprised discords, her scale contained twelve tones. Her voice, with its warped, homely, Cockney vowels and random aspirates. Her dark, rusty, dipping, swooping voice, imperious as a siren's. (Carter, [1984] 1985: 43)

The novel rings with Fevvers' expansive laughter, guffawing 'uproariously' on the first page, and spilling out in a 'spiralling tornado' from the last.[26] The singing and dancing Chance Sisters, in *Wise Children* (1991a), are among Carter's most vocal characters.

Women's silence in patriarchal discourse is correlative with their marginalised position within the specular regime. As Luce Irigaray has argued, the scopic bias inherent in theoretical and philosophical discourse is gendered:

> Woman's desire has doubtless been submerged by the logic that has
> dominated the West since the time of the Greeks. Within this logic, the
> predominance of the visual, and of the discrimination and individual-
> isation of form, is particularly foreign to female eroticism. Woman takes
> pleasure more from touching than from looking, and her entry into the
> dominant scopic economy signifies, again, her consignment to passivity:
> she is to be the beautiful object of contemplation. (1985: 25–6)[27]

It is useful to return to the theorisation of sound in film theory and in
particular an area of feminist film theory and practice which attempts to
challenge the conventional configuration of sound/image and the
privileging of the visible in the hierarchy of the senses (see Doane, [1978]
1980: 47–60, [1980] 1986: 335–48). Silverman locates the specificity of
the female voice as point of resistance to the dominant ideology of the
visible, arguing that to allow woman 'to be heard without being seen ...
would disrupt the specular regime upon which mainstream cinema
relies; it would put her beyond the control of the male gaze' (1990: 313).
Silverman goes on to examine the ways in which feminist cinema has
attempted to 'exhume a female voice which has been repressed by
patriarchy'.[28] She argues that feminist film makers generally 'resort in
one way or another to the principle of non-synchronization, devising
various strategies for divorcing the female voice from the female body'
(Silverman, 1990: 315).[29] Silverman's theory has interesting implications
when it comes to radio with its dependence on the disembodied voice.

In a sense radio can be seen to occupy a similar position within the
ideology of the visible to that of woman within patriarchal discourse. Both
represent a blindspot which paradoxically operates both as a lack and an
excess within the dominant ideology.[30] Evoking Luce Irigaray's thesis that
'patriarchal culture has a heavier investment in seeing than in hearing',
Mary Ann Doane posits that 'the voice appears to lend itself readily as an
alternative to the image, as a potentially viable means whereby the woman
can "make herself heard"' (Doane, [1980] 1986: 346).[31] It would appear,
then, that radio might offer a unique space for the articulation of (female)
subjectivity because of its reliance on the voice.

In the radio plays, the 'inner confessional narrative' identified by
Lewallen in the The Bloody Chamber, is indeed given a material voice
through the use of dramatised interior monologues.[32] In Vampirella, for
example, most of the characterisation of the Countess takes place on the
thoughts microphone, which uses a back echo to make the voice seem
nearer and more intimate. Interior thoughts are spliced into the middle of
dialogue and characters break out of the action, speaking directly to the
audience. Carter encourages us to identify with the world of the Countess,
allowing us to witness her self-development and internal thought

processes, as well as her relationships with her father, Count Dracula, her governess and keeper, Mrs Beane and the Hero. The narrative flashes back and forth between the present and her childhood experiences as she tries to come to terms with her vampiric 'condition'. Mrs Beane tries to console her charge:

> COUNTESS. I am the lady of the castle. My name is exile. My name is anguish. My name is longing. Far, far from the world on the windy crests of the mountain, I am kept in absolute seclusion, my time passes in an endless revery [sic], a perpetual swooning. I am both the Sleeping Beauty and the enchanted castle; the princess drowses in the castle of her flesh.
> MRS BEANE. Hush, hush my dearie, don't distress yourself.
> COUNTESS. (Shivers.) Cold, so cold, Mrs Beane ... the wind creeps in through the cracks in the old stone and the fire never warms me.
> MRS BEANE. (To a child.) Now, you just stop feeling sorry for yourself and eat up your egg. Look, I've cut up your bread and butter into soldiers for you.
> COUNTESS. (As a child.) Shall I eat up the nice soldiers?
> MRS BEANE. Like a good girl, now ... och, your hands are like ice! (Carter, 1985: 90–1)[33]

We are also given apparently unmediated access to female subjectivity in the radio version of *The Company of Wolves*. Red Riding Hood describes herself, directly addressing the audience. This description occurs in the middle of Granny's old wives' tale about a werewolf who attacks a 'little girl just as old as you are' (Carter, 1985: 61). Red Riding Hood mentally rejects Granny's identification and the narrative is interrupted whilst she describes her own burgeoning sexuality. She has not yet started bleeding, on the cusp of womanhood, like the werewolf a "twixt and 'tween thing' (Carter, 1985: 64), neither adult nor child:

> RED RIDING HOOD. (Getting close. Far right.) Twelve. Going on thirteen, thirteen going on fourteen ... not such a little girl, for all that you baby me, Granny. Thirteen going on fourteen, the hinge of your life, when you are neither one thing nor the other, nor child nor woman, some magic, inbetween thing, an egg that holds its own future in it.
> An egg not yet cracked against the cup.
> I am the very magic space that I contain. I stand and move within an invisible pentacle, untouched, invincible, immaculate. Like snow. Waiting. The clock inside me, that will strike once a month, not yet ... wound ... up ...
> I don't bleed. I can't bleed.
> I don't know the meaning of the word, fear. Fear? (Carter, 1985: 61)

In the equivalent scene in the short story the theme of the girl's puberty is explored through the impersonal narrator. She exhibits the visible signs of puberty, 'her breasts have just begun to swell' and she has just started her menses, 'the clock inside her that will strike, henceforward, once a month'. She is full of potential, as yet untapped:

> She is an unbroken egg; she is a sealed vessel; she has inside her a magic space the entrance to which is shut tight with a plug of membrane; she is a closed system; she does not know how to shiver. She has her knife and she is afraid of nothing. (Carter, [1979] 1981: 113–14)

The radio play retains the 'literary' quality of the short story, sharing much of the same imagery, such as the egg and the clock, but an important change has occurred – namely the shift from narrative to drama. Rather than being described externally by the omnipresent, anonymous, third-person narrator of the short story, which implicitly situates the girl as the passive object of a (masculine) gaze, the radio play gives us access to Red Riding Hood's subjectivity as she describes herself on the thoughts microphone.[34] In 'vocalising' the 'inner confessional narrative' inferred in the short story and giving it a material voice, the radio plays could be said to offer a privileged space for the articulation of female subjectivity and desire.

## Problematics of a feminist politics of the voice

In Carter's radio plays, then, the female voice appears to offer an attractive alternative to the dominance of the specular economy in which women have been denied a role in discourse. But while it is tempting to read the female voice, and by extension radio, as offering an inherently radical alternative, as Doane warns, 'the notion of a political erotics of the voice is particularly problematic from a feminist perspective':

> to mark the voice as an isolated haven within patriarchy, or as having an essential relation to the woman, is to invoke the specter of feminine specificity, always recuperable as another form of 'otherness'. (Doane, [1980] 1986: 346)

Within feminist theory there has been a great deal of hostility towards that branch of feminism which calls on the female body or the voice as an alternative to patriarchal discourse. Toril Moi, for example, argues that Irigaray's 'attempt to establish a theory of femininity that escapes patriarchal specul(ariz)ation necessarily lapses into a form of essentialism' (Moi, 1989: 143, 147; see also Butler, 1993). She similarly criticises Cixous' 'lyrical, euphoric evocation of the essential bond between feminine writing and the mother as source and origin of the voice to be heard in all female texts'.[35] This privileging of the female voice, she argues, is consonant with Cixous' configuration of the pre-Oedipal maternal voice as a source of innate good (Moi, 1989: 114–15).[36] While Moi finds her biologism problematic, she also suggests that 'Cixous's vision of female/feminine writing as a way of reestablishing a spontaneous relationship to the physical *jouissance* of the female body may be read positively, as a utopian vision of female creativity in a truly non-oppressive and non-sexist society' (Moi, 1989: 121). However, for Moi, both Irigaray and Cixous neglect the material conditions of women's oppression, and consequently their utopian projects ultimately fall short.

Delineating the 'diversity of the feminist critique of language', Deborah Cameron argues that for some feminist critics, 'notions of women's or feminine language just aid and abet anti-feminist thinking' (Cameron (ed.), 1990: 10–11), ensuring that the female voice remains marginalised from rational, patriarchal discourse. She further suggests that for many feminists 'much of the feminist project of Irigaray *et al.* is completely utopian' with 'little concrete pay-off' (Cameron (ed.), 1990: 11). However, as Jean Grimshaw argues, whilst Irigaray is often accused of such 'biological essentialism' and 'regressive Utopianism', she is in fact more concerned with 'how it might be possible to "deconstruct" or expose that which is "hidden" in Western philosophy' (1992: 112). For Grimshaw, Irigaray's evocation of the body is a risky, but nevertheless subversive strategy.[37] By drawing attention to the marginalisation of woman within patriarchal culture, and foregrounding their exclusion from the specular economy, she posits the possibility of challenging the dominant ideology of visible. Thus, although it is necessary to problematise the essentialising tendencies of 'French feminisms', it is also important not to dismiss their utopian potential.[38]

Carter herself has an equivocal relationship with this area of feminist theory, as Sally Keenan has observed, offering a challenge,

> albeit an oblique one, to the revisionary psychoanalytic theories of the French feminists, especially Hélène Cixous and Julia Kristeva, in whose work, during the 1970s, motherhood and the maternal body assume crucial significance in a variety of ways. (Keenan, 1997: 134)

Citing *The Sadeian Woman*, Keenan suggests that Carter rejects 'the recreation of mother goddesses or the eco-feminists' reassertion of Nature as Mother' inherent in much 1970s feminist theorising (Keenan, 1997: 134). It is possible to read the many-breasted, castrating figure of Mother and her female commune, Beulah, in *The Passion of New Eve* ([1977] 1990) as an overt parody of the biologism of French feminisms and radical feminist separatism alike. But Carter's attitude towards these feminisms is more complicated than this analysis suggests. As demonstrated in the Introduction, there has recently been a growing recognition of Carter's oscillation between a variety of feminist perspectives, from utopian to materialist, in her own writing practice. This oscillation, which marks a refusal to come to rest in a definitive feminist position, is demonstrated in Carter's treatment of the voice in radio.[39]

## Colluding with the voice of patriarchy

Carter is clearly aware of the problematics of a feminist politics based on the specificity of the female voice. While she attempts to create a productive space for female subjectivity, with the interior monologues of the central female protagonists, she also gives material voice to the mouthpieces of patriarchal culture. As Doane asserts:

> it must be remembered that, while psychoanalysis delineates a pre-oedipal scenario in which the voice of the mother dominates, the voice, in psychoanalysis, is also the instrument of interdiction, of the patriarchal order. ([1980] 1986: 346)

The patriarchal figure of Count Dracula haunts *Vampirella* with the 'faint rumble' of his 'posthumous chuckle' (Carter, 1985: 92). His sinister tones loom over the entire play, opening with his description of the ritual used to track down vampires: 'they choose a young virgin boy who is a pure maiden, that is to say, who has not yet known any woman, and set him bareback on a stallion that has not mounted its first mare' (Carter, 1985: 84), and ending with his last words: 'The shadow of the Fatal Count rises over every bloody battlefield. Everywhere, I am struck down; everywhere, I celebrate my perennial resurrection' (Carter, 1985: 116). At the climax of the play, the moment of the Countess's transformation, the Count moans in the background as he witnesses the end of his line:

> COUNT. ... Choking ... Airless ...
> HERO. (*Thoughts microphone.*) She's rich enough to pay for treatment, in all conscience. Oh the poor girl. A ghastly affliction.
> *Bedroom.*
> COUNTESS. I feel ... almost a healthy sleepiness come upon me. Will you ... would you ... could you give a goodnight kiss?
> [...] *The Count moans and gurgles.*
> COUNT. Is a millennium of beastliness to expire upon a *kiss*? (Carter, 1985: 114–15)[40]

Working in tandem with voice of the Count, the Hero's commentary attempts to contain, to a certain extent, the expression of the Countess' subjectivity. His diagnosis of the Countess as 'a poor, sick girl' in need of the 'therapeutic couch' of a Viennese doctor, deliberately recalls the patriarchal discourse of Freudian psychoanalysis in which female deviance is configured as madness (Carter, 1985: 112–13). But we are later invited to enter into the Countess' subjectivity and reject his classification.

The Hero and his bicycle are the modern-day equivalents of the virgin and the stallion. Based on a *Boys' Own* stereotype, he is portrayed with an abundance of 'stiff-upper-lip', and boyish optimism: 'my colonel assures me I have nerves of steel' (Carter, 1985: 86). He is embarking on a cycling adventure in the Carpathians:

> HERO. (*Brisker, less introspective tone.*) [...] On two wheels in the land of the vampires! A suitable furlough for a member of the English middle classes. [...]
>
> Nobody is surprised to see me, they guess at once where I come from. The coarse peasants titter a little behind their hands. Le Monsieur Anglais! But they behave with deference; for only a man with an empire on which the sun never sets to support him would ride a bicycle through this phantom-haunted region. (Carter, 1985: 87)

The irony of the Hero's faith in empire is fuelled both by our postcolonial perspective and his impending death in a war which, as Carter points out, 'was more hideous by far than any of our fearful superstitious imaginings' (1985: 9–10). He is unable to understand the 'coarse peasants', expecting them to be able to speak his language, 'No spik English, eh?' (Carter, 1985: 87, 89). His assumed social superiority is revealed as much by the content of his speech, as his tone of voice.[41] Carter was well aware of the power of aural suggestion, maintaining that 'the rich textures of radio are capable of stating ambiguities with a dexterity over and above that of the printed word. The human voice itself imparts all manner of subtleties in its intonations' (1985: 10). The dramatic representation of character on radio is firmly linked with tone of voice. Gill Branston and Roy Stafford acknowledge the importance of the cultural codes of the speaking voice in radio, arguing that pitch, texture and shape, together with accent, dialect and language registers all contribute to the cultural signification of the voice. (Branston and Stafford, 1996: 21–5). As psychologists G. W. Allport and H. Cantrill demonstrate, the accent, intonation and pitch of the voice trigger both psychological and social assumptions about character:

> most people who listen to radio speakers feel assured that some of their judgments are dependable. Often the impression is nothing more than a feeling of favour or aversion, but sometimes it represents a surprisingly definitive judgement concerning the speakers' physical, intellectual, and moral qualities. (Allport and Cantrill, 1972: 155)

If the listener's identification process is affected by tone of voice, then the short and clipped voice of the Hero does not invite a positive identification. In fact, whereas we are encouraged to identify with the Countess through her interior monologues, Carter consciously alienates us from the Hero. His speech patterns are simultaneously nervous and smug, conjuring up a complacent young man, who represents a patriarchal order completely at home in the belief of its own ascendancy.[42]

However, for Carter the male voice is no more inherently patriarchal than the female voice is liberatory. In *Puss in Boots* the Hero and Puss counterbalance the patriarchal Pantaleone, and *The Company of Wolves* ends with Red Riding Hood falling asleep in the arms of the tender Werewolf as he tells her a story: 'Are you listening? Are you sleeping?' (Carter, 1985: 81).[43] Furthermore, far from upholding the female voice as some inherently utopian space from within which women's discourse can finally be heard, Carter acknowledges what Warner has described as 'women's collusion in their own subjection' in her introduction to *The Virago Book of Fairy Tales* (Carter (ed.), [1992] 1993: xv). Indeed, the voice of patriarchy often speaks directly through the female characters in the radio plays. If the Count and the Hero represent the voice of interdiction in *Vampirella*, then so, to a certain extent, does Mrs Beane. Similarly, the Hag in *Puss in Boots* acts as Pantaleone's willing gaoler, safeguarding the chastity of his young wife.[44]

The voice of interdiction also spills forth from the mouth of Granny in the radio version of *The Company of Wolves*, which will form the focus of the remainder of this chapter. Granny's old wives' tales are designed to frighten Red Riding Hood:

> GRANNY. Fear and flee the wolf, my little one. [...] Oh, my sweet grandchild, whatever you do in the winter weather, never stray from the path through the forest or –
> RED RIDING HOOD. (*By Granny.*) What will happen to me, then, Granny?
> GRANNY. You'll be lost, instantly, and the wolves will find you! And always be home by nightfall or the wolves will ...
> RED RIDING HOOD. What will they do if they catch me?
> GRANNY. Why ... gobble you up!
> *Making a game of it, she growls at Red Riding Hood, who giggles delightedly.*
> RED RIDING HOOD. (*Running to right.*) Stop it Granny, you're tickling!
> GRANNY. Grrr!
> *Granny's growls get closer and more menacing. Take down background as the growls crossfade to rending sounds. A piercing scream cuts rending sounds and we are left with cold wind.* (Carter, 1985: 59)

Warning Red Riding Hood about the dangers in the forest, Granny pretends to gobble her up. As Carter maintains, this interaction with the listener, in which the story-teller jumps on the child pretending to be the wolf, is part of the tale's history as a 'rough nursery game with a real moral' (Haffenden, 1985: 84).[45] But, disturbingly, Granny's playful gobbling noises turn into sinister growls and then the sounds of flesh rending and bones crunching, implicating her in beastliness. If we return to 'The Werewolf', another retelling of Red Riding Hood which precedes 'The Company of Wolves' in *The Bloody Chamber* ([1979] 1981), it becomes clear that if wolves are not always what they seem then neither are grannies. In fact, Granny turns out to be the werewolf.[46] Elaine Jordan argues, effectively, that Carter's 'revision of the fairytale has one obvious project':

> to question and reverse the age-old wisdom that wolves rather than prohibitive mentors are to be feared, and that sexual initiation is a kind of extinction. (Jordan, 1990: 28)

By conflating the roles of Granny and the wolf, Carter foregrounds Granny's collusion in the patriarchal oppression of female sexuality: Granny symbolises 'Mother Goose as agent for repression' (Carter, 1983e: 368). Thus Carter demonstrates that the female voice is no safe haven from patriarchal order, however attractive an utopian politics of the female voice may appear.

## Interactive story-telling

Oral story-telling, however, is a two-way process, in which the listener is able to affect the outcome of the tale. As Carter maintains, 'The narrative drive is powered by the question: "What happened then?" The fairy tale is user-friendly; it always comes up with an answer to that question' (Carter (ed.), 1990: xxi). In the radio version of *The Company of Wolves*, Carter dramatises the dialogue between Granny and Red Riding Hood, recreating the oral tradition in such a way as to recognise the agency of the listener. Red Riding Hood's subjectivity offers a point of resistance to Granny's prohibitive voice:

> GRANNY. [...] If you spy a naked man among the pines, my dearie, you must run as if the devil were after you.
> RED RIDING HOOD. A naked man? In *this* weather? He'd have his thinguma-jigs frozen off, Granny!
> *She laughs.*
> GRANNY. Well, just watch out!
> *But Red Riding Hood continues to laugh.* (Carter, 1985: 69)[47]

The patriarchal voice of interdiction may speak but, as Carter demonstrates, we do not have to heed it. In fact we can talk back. In the introduction to *Expletives Deleted*, she writes 'I spent a great many years being told what I ought to think, and how I ought to behave, and how I ought to write, even, because I was a woman … but then I stopped listening to them and tried to figure it out for myself but they didn't stop talking, oh, dear no. So I started answering back' (Carter, 1992: 5). Carter dramatises this 'back talk' in the radio version of *The Company of Wolves*. It is the interchange between the articulation of female subjectivity, and the voice of interdiction wherein lies the most productive reading of the voice in Carter's writing for radio.

In order to illustrate the dialogue between these two voices it is fruitful to make a detailed textual analysis of the radio play. Comparing the same sequence in the two versions, it is possible to argue that the radio play develops and extends the radical feminist message of the short story. In the short story, what I shall call the Hunter scene occurs in the middle of a series of anecdotes about werewolf lore which form the first half of the tale:

> So this hunter dug a pit and put a duck in it, for bait, all alive-oh; and he covered the pit with straw smeared with wolf dung. Quack, quack! went the duck and a wolf came slinking out of the forest, a big one, a heavy one, he weighed as much as a grown man and the straw gave way beneath him – into the pit he tumbled. The hunter jumped down after him, slit his throat, cut off all his paws for a trophy.
>
> And then no wolf at all lay in front of the hunter but the bloody trunk of a man, headless, footless, dying, dead. (Carter, 1985: 111)

The short story already exhibits elements of an oral story-telling tradition with the colloquial language 'all alive-oh', the onomatopoeic 'quack' of the duck and repetitive rhythm of the sentence structure.

The radio play utilises a number of narrative voices in addition to the short story's detached, omnipresent, third-person narrator. Granny, the Hunter, Red Riding Hood and the Werewolf also contribute, each offering a different perspective on the tale. This multiplication of narrative points of view foregrounds the act of story telling, aligning the radio play even more closely with the oral tradition.[48] In the short story the Hunter scene is one of many in a series of werewolf stories; in the radio play it becomes a dramatic space in which the dynamic of story-telling itself is acted out. Where no specific audience is implied in the short story, in the radio play Granny tells the tale to Red Riding Hood. In both versions, rather than perpetuating the fixed narrative transaction of the literary fairy tales, Carter's story-telling acknowledges and makes space for the interpretative act. Where the short story invites an interrogative reading because of its positioning in relation to the other werewolf stories in *The Bloody*

*Chamber,* this technique is exaggerated in the radio play where the various narrative voices compete within the text to give different and sometimes conflicting points of view.

As Granny narrates the story we hear distant shouting, sheep bleating and dogs barking. Then Red Riding Hood interjects: 'So, what happened to the poor wolf, then?' (Carter, 1985: 62), emphasising the interactive nature of oral story-telling. Continuing the narrative, Granny is indicated by the domestic sounds of the crackling fire, the ticking clock and clicking knitting needles – which create an interior ambience. Temporal and spatial movement is created using sound-effects and acoustic images. We move to an exterior background – the wind rises, we hear digging – and the Hunter takes over the narration of his own tale in mid-sentence:

> *Fade in digging. Exterior acoustic from fireplace and spread to cover stereo*
> *picture. Fade domestic noises.*
> GRANNY. And this hunter dug –
> HUNTER. (*Centre. Close.*) – a pit, with steep sides. A deep pit. A wolf-trap.
> And in this pit I stuck a sharpened stake and tied to this stake by a
> string around its left leg a fine –
> *Quacking, fluttering of wings.*
> (*With fluttering of wings.*) Now, you just stop that flapping and hold still!
> (Carter, 1985: 62)

The narrative slips into the present tense – the action occurring in 'real time' – with the invisible duck conjured up out of thin air by sound-effects and the Hunter's words: 'now, you just stop that flapping and hold still!'. While the Hunter narrates we hear the duck flapping, followed by undergrowth stirring, duck quacking, grass rustling, barking and growling, screaming, throat slitting, and the 'thwack and dull thud' of a paw being lopped off (Carter, 1985: 63). The Hunter shifts from the role of narrator to participant in the action, the narrative cutting from past to present and back again, with Granny intervening in the story-telling. The scene climaxes with the description of the werewolf transformation from three narrative points of view, culminating with the Narrator's detailed description of the paw changing back into a hand. The use of the 'close' microphone, with no background acoustics, creates a very chilling effect:

> GRANNY. (*Far left.*) Upon the ground the hunter saw there fall no paw at all
> but –
> HUNTER. (*From the pit.*) A hand! A man's hand!
> *Wind faded out:*
> NARRATOR. (*Centre. Close.*) The desperate claws retract, refine themselves as
> if attacked by an invisible emery board, until suddenly they become
> fingernails and could never have been anything but fingernails, or so it
> would seem. The leather pads soften and shrink until you could take

fingerprints from them, until they have turned into fingertips. The clubbed tendons stretch, the foreshortened phalanges extend and flesh out, the bristling hair sinks backwards into the skin without leaving a trace of stubble behind it. (Carter, 1985: 63)[49]

In the radio play, before the scene reaches its final denouement, a strange sequence occurs which appears to take place in the mind of Red Riding Hood as she listens to Granny's story-telling. The Werewolf (whom she later meets in the forest) invites Red Riding Hood to identify with him: 'Now my skin is the same kind of skin as your skin, little sister. There! my hand ... won't you take hold of my hand?' (Carter, 1985: 63). The atmosphere is sexually charged. The Werewolf's voice is deep, low and suggestive. Red Riding Hood gasps at the invitation, a sound which can at once be interpreted as surprise and sensual arousal. This unexplained sequence interrupts the flow of the narrative. In the act of listening to Granny's story (which is intended to scare her), Red Riding Hood reappropriates the tale and instead of fearing, she identifies with, and possibly desires, the wolf. The tale has its own resonance in her imagination and she goes on to explore this identification/desire through the narration of a brief story about her own experience with wolves. Interrupting Granny's tale, she addresses the audience directly on the thoughts microphone:

> RED RIDING HOOD. (*Close. Far right.*) Once, one winter when I was little, my father took me out into the wood and we found the track of a wolf, prints as big as dinner-plates, and my father took a good grip of his rifle and peered around but I put my little foot into the print, to match it for size, and I felt all the warmth that lies under the snow swallow me up. (Carter, 1985: 63–4)

The action of mirroring the wolf's footprint and the feelings of warmth and incorporation exhibit a strong identification with the wolf, which runs counter to both the father's protective instincts, and the acculturating intentions of Granny's cautionary tale. Carter uses the full breadth of the sound screen, situating Red Riding Hood on the close microphone, 'far right', further distancing her from Granny who, situated 'far left', continues her narration, using almost the exact words of the short story: 'And now no wolf at all lay before the hunter but the bloody trunk of – ' and again the Hunter picks up mid-sentence, 'So I may never touch another drop, it was a man, with his throat cut and handless, bleeding, dying ...' and the Narrator finishes with an abrupt and hollow 'Dead' on close microphone (Carter, 1985: 64).

The radio play uses the extra dimension of sound to achieve dramatic shifts in time and space – from the narrative present of Granny's fireside story-telling indicated by the 'domestic background' (Carter, 1985: 64), to the imagined forest of the story suggested by an exterior acoustic and spot-effects of rustling grass and crashing branches (Carter, 1985: 62) and Red Riding Hood's interior thoughts on close microphone. Thus we are given extensive access to Red Riding Hood's subjectivity in the radio play. In addition to her imaginative engagement with the tale, Carter also allows her to comment out loud at the end of Granny's narrative. Again, she responds by empathising with, rather than fearing the wolf, her continued identification once more throwing Granny's instructive intentions into relief:

> *Bring up and fade domestic background.*
> RED RIDING HOOD. (*Thoughtful.*) But I would be sorry for the poor thing, whatever it was, man or beast or some benighted 'twixt and 'tween thing, trapped by a mean trick and finished off without its supper. (Carter, 1985: 64)

By putting the werewolf lore in Granny's mouth, Carter highlights the practice of using myth and legend in the process of acculturation, and more specifically the role of women in the perpetuation of these patriarchal systems of signification. But by dramatising the process of narrative transmission and inserting an audience for the story, Carter is able to juxtapose Granny's intention with Red Riding Hood's reception of the tale, foregrounding the agency of the listener in that transaction. Red Riding Hood is given an active voice with which to negotiate an independent path through Granny's narrative. She takes part in the telling of the tale, both on an imaginative level and via direct interjection. Refusing to subscribe to Granny's interpretation, she mentally and verbally contributes her own alternatives.

Thus the radio play could be seen to develop and extend the radical project of the short story – both thematically and on a formal level – because of this foregrounding of the interactive process of narration which creates a transformative space in which the listener can contribute to the meaning of the tale.[50] Carter recognises the voice both as the site of interdiction and resistance. As she argued in 'Notes From the Front Line', 'language is power, life and the instrument of culture, the instrument of domination *and* liberation' (1983d: 77, emphasis mine). The real radical potential of the voice in Carter's radio, therefore, stems not from a straightforward privileging of the female voice, nor from a simple recognition of the role of women in processes of acculturation, but from the negotiation between these two configurations of the female voice.

## Notes

1 As Marina Warner asserts, Carter 'first began developing her interest in folklore, discovering with her husband the folk and jazz music scenes of the 1960s' (Carter (ed.), [1992] 1993: xiii).

2 See Carter (1976: 188–9, 1983e: 367–8, 1997: 465–7, 473–5, 476–7), Carter ((ed. and trans.), 1977, 1982), Carter ((ed.), 1990, [1992] 1993). This final posthumous collection is introduced by Marina Warner, who writes that Carter 'did not have the strength, before she died, to write the introduction she had planned to this volume, but she left four cryptic notes among her papers' (Carter (ed.), [1992] 1993: xi).

3 While the influence of fairy tale can be traced back to her early fiction, particularly *The Magic Toyshop* (1967), Carter's explicit political engagement with the genre can be traced from her 1977 translation of Charles Perrault and *The Bloody Chamber* (1979).

4 As argued in Chapter 1, those critics who do mention the radio plays use them to elucidate the short stories, without understanding the mutual relationship between Carter's writing for radio and her engagement with fairy tale.

5 Carter writes, 'I sweated out the heatwave browsing through Perrault's *Contes du temps passé* on the pretext of improving my French' during the drought of summer 1976 (1976: 189). Much of this article makes it into the foreword of *The Fairy Tales of Charles Perrault* (Carter (ed. and trans.), 1977). See Table 1.1 (p. 28) for full transmission details of the radio plays.

6 Radio is also an amplification in the sense that, as a medium of mass-communication, it expands the close-knit, familial audience of the oral tradition to include a larger radio community.

7 As Jack Zipes argues, 'feminist discussion about the social and cultural effect of fairy tales began in the early 1970s' (Zipes (ed.), 1986: 4).

8 For the Marxist Zipes, feminist rewritings of fairy tales are 'socially symbolic acts to pursue alternatives to the destructive and also self-destructive processes in American and British child rearing and socialisation ... As a cultural phenomenon, the new feminist fairy tales seek to break boundaries and speak in the name of future generations which may not need a feminist literature of this kind in the future' (Zipes (ed.), 1986: 13–14).

9 Merja Makinen comments on Carter's reputation as the 'high-priestess of post-graduate porn' (Makinen, 1992: 3). Carter's exploration of de Sade is part of a broader investigation of pornographic representation in her fiction and journalism. See 'Once More into the Mangle', 'Lovely Linda', 'A Well-Hung Hang-Up', 'Japanese Erotica' and 'Titillation' all collected in *Nothing Sacred* (1982d). 'I owe a great deal to pornography' she writes in 'The Power of Porn' (1977: 9), blaming her higher education on the lifting of the *Lady Chatterley* ban.

10 She identified the relationship between the two in her earliest journalism on fairy tale. 'The wolf consumes Red Riding Hood' in the original tale, she asserts 'what else do you expect if you talk to strange men, comments Perrault briskly. Let's not bother our heads with the mysteries of sado-masochistic attraction, we must learn to cope with the world before we can interpret it' (Carter, 1976: 189). A similar line appears in the foreword to *The Fairy Tales of Charles Perrault* (1977: 17–18). Remarking on the sexual violence implicit in Hans Christian Andersen's stories, Carter blithely suggests that a 'sensitive child might come to less harm if he sticks to soft-core porn, rather than Andersen. That extraordinary series of French comic books called *Contes Féerotiques*, for example, in which the seven dwarfs sport erections larger than themselves, and one is left in no doubt as to exactly what kind of Beast it was the Beauty married' (1976: 188).

11 One of Duncker's main criticisms is what she sees as Carter's heterosexual bias: 'some things are unthinkable. She could never imagine Cinderella in bed with the Fairy God-mother' and her failure to break out of the 'power imbalance inherent in all heterosexual relationships' (1984: 11).

12  As Makinen asserts (1992: 4), Duncker and Lewallen read Carter as failing to 'revision the conservative form for a feminist politics, and so her attempts at constructing an active female erotic are badly compromised – if not a reproduction of male pornography'. But, as she goes on to argue, it is not Carter, but 'the critics who cannot see beyond the sexist binary opposition'.

13  See Dworkin (1974, 1982). More recent feminist research indicates that the dynamics of pornographic identification are more complicated than Dworkin's analysis suggests. See, for example, Wicke (1993: 62–80).

14  I borrow Elaine Jordan's terminology here (1992: 119). Taking issue with Duncker, Susanne Kappeler and Robert Clark, among others, Jordan offers a sustained resistance to this 'anti-pornographic' reading of Carter's work in a series of three essays: 'Enthralment: Angela Carter's Speculative Fictions' (1990), 'The Dangers of Angela Carter' (1992) and 'The Dangerous Edge' (1994).

15  Zipes argues that while raising 'important questions about classical fairy tales', she fails to address 'their Utopian allure and historical evolution' (Zipes (ed.), 1986: 6).

16  Makinen quotes feminist artist, Mary Kelly, who argues 'there is no such thing as a homogeneous mass-audience. You can't make art for everyone. And if you're enjoyed within a particular movement or organisation, then the work is going to participate in its debates' (Makinen, 1992: 6, citing Kelly, 1984).

17  Ellen Cronan Rose (1983: 222–5) offers an insightful analysis of the ways in which these two retellings inform each other.

18  In the dialogue between 'The Werewolf' and 'The Company of Wolves', Carter is able to suggest that wolves do not automatically symbolise male sexual aggression, which is how the wolf is often read by feminist critics. For example, Avis Lewallen argues 'another beast that rears its sexual head in various guises is the wolf … in "The Company of Wolves", sexual choice becomes a question of straightforward survival in a seemingly natural, brutally physical male world' (1988: 53); similarly Maggie Anwell suggests that 'if it is seen as a moral fable in the Perrault vein, then its message can only be that willing acceptance of male aggression is the best way to guarantee survival' (1988: 78).

19  Carter argues that Bettelheim is 'terrific with children, but I think he is sometimes wrong' (Haffenden, 1985: 82).

20  In interview with John Haffenden (1985: 83), Carter states that 'some of the stories in *The Bloody Chamber* are the result of quarrelling furiously with Bettelheim'.

21  As argued in Chapter 1, she was attracted to the 'open-endedness' of radio as a medium, with its space for the listener's imagination (Carter, 1985: 7). As I go on to demonstrate in this chapter, Carter's radio drama foregrounds the interactive nature of fairy tale and the active role of the listener in the narrative transaction.

22  This title is appropriated from 'The Voice of Fairy Tale', a conference at Birkbeck College, University of London, November 1994, at which Marina Warner, author of *From the Beast to the Blonde: On Fairytales and Their Tellers* (1994), was a keynote speaker.

23  Silverman refers specifically to women's exclusion from mainstream cinematic discourse, but her argument is also current in feminist theory as a whole.

24  As ever refusing to toe the politically correct feminist line, Carter simultaneously mocks the jargon of sisterhood while recognising its radical potential: 'The language of my militant sisters reflects reality in the way that the language of any politico-religious subgroup does, partially, with its own polemical, subversive bias' (1980b: 234).

25  The abused Mignon, too, finds her singing voice (Carter, [1984] 1985: 142).

26  Fevvers' laughter recalls Hélène Cixous', 'The Laugh of the Medusa' ([1976] 1980: 264), in which she calls on feminine writing 'to smash everything, to shatter the framework of institutions, to blow up the law, to break up the "truth" with laughter'. Conversely, Paulina Palmer reads this via Bakhtinian Carnivalesque, commenting on the 'subversive potential of laughter': 'As well as irreverently mocking the existing political order, it is socially and psychically liberating' (1987: 201). Significantly, Aunt Margaret

breaks her silence with laughter, in the film, *The Magic Toyshop*, see Chapter 6.

27 This 'discrimination and individualisation of form' refers to the construction of sexual difference in which the woman's lack of visible genitals provides the moment of 'revelation' in Freudian psychoanalysis, one of those 'patriarchal models of knowledge' which has its locus in the scopic realm. As Toril Moi argues, 'Freud's theory of sexual difference is based on the *visibility* of difference: it is the eye that decides what is clearly true and what isn't' (1989: 132).

28 Silverman quotes Laura Mulvey describing her avant-garde feminist film, *Riddles of the Sphinx*, 'I felt the time had come not to deal with that kind of silence which so many in the women's movement had felt and talked about, a kind of cultural silence, essentially. Having taken that as a fact, one had to go ahead and try to fill in the gaps and think of ways one would give voice to female desires' (Silverman, 1990: 315, citing Mulvey and Wollen, 1979: 24). It is notable that Mulvey, the seminal theorist of the male gaze, should be interested in the voice in her own cinematic practice. Theories of the gaze are discussed in detail in Chapters 4–6.

29 While Silverman's article is useful, the limitations of this feminist strategy are clear. Her configuration of the subversive potential of the disembodied female voice implies that women cannot have authority as coherent speaking subjects. Whilst this tactic successfully avoids both the male gaze and the biologism of 'French feminisms', to deny woman a physical presence seems, to me, to be equally ghettoising.

30 One of the reasons for the marginalisation of the medium may well be that it is gendered as female, with its association with the domestic (think of 'Listen with Mother' and 'Woman's Hour', for example).

31 Doane does not directly cite Irigaray, but refers the reader to Heath (1978: 83–4) for a 'fuller discussion of the relationship some feminists establish between the voice and woman' (Doane, [1980] 1986: 348). See also Cixous' evocation of the maternal voice in 'The Laugh of Medusa' in this connection ([1976] 1980).

32 As David Wade argues 'a prominent feature of radio's dramatic structure became the interior monologue, conveying to the listener pictures which are, by definition, solely of the mind' (1981: 238).

33 It is necessary to reiterate the difference between text and performance, and to foreground the inherent difficulties in describing an aural medium using words. I have had to rely on detailed description of the performance, in addition to extensive quotation from the written script, in order to give some idea of the richness of the play. Note the irony of the buttered soldiers referring to her potential victim, the Hero, himself a soldier, who will 'animate' her with his blood: 'nothing – nothing, I assure you! – animates me half so much as the presence of a stranger ... My castle is famed for its hospitality', the black humour reinforced by the 'faint rumble of the Count's posthumous chuckle' (Carter, 1985: 92). To avoid confusion with authorial ellipses, my own ellipses will appear in square brackets when quoting from the radio plays.

34 The film finds alternative ways of representing female sexuality, as discussed in Chapter 5.

35 Moi goes on to argue that for Cixous, 'femininity in writing can be discerned in a privileging of the *voice* ... The speaking woman *is* entirely her voice ... Woman, in other words, is wholly and physically present in her voice – and writing is no more than the extension of this self-identical prolongation of the speech act' (Moi, 1989: 114). Jacqueline Rose (1986: 4) similarly warns against the 'too easy assimilation of the underside of language to an archaic femininity gone wild'.

36 Moi suggests that for Cixous, the 'voice in each woman moreover, is not only her own, but springs from the deepest layers of her psyche: her own speech becomes the echo of the primeval *song* she once heard ... It is, in short, the Voice of the Mother, that omnipotent figure that dominates the fantasies of the pre-Oedipal baby' (Moi, 1989: 114). As I go on to argue this Kleinian figure of the Good Mother fails to acknowledge the role of women in the acculturation process.

37 Irigaray's strategy of mimesis could be linked to Carter's risky appropriative strategies discussed in the Introduction.

38 I am conscious of being guilty of reductionism in using this term. While it is useful shorthand to refer to notions of writing the female body, and feminine writing associated with theorists such as Cixous/Irigaray/Kristeva, I do not wish to elide the differences between them.

39 As outlined in the Introduction, Carter's oscillating feminist strategy informs my own multiperspectival approach to her work.

40 The pun on airless/heirless, more conspicuous in performance, must be intentional in this play which foregrounds the patriarchal basis of vampirism.

41 Carter had considerable input on the language registers of her characters, as demonstrated by the detailed dialect instructions in her character notes for *A Self-Made Man*. Augustus John, for example, is 'bluff; upper class', Siegfried Sassoon, 'upper class but less offensively so', even stipulating that the 'upper class characters talk with "Edwardian" accents. Please listen to Archive records if you feel you need guidance' (Mark Bell, editor of Carter, *The Curious Room*, 1996, has generously given me access to this unpublished archive material).

42 Reformulating the radio play, Carter chose to downplay this aspect of the Hero's character. In 'The Lady of the House of Love' the first-person point of view of the soldier exists to a limited extent – we get some interior monologue – but most of the character-isation is filtered through the impersonal narrator. This paradoxically serves to heighten identification with the soldier, whereas you might expect it to make us less sympathetic. The absence of the short, clipped, military voice leaves more to the reader's imagination than in the radio play, where the voice is already blueprinted. In the story the soldier is portrayed as an object of physical desire, 'blond, blue-eyed, heavy-muscled' ([1979] 1981: 97). Elaine Jordan describes him as the Countess' 'lovely young lover' doomed 'to the carnage of the First World War' (1992: 126). In the radio play the Hero is rather more implicated in that carnage by his more explicit association with the officer class.

43 The Werewolf tells a reconciliatory tale, reminiscent of 'Peter and the Wolf' (1982) in Carter ([1985] 1986) and the almost identical, uncollected 'Cousins' (1980a).

44 Though, Mrs Beane is a more equivocal figure than the Hag. A 'free-thinker' with 'pawky Scots humour', she has her own bloody past with the cannibal Sawney Beane. An independent, working woman, Mrs Beane's pragmatism offsets the passivity of the Countess, even if she is in the pay of the patriarchal Count. By replacing her with a dumb crone, the short story downplays the often ambivalent and contradictory role of women's collusion with patriarchal power (Carter, 1985: 116, 90).

45 Carter describes her grandmother reading Red Riding Hood to her as a child, 'when she came to the part about the wolf jumping on Little Red Riding Hood and eating her up, she used to jump on me and pretend to eat me. Like all small children, I loved being tickled and nuzzled: I found it bliss, and I'd beg her to reiterate the story to me just for the sake of this ecstatic moment. When I was researching the story I looked at a facsimile of Perrault's manuscript, and I found that when he comes to the bit about the wolf jumping on Little Red Riding Hood, it says in the margin "The story-teller should do likewise" – so that acting out the story has always been part of the story, traditionally' (Haffenden, 1985: 83).

46 Some critics have found the grandmother's violent death problematic (particularly Clark, 1987: 147–61), but Carter is clearly not suggesting that all grannies are to be mistrusted.

47 This of course recalls both Cixous', 'The Laugh of Medusa' ([1976] 1980), and Fevvers' laughter at the end of *Nights at the Circus* ([1984] 1985).

48 The radio play as a whole is more concerned with the process of story-telling than the short story, and this also forms the basis for the emphasis on story-telling in the film, where the Red Riding Hood figure, Rosaleen, is given an active role as story-teller, see Chapter 5.

49 There is a significant shift in emphasis in the handling of the werewolf transformation in the radio play. I will discuss this aspect of the scene in more detail in Chapter 5 in relation to the graphic animatronic metamorphoses in the film adaptation.

50 This emphasis on the interactive nature of story-telling is sustained and extended in the film adaptation, which receives further attention in Chapter 5.

# 3

# 'Artificial biography': *Come Unto These Yellow Sands* and *A Self-Made Man*

This chapter focuses on Carter's radical experimentation with biography in *Come Unto These Yellow Sands* ([1979] 1992a) and *A Self-Made Man* (1984a), two radio plays which deconstruct the lives of Victorian painter, Richard Dadd, and Edwardian novelist, Ronald Firbank, respectively. The first half of the chapter is concerned with establishing this deconstructive technique, examining the generic conventions of traditional life-writing and investigating Carter's political project in parodying these conventions in her two 'artificial' biographies (Carter, 1996: 504).[1] The second half of the chapter expands on these issues through a detailed discussion of the formal and thematic structure of the two plays.

## Life-writing in the realist mode

Before delineating Carter's deconstructive 'artificial' biography, it is necessary to outline the development of the genre in order to identify her project in deconstructing it. Traditional biography aims to order and structure material into a coherent and comprehensible whole, constructing a seamless 'Life' in which the subject is recognisably 'characterised' within a logical sequence of events. As Alan Shelston suggests, the traditional biographer will seek to find 'actions and patterns of behaviour which will contribute to a consistent explanation of the overall life of his subject' (1977: 13).[2] Traditional biography upholds the formal and philosophical unities of time, place and character – the 'definition of self as a coherent, indivisible and continuous whole' – which Rosemary Jackson maintains 'has dominated Western thought for centuries and is celebrated in classic theatre and "realistic" art alike' (1981: 83). As Liz Stanley similarly argues, traditional biography 'proposes that there is a coherent, essentially unchanging and unitary self which can be referentially captured by its methods' (1992: 8). Like other rationalistic forms, traditional biography aims to conceal these methods, passing itself off as the 'truth' about the biographical subject. Thus traditional biography can be seen as the logical extension of a particularly didactic strain of realist fiction – life-writing in the realist mode – a style of writing which, as we have seen, Carter consciously tried to avoid in her own practice (see 1983d: 76–7).

## The new biography

Shelston (1977: 63) identifies an ideological shift in biographical writing exemplified by Virginia Woolf's review of Harold Nicholson's *Some People*, which he argues, signals a change 'in attitude in the mood and priorities of twentieth-century biographers'. In her 1927 essay, 'The New Biography', Woolf contrasts traditional biography with the emergence of a 'new school' (1994: 478). 'The days of Victorian biography are over', she suggests, 'with the twentieth century ... a change came over biography, as it came over fiction and poetry ... the point of view had completely altered' (Woolf, 1994: 475). Woolf's concept of the 'new biography' can be seen as an extension of her critique of the tyranny of the realist novel in her 1925 essay 'Modern Fiction':

> The writer seems constrained, not by his own free will but by some powerful and unscrupulous tyrant who has him in thrall, to provide a plot, to provide comedy, tragedy, love interest, and an air of probability embalming the whole so impeccably that if all his figures were to come to life they would find themselves dressed down to the last button of their coats in the fashion of the hour. The tyrant is obeyed; the novel is done to a turn. But sometimes, more and more often as time goes by, we suspect a momentary doubt, a spasm of rebellion, as the pages fill themselves in the customary way. Is life like this? Must novels be like this? (Woolf, 1994: 160)

Modernist interventions in biography extended the question – 'must biography be like this?' Woolf herself experimented with the genre in *Orlando* (1928), her pseudo-biography of Vita Sackville West in which, as Shelston argues, 'she parodied the activities of the traditional biographer, and taunted him with his inability to capture the essentials of the life which he recorded' (1977: 64). In this parodic biography Woolf draws attention to the traditional biographer's artificial construction of the life of his (and the traditional biographer is emphatically a he) subject: 'directly we glance at eyes and forehead, we have to admit a thousand disagreeables which it is the aim of every good biographer to ignore' ([1928] 1993: 12). As Shelston argues, 'the inescapable characteristics of personality, its irrationality and its variety, are seen here as a direct challenge to the orderly proceedings of the biographical method' (1977: 65). As Sandra Gilbert argues in her introduction to *Orlando*:

> Woolf wittily parodies the intrusive and often absurd speculations of the scholar who presumes to know the 'truth' about the 'life' and 'self' of his subject. Each of us ... has many 'lives' and many 'selves'. Nor can they ever, in their multiplicity, be properly understood by the voyeuristic researcher. (Woolf, [1928] 1993: xxix–xxx)

As Gilbert posits, in *Orlando* Woolf was attempting to create 'a new kind of record – an exuberant account of a life which, though apparently lived on the edge of patriarchal history, nevertheless appropriates and transforms that history' (Woolf, [1928] 1993: xxv).[3] This appropriative strategy works to critique traditional biography from within. Gilbert's description of Woolf as 'metabiographer' is useful here – 'a writer who both deploys and criticizes the form in which she is working' (Woolf, [1928] 1993: xxv). But, while challenging the conventions of Victorian biography in *Orlando*, and 'The New Biography', Woolf's 'impressionistic' approach still has the ultimate objective of reaching some 'truth' about the subject:[4]

> the biographer's imagination is always being stimulated to use the novelist's art of arrangement, suggestion, dramatic effect to expand the private life. Yet if he carries the use of fiction too far, so that he disregards the truth, or can only introduce it with incongruity, he loses both worlds; he has neither the freedom of fiction nor the substance of fact. (Woolf, 1994: 478)[5]

Thus, even within changing modernist concepts of 'personality', the emphasis is on structuring a coherent life, on pattern, selection, prioritisation and interpretation, and on the unique individuality of experience.[6]

Despite Woolf's hailing of the 'new biography', and the more recent developments in the theorisation of the postmodern subject, modern life-writing remains overwhelmingly founded upon the very 'realist fallacy' (Stanley, 1992: 8) of Victorian biography which Woolf had earlier critiqued. Commenting on a Modern Biography conference held at the University of East Anglia in 1985, Stanley maintains that:

> the fundamental task of the biographer remains unchanged. Indeed, this task was seen as *unchangeable*: to assemble as far as possible 'the truth about subject X or Y' ... Now as much as in Boswell's *Johnson* or Froude's *Carlyle*, the modern biographer's task is marked out as an essentially social psychological one. (Stanley, 1992: 6)

Stanley notes delegates' dismissive response to the postmodern critique of the realist fallacies of traditional biography as the 'denigration' of the genre, at a conference at which 'classical modernist ideas about biography were stated rather than argued' (1992: 6).

More recently Valentine Cunningham (1995: 17) was still remarking on the 'glorious false coherence of the art of life' in a review of John Batchelor's *The Art of Literary Biography* (1995).

## Life after death of the author

How, then, should we read this persistence of traditional biography after the supposed 'death of the author' (Barthes, 1977: 142–8)? As Lorna Sage observes, Carter 'had a position on the politics of textuality. She went in for the proliferation, rather than the death, of the author' (1994: 58). She recognised the importance of biography in grounding identity in socio-historical contexts.[7] That she was fascinated by the genre is evidenced by the extent to which she reviewed biographies in her journalism.[8] An examination of these reviews reveals an equivocal relationship with the genre; at once critical of the act of biographising and fascinated by the lives of the predominantly female biographees. She admires Michèle Sarde's biography of Colette, arguing that 'however besotted, however uncritical, however willing to draw illegi[ti]mate parallels between art and life' it 'nevertheless demonstrates how it was the passionate integrity of Colette's narcissism that rendered her indestructible' (Carter, 1982d: 176).[9] She pokes fun at Anthony Alpers' equally 'loving, even besotted biography' of Katherine Mansfield, which 'impeccable in every other respect, suffers from a prurient intimacy of tone' (1982d: 160–1).[10] And, it is not only male biographers who come in for this type of criticism – she equally derides the 'richly fatuous self-regard that gleams off every page' of Carol Ascher's biography of Simone de Beauvoir (1997: 530).

While Carter preferred to review the lives of women, in her artificial biographies she chose to examine the lives of two male figures. But her interest in the fragile masculinities of Dadd and Firbank does not signal a departure from her feminist project, indeed it is part of her wider political examination of identity. In one of her last interviews, she states:

> I do think fiction ought to be asking the great unanswerable adolescent questions. Why are we set upon this planet? For what purpose? And I know that my own fiction doesn't look as if it's asking these questions precisely, but I am asking myself versions of questions that I think are even more basic ... like how do we know we are here? Who *do* we think we are? (Evans and Carter, 1992: 41) [11]

Significantly she does not ask 'who are we?' which implies an essential, lost 'we' or an 'I' to discover, but 'who do we think we are?' 'I never believe that I'm writing about the search for self' she argues, insisting that she is not concerned with the "self" as a 'mythical beast which has to be trapped and returned, so that you can become whole again', but instead seeing identity in terms of 'negotiations that we have to make to discover any kind of reality' (Evans and Carter, 1992: 39–40).

For Carter, then, the purpose of fiction and art is not the search for a coherent, unified self, but to reveal the subject in process and to posit the political possibilities of self-creation. In her artificial biographies she radically experiments with the genre in order to release identity from rationalistic modes of representation which are dominant in Western European culture. By subverting traditional biography, she aims to challenge the concept of stable (masculine) subjectivity, revealing the incoherent, contingent nature of identity. This is a political project which, in recognising the cultural construction of identity, suggests we can have some agency in that construction, freeing us to construct alternative selves.[12] As Jackson argues, the disruption of the unity of character offers a particular challenge to the 'dominant philosophical and epistemological orders' (1981: 175–6) which are inherent in traditional biography:

> character deformation suggests a radical refusal of the structures, the 'syntax' of cultural order. Incoherent, fluid selves exist in opposition to precious portraits of individuals as whole or essential. (Jackson, 1981: 86–7)

It is just such 'precious portraits' which Carter deconstructs in her artificial biography in order to reveal the cultural construction of identity as whole, stable, fixed and centred. As Jackson suggests (1981: 175–6), this refusal of 'the "syntax" of cultural order' is potentially radical because it dismantles this 'concept of "character" and its ideological assumptions, mocking and parodying a blind faith in psychological coherence'. As observed in Chapter 1, Carter found radio the ideal medium with which to disrupt the traditional unities which uphold rationalistic texts. The amorphous nature of radio, its ability to deal with many overlapping and sometimes conflicting ideas, makes it particularly adept at playing with the unity of character, lending itself to the representation of those elements traditionally repressed or marginalised by mainstream culture. As John Drakakis argues (Drakakis (ed.), 1981: 21), 'soliloquy, flashback, the cross-cutting of scenes, all became part of the "grammar" of the radio play', and these formal properties facilitate Carter's radical experimentation with identity in both plays, allowing her to parody the conventions of traditional biography.

As Jackson asserts, albeit rather tautologically, 'it is important to understand the radical consequences of an attack upon unified "character", for it is precisely this subversion of the unities of "self" which constitutes the most radical transgressive function of the Fantastic' (1981: 83). While she acknowledges, importantly, that 'this does not imply that subjects can exist outside of ideology and of the social formation', Jackson argues that fantasies can nevertheless, 'image the possibility of radical cultural transformation through attempting to dissolve the boundary lines between the imaginary and the symbolic' (1981: 178). Elaine Jordan's evocation of Kristeva's 'speaking subject' is useful here, because it gives a sense of both the possibilities and the limitations of this writing strategy: 'we are speaking or writing subjects, in discourses that precede us and go on; we participate in them and can produce new ones ... the production of new selves, as well as the deconstruction of old fixed identities, is very much a part of Angela Carter's discourse' (1990: 27). Acknowledging the fact that as speaking and writing subjects we can write only from within the dominant discourse, Carter's political stance – her oscillation between the utopian and the pragmatic, the liberatory and the materialist – is one which also recognises room for agency and resistance within these existing cultural and social limitations.

Jackson's theory of the fantastic as a literature of subversion can, of course, be usefully extended to include those texts which disrupt rationalistic discourse, as is the tendency in much postmodern writing. As Paul Magrs suggests, feminism has an important stake in such redefinitions of subjectivity:

> In the cultural context that has been labelled postmodernism, the redefinitions of this generic 'subject' have actually been at the expense of that stable self. The 'subject' is undermined, fragmented, shown to be in an untenable position. The 'subject' is an apocryphal being; and in the era of postmodernity, it is feminism which has set about unsettling the unfair assumption that a universalized application of a male model of experience will do for everyone. (1997: 186)

A redefinition of the subject is necessarily gendered, Magrs points out, citing Marjorie Garber's theorisation of the dominant subjectivity as presupposedly male: 'to be a subject is to *be* a man' (Garber, 1992: 94). As Magrs maintains (1997: 185), Carter was keen to trouble heterosexual male 'blindness to their own contingency and their bland belief in their own cultural centredness'. In an interview with John Haffenden she responded to a question about 'myths of femininity' by insisting that:

> men live by the myths you've mentioned as much as women, because there has been the idea that fiction that demythologizes them is only of interest to women – as though the dichotomy in our culture is so vast that only women are interested in certain kinds of social fiction, whereas they affect us all very profoundly. Indeed, they affect men much more than women, because women know in their hearts that they're not true. (1985: 91–2)

Much of Carter's later fiction is concerned with representing 'men in flux' (Magrs, 1997: 193), as evidenced in Walser's self-reconstruction in *Nights at the Circus*, and the butterfly collecting, metamorphosising Uncle Perry in *Wise Children*.[13] *Come Unto These Yellow Sands* and *The Self-Made Man* similarly work to reveal the contingent and shifting nature of identity in opposition to the ideology of the stable (masculine) subject. In these two plays Carter foregrounds the constructedness of male subjectivity, suggesting that masculinity is just as constructed as myths of femininity. Carter's artificial biography, like her 'demythologising' practice, parallels Barthes' appeal for 'experimental myth' and 'artificial mythologies' in 'Myth Today' ([1957] 1993: 135). Barthes suggests 'the best weapon against myth is perhaps to mythify it in its turn, and to produce an *artificial myth*: and this reconstituted myth will in fact be a mythology' ([1957] 1993: 135).[14] Carter draws attention to the myth of identity as essential and natural, denaturalising the ideological project implicit in traditional biography by parodying the conventions of the genre: remythologising it in effect.

## Artificial biography

Before going on to discuss the plays individually, it is essential to explore their structural similarities. Both plays are generic hybrids, combining drama, documentary, art history and literary criticism, in order to deconstruct the 'Lives' of their two central figures: Richard Dadd and Ronald Firbank, respectively. This hybridity is demonstrated in Carter's apparent confusion about exactly what she is doing when she describes *Come Unto These Yellow Sands*. She offers two contrary perspectives in two consecutive paragraphs in the Preface to her play anthology. In the first paragraph she explores her fascination not only with the culture that produced Dadd and his work, but also with his life and work as 'expressions' of that culture: '*Come Unto These Yellow Sands*, my play about Dadd, isn't precisely story-telling for radio, nor is it art or cultural criticism, although there is a lot of that in the script', Carter asserts (1985: 12). In the next paragraph she asserts that it, 'isn't a documentary at all, nor really, a play, but a piece of cultural criticism in the form of a documentary-based fiction' (1985: 12). In her attempt to define the play, Carter finds only negative descriptions (it is not story-telling, documentary, art history, cultural criticism, or even a play) and then flatly contradicts herself. But the contradiction seems to arise precisely because she is attempting to describe such a complex, richly layered narrative. Looking at the structure of the play, it is clear why she has so much difficulty in reaching a 'definitive' definition. Her difficulty in defining *Come Unto These Yellow Sands* is significant because it signals a conscious refusal to limit the play to any one interpretation. Even when she arrives at a positive definition it is a hybrid of a number of genres: 'a piece of cultural criticism in the form of a documentary-based fiction' (1985: 12). It is as if she does not want to give any one element priority, and sees all of these diverse elements melding together to form a genre-transgressing whole.

It is important to address the issue of how far Carter reworks existing biographical materials. The announcer introduces *Come Unto These Yellow Sands* as 'an imaginative reconstruction for radio of the life and surviving paintings of Richard Dadd' (1985: 16); and *A Self-Made Man* is introduced as 'an exploration for radio of Ronald Firbank in which he speaks mostly in the words of his own fiction and letters and his contemporaries also speak mostly in their own words, written and compiled by Angela Carter' (1984a).[15] Significantly, both descriptions are qualified by tentative language: 'an imaginative reconstruction' and 'an exploration', rather than claiming to be final, complete and irrefutable versions of events. The words 'written and compiled' are key here – Carter goes beyond merely regurgitating other authors' research, positively reappropriating the available biographical material in order to explore the cultural implications of the lives of biographical subjects, splicing different sources with her own imaginative interpretations, and using radio to piece together a rich and complex text. In the published version of *Come Unto These Yellow Sands* she gives special thanks and acknowledgement to Patricia Allderidge (1974), Dadd's archivist, whose book on Dadd Carter uses extensively as a source material. Similarly, in *A Self-Made Man*, Carter reworks biographical material from a number of different sources.[16]

Carter radicalises biography by letting the characters speak for themselves. Obviously most biographers quote their subjects at length, so in this sense they are given a voice, but Carter allows multiple points of view to reveal the different possibilities of interpreting events, drawing attention to the artificial construction of biography. Although she uses the tools of traditional literary biography, such as critical comment, anecdote and personal accounts, she does so not to build unified character, but to deconstruct it; not to create a whole picture, but to fragment the image. *Come Unto These Yellow Sands* is made up of a combination of narrative voices: the objective narration from both male and female narrators in the style of art historical critique and biographical history; personal commentary from Dadd's family, friends, his landlady and his doctor; characters in his paintings coming to life, and two imaginary academic lectures. A similar multiperspectival structure is utilised in *A Self-Made Man* where Firbank comments ironically on the various narrators as they attempt to biographise him. This polyvalent, polysemic approach, offers a multi-perspectival, rather than limited, view of the lives of her biographees.

Thus Carter's artificial biographies invite the listener to build up his or her own picture of lives of Dadd and Firbank from the various narrative points of view. In both plays meaning is produced in the negotiations between these different narrative voices. In a letter to Glyn Dearman, Carter explains the reason behind this doubling of narrative voices in *Come Unto These Yellow Sands*:

> The cast list looks a bit daunting but the doubling (indeed, trebling) that I suggest isn't for economic reasons so much as to create a certain kind of linking. It worked very well in *Vampirella*, after all; Oberon and Henry Howard (a one-line part) and the Shopkeeper are all basically lecturers, art-critics, while the four female principles can do psychologically very well as aspects of one woman.[17]

Similar in structure to *Come Unto These Yellow Sands*, *A Self-Made Man* uses the same kind of interdisciplinary method to explore the life and work of Ronald Firbank. In another letter to Dearman, Carter describes the play as a generic hybrid, 'partly a dramatisation of Firbank's life, partly a fictional debate of his work ... a fake radio documentary, plus a fake literary critical seminar' (1996: 504). Once again Carter utilises both a male and female narrator, giving equal authority to both sexes. She explains that she used the 'split narrator again' in order create 'a different texture of voices and the male narrator is a *bit* like Daddy, the female narrator is a *bit* like Baba' (1996: 504). It is productive, here, to refer to Stanley's call for an 'auto/biographical' practice which recognises the biographer as socially-located:

> We should ask of biography the question 'who says?'. And 'who says' is someone who has produced one more interpretation from among a range of possibilities, and who has produced it from one particular angle rather than any other. In other words, 'the biographer' is a socially-located person, one who is sexed, raced, classed, aged ... once we accept that ideas are not unique but socially produced even if individually expressed by members of particular social, cultural and political milieux, then we can also extrapolate this to the ideas and interpretations produced by the biographer. (1992: 7)

Carter situates biographical perspective in the mouths of gendered narrators and socially located specific speakers.[18] Dramatic dialogue is interspersed with anonymous, 'objective' documentary narration and personal accounts of Firbank's contemporaries.

This 'fake' biography runs parallel with an imaginary academic seminar entitled, 'Elementary Structures in the Life and Art of Ronald Firbank'

(Carter, 1996: 140). Hosted by 'the literature department of the University of Pisuerga at Kairoulla, held, for reasons of immediate convenience, in a room with dreadful wallpaper in the Hotel Quirinal, in Rome', the seminar parodies the attempts of traditional literary biography to 'explain' Firbank via his fiction and vice versa. The seminar is divided into five sections: Dandyism, Religion,[19] Decadence, Ragtime and Elsewhere; each introduced with an ironic drum roll. Here Carter radically criticises the attempts of literary biography to pin down character and identity. The seminar refers to Baudelaire, Wilde and Beardsley, compares Firbank to characters in his own novels and we are offered conflicting accounts of his habits, dress and epigrams. To whom did he originally claim that he was Pavlova chasing butterflies whereas Siegfried Sassoon was Tolstoy digging for worms? Was it to Sassoon himself (1996: 139–40)? Was it a bowler or a trilby that he always wore (1996: 141)? Carter juxtaposes the multiple points of view of characters, narrators (who now take on academic personae) and Firbank himself, who repeatedly interrupts the seminar – 'by the way, 'I wish you wouldn't call me Firbank; it gives me a sense of galoshes' (1996: 139).

In both plays, then, Carter uses radio as a vehicle for her demythologising practice, taking the lives of Dadd and Firbank as a point of departure for imaginative explorations into specific culture(s) that produced them. She exposes the darker side of Dadd's fairyland and dissects Firbank's artificial persona, rewriting their personal histories to reveal the unwritten and the taboo. The remainder of this chapter will focus on a more detailed discussion of the two plays.

### 'As if the fairies had touched him': *Come Unto These Yellow Sands*

*Come Unto These Yellow Sands* explores the life of the Victorian painter Richard Dadd, who murdered his father and was incarcerated at Bethlem Royal Hospital, where he continued to paint, surviving well into old age. Working on 'the fruitful paradox, that radio is the most visual of mediums because you cannot see it' (1985: 11), Carter truly pushes the medium to its limits, using radio's 'blindness' to recreate a picture gallery in words.[20] She argues that she would have been unable to consider Dadd in the way that she wanted in any other medium but radio, because it enabled her to 'cross-cut from subjective to objective reality, from the inner personal voice to the conflicting voices of those bearing witness to the diverse manifestations of that inner voice' in *Come Unto These Yellow Sands* (1985: 12). As previously observed, Carter suggests that radio is particularly adept at representing interiority and is hence '*par excellence*, the medium for the depiction of madness; for the exploration of the private worlds of the old, the alienated, the lonely' (1985: 8). Carter dismantles the traditional approach to her biographical subject in order to give voice to those elements which have been silenced by the dominant culture:

> the listener is invited inside some of Dadd's paintings, inside the 'Come Unto These Yellow Sands' of the title and into that eerie masterpiece, 'The Fairy Feller's Master Stroke', to hear the beings within it – the monsters produced by repression – squeak and gibber and lie and tell the truth. (Carter, 1985: 12)

Carter decodes the cultural messages behind Dadd's paintings: the fashion for sentimentalising children during a period of child labour, the fascination with fairy nudity in an era of puritanical prudery, the obsession with the exotic other at a time of colonial domination. She does this by subverting a number of generic conventions, the most prominent of which are those of the art historian. The characters in Dadd's paintings are given a voice with which to 'talk back', taking issue with the way in which Dadd has represented them. 'I am pictured in a kind of grotto', Titania describes herself in the early *Titania Sleeping* (1841). Other characters in Dadd's paintings hypothesise about the context of their own creation. Puck introduces Oberon's lecture on Victorian fairyland, to a heckling audience of creatures from the unconscious:

> PUCK. [...] (*Officious.*) Settle down, please, settle down ... emanations of the id to the back of the room, apparitions from the unconscious and preconscious in the gallery. Pre-Christian survivals, fertility symbols, nightmares and ghouls in the pews to the right, death-signs, stormwarnings, to the left. Oedipal fantasies in the front row, please. And I'll thank you poltergeists to keep a firm hand on your impulses during the lecture.[21]

Oberon's lecture which follows captures the richness, humour and intelligence of Carter's radio drama.

> OBERON. Thank you, friends, thank you.
> *Rustles papers, coughs.*
>    The vogue for paintings of fairy subjects during the mid-Victorian period might be regarded as the manifestation of a compensatory 'ideology of innocence' in the age of high capitalism, a period when the relations of man with his kind were increasingly under stress and the art which reflected these relations became increasingly fraudulent.
> *Hobgoblin chorus of cheers. Hear, hear! Well said!* (1985: 22–3)

But the irony of Oberon, King of the fairies, delivering a Marxist critique of the compensatory ideology of the 'pastoral exotic' is lost on one critic.

Guido Almansi takes issue with what he sees as 'the facile sociological conclusions offered by Carter in her analysis of complex phenomena such as the cult of exoticism, the nature of the "pastoral exotic", repression and Victorianism' (1994: 228).[22] But in her critique of Victorian repression Carter is clearly not, as Almansi suggests, claiming that twentieth-century society is somehow unrepressed. She would argue that today's repression simply takes a different form – 'repressive desublimation – i.e. permissiveness' (1982d: 123).[23] In his eagerness to accuse Carter of 'jargonism', Almansi fails to read the irony of this speech being situated in the mouth of Oberon, and the humour of its intended audience: this is 'not a *normal* crowd' (1985: 22). Almansi is also wrong, I think, in reading Oberon as such a straightforward mouth-piece for Carter. Indeed, his lecture is gradually faded out: 'Oberon's voice is blown away by the wind, gets smaller and smaller from now on, until it fades away altogether' (1985: 25), undermining his already shaky 'academic' authority. Oberon's lecture is a direct comment on the Victorian appropriation of fairies, an analysis of the period in which fairy tale became fully integrated into the middle-class nursery and all sexual and bestial elements, if not actually censored, at least brushed under the (Turkish) carpet. Carter unpicks Dadd's apparent obsession with Shakespearian fairy subjects by having Oberon quote Hamlet's 'offensive epitaph on the mad Ophelia' in his lecture: 'Death and affliction, even hell itself,/She turns to favour and to prettiness' (1985: 24).[24]

It is worth comparing *Come Unto These Yellow Sands* with 'Overture and Incidental Music for *A Midsummer Night's Dream*' ([1985] 1986: 63–76) in which the changeling speaks directly to audience just like the characters in Dadd's paintings in the radio play. As Sage notes:

> Shakespeare's play is subjected to a cunning transformation by means of a sort of pre-script. We are behind the plot before the curtain rises, eavesdropping on the suppressed subtext ... Shakespeare's text is reattached, via this umbilical cord of a narrative, to an imaginary matrix. Going 'behind' his text you free up the future, patch him into the quilt of writing once again. (1994, 45–6)

The same thing occurs in *Come Unto These Yellow Sands*. We are allowed 'behind' the static surface of the canvas into the 'real' world of the fairies, who cogently comment on how they have been represented by Dadd in his paintings and the culture that produced him. By putting the words of art history into the mouths of the figures within the frame, Carter draws attention to the very act of historicising art, thus commenting on the very act of cultural criticism that she is perpetrating herself.

Carter also foregrounds the disjunction between Dadd's depiction of

Victorian fairyland and his Oedipal crime. As observed in Chapter 2, Carter took a great scholarly interest in the history of the fairy tale, from its origins in the oral tradition to its evolution as a literary genre. In 'The Better to Eat You With', she suggests,

> It doesn't need the horrid example of the painter Richard Dadd, the aptly named parricide, to suggest there is something peculiar about a grown man who devotes his life to an obsessional exploration of fairyland. The realm of faery has always attracted nutters, regressives and the unbalanced ... Tellers of fairytales must have felt they could perpetrate the most excessive fantasies without fear of censure, provided everything took place in that domain of psychoanalytic privilege, fairyland. (1976: 188)

This is made explicit in the radio play, where, the 'innocent' fairy subject matter is at odds with Dadd's delusions and persecution complex. Puck illustrates the compensatory ideology of innocence which Oberon goes on to discuss in his lecture: 'Ravishingly pretty ... but so much, so very much prettiness suggests the presence of far too many ugly beings gibbering away behind the painted screen where he pushed them' (1985: 22). Carter proposes that the fairy subject matter becomes more disturbing in Dadd's later works which were painstakingly executed over a period of many years in mental hospital. She points out that all is not quite so pretty and harmonious as Dadd would have us believe in these paintings, interpreting *The Fairy Feller's Master Stroke* as a freeze frame of the fatal moment before Dadd committed parricide. The Fairy Feller knowingly suggests that 'the blow I am about to strike, which he prevents me from, is the very blow he struck hisself!' (1985: 47).

Another important and interconnected theme throughout the play is the aesthetic influence of Dadd's tour of the Middle East which contributed to his breakdown. Carter maps Dadd's transformative experience in the East, incorporating his subjective point of view with the 'objective' account of his travelling companion and patron, Sir Thomas Phillips. Both of these Western perspectives are further qualified by the voice of an Egyptian shopkeeper: 'I knew immediately I saw him that this young man would buy anything I chose to sell him':[25]

> *Cash register*
> SHOPKEEPER. [...] What's this? (*To inaudible voice over his shoulder.*) What? You want my lecture on orientalism?
> *Coughs, clears throat. Crossfade to rustling of lecture theatre audience.*
> My lecture on orientalism ... are you attending? Very well. Throughout the nineteenth century, the Orient exercised a magnetic attraction upon the European middle class, to whom my distinguished visitors purveyed the aesthetic, the sense of style, the taste. [...]

OBERON. ... a compensatory ideology of innocence ...

SHOPKEEPER. (*Tetchy.*) No, no, no, no! Innocence? Never! These were the lands of the harem, of the assassin, of the naked blonde slave-girl in the market ... the cult of the exotic was a compensatory ideology of sensuality, of mystery, of violence. Of the *forbidden*, which the customers of my customers could enjoy vicariously, without any danger of their souls. (1983: 30–2)

The Shopkeeper's lecture reminds Almansi 'a bit too closely of certain lectures of a sociological nature which I had the misfortune to hear thirty years ago, plus the distant echo of a perfunctory reading of Edward W. Said's *Orientalism*' (1994: 228). That this is clearly not a 'distant echo' but an explicit reference to Said (1978) bypasses Almansi here, and he further misses the subversive irony of the shopkeeper, as colonised subject, theorising about his own construction within the Western European imagination: 'we are not responsible for their fantasies about us' (Carter, 1985: 33).[26] Carter's astute awareness of the complicated nexus of power, domination and exploitation, which is implicit in the capitalist consumer culture of tourism, anticipates the recent resurgence of postcolonial theory, in which Said has continued to play a significant role.[27]

Dadd continued to paint after his incarceration in Broadmoor Hospital, drawing on his Middle Eastern sketch books for inspiration. These later paintings incorporate both the pastoral and Eastern exotic; the fairy subjects take on the costume and attributes of the East. In *Contradiction: Oberon and Titania* (1858), Oberon comments, 'he has decided to give to me, Oberon, the fierce, proud air of an Arab chieftain or a Kurdish brigand' (Carter, 1985: 42). Describing her depiction in the same painting, Titania comments on her transformation from lithe nymphet, reclining in a glade, to her now imposing figure in the later painting:

TITANIA. And he has learned some respect for the Queen of the Fairies. Now I dwarf my court!

*Thumping footsteps; humming, buzzing.*

Here come I, Titania, with my gigantic stride! How big I've grown, since the time he took my picture when I was sleeping in the glade. I tower over my fairy subjects like Gulliver in Lilliput; I trample them underfoot –

*Particularly thumping footstep; tiny fairy scream.*

There! I've flattened her, that winged creature no bigger than my little finger who nestled in the flower bell. (1985: 40)[28]

Carter foregrounds the violence of these later paintings, with Titania stepping on the hapless fairy and the tiny figures in war-dress carrying weaponry.

Allowing one of the characters in Dadd's paintings to have the final word, the play culminates with the finale of Oberon's lecture in which he draws parallels between the 'quaint pornography of never-never-land' and 'the infection of the mystic East' in Dadd's later work (Carter, 1985: 53). In the preface to the play anthology, Carter comments on the cultural significance of Dadd's continued fascination with the 'innocent' Victorian fairy land:

> The contradiction between the kitsch content and the distorted style of the paintings of Dadd's madness, together with his archetypal crime of parricide ... seem to me expressions of the dislocation of the real relations of humankind to itself during Britain's great period of high capitalism and imperialist triumph in the nineteenth century, during Dadd's own long, alienated lifetime. (Carter: 1985: 12)

Carter reads Dadd's inability to resolve Oedipal conflicts as symbolic of his status within a repressive Victorian society, 'the terrible glamour of parricide, a crime which struck at the very root of the patriarchal order of his time' (1985: 53). Dadd's problematic identity formation can lead only to madness in the context of his repressive times; Oberon concludes that Dadd 'contrived in some measure, in spite of or, perhaps, because of, his absolute seclusion from it, to capture the essential spirit of his age' (Carter, 1985: 53).

### 'How can one dissect a butterfly?': *A Self-Made Man*

*A Self-Made Man* continues the demythologising project of *Come Unto These Yellow Sands*, offering an even more radical exploration of the subject in process. The 'self-made man' of the title refers to Firbank, whose self-creation is the main focus of the play. But it also refers to his grandfather, Old Joseph Firbank, whose rapid rise from the dark depths of the coal mine to the height of bourgeois respectability as a wealthy railway pioneer epitomises the self-created fortunes of the rising middle classes of industrial England, which forms the background to Firbank's existence. In the following scene, music and sound-effects are used to disrupt the ideological operation implicit in traditional biography:

> MALE NARRATOR. The grandfather, a self-made man [...] who went to work in the mines at Bishop Auckland, County Durham, at the age of seven; and then –
> (*First line of song, 'Poor Paddy works on the railways' [...]'In eighteen hundred and forty-one, my corduroy britches I put on, to work upon the railways' – cut off at this point, sharp.*)

– he went to work upon the railways. Soon, by dint of hard work –
(*Pick and shovel; cut off*)
– he prospered sufficiently to enable him to contract the labour to build railways for himself.
(*Lots of picks and shovels; cut off.*) (Carter, 1996: 125)

Once again, the printed text does not recreate the experience of listening to the play. In performance, the abrupt jump-cut from the railway song to the narrator's voice, and the ironic insertion of the spot-effects of picks and shovels within his monologue, work to draw attention to the constructedness of the medium. Carter takes the conventions of both radio drama and traditional biography and exaggerates them. This defamiliarising tactic upsets the traditional biographical process, unsettling the dominant ideology of the subject as coherent, fixed and whole.

Carter uses Firbank's family history to explore issues relating to the massive social and cultural changes occurring at the turn of the century.[29] She derives great pleasure from foregrounding the fact that the Firbank fortune was originally founded on railways: 'brand-new money, a very nineteenth-century fortune; a fortune of the Age of Steam and mass transportation' (1996: 124). Firbank's father, Sir Thomas Firbank, mismanaged the family fortune so that, brought up with 'great expectations of immense wealth', Firbank was 'put out to find he would be only rather rich' (Carter, 1996: 125). The social insecurity of the upper middle class is illustrated by a dramatised sketch in which Firbank practices an imaginary libel case against Osbert Sitwell who, he claims, has insulted the family name by suggesting that 'the Firbank fortune had been founded on boot-buttons' (Carter, 1996: 124). Firbank is depicted as being highly conscious of his working-class roots, while at the same time drawing attention to them in the public arena of the Eiffel Tower Restaurant.

It is significant that Firbank was born in 1886, the same year that Dadd died, because in many ways, *A Self-Made Man* continues the critique of Victorian culture begun in *Come Unto These Yellow Sands*. Firbank is the fragile product of that century of rapid social and industrial change, as outlined in the following scene (Carter, 1996: 132–3):

MALE NARRATOR. [...] The grandchildren of a self-made man exist, perhaps, at a third remove from reality. Of the four grandchildren of the hard-headed, horny-handed railway pioneer, who built himself up out of his own sweat and labour and the sweat and labour of others, only the very frailest –

OLD FIRBANK. (*Faint – on echo.*) 'Eh lad! That woarn't pull a load of muck!'

MALE NARRATOR. – was sufficiently moved by the will to live to make himself, in *his* turn, as if from nothing, or from the shards of ideas, from brilliant fragments, of illusion, from his irretrievable sense of his own

difference – only frail Artie was able to reconstruct out of these
intangibles an artificial temperament –

FEMALE NARRATOR. Who was it said: 'The first duty in life is to be as artificial
as possible?'

FIRBANK. Oscar Wilde.

MALE NARRATOR. – to construct an artificial temperament durable enough to
withstand the buffetings of the world; to create himself a crust, a
portable home like that of jewelled mollusc –

FIRBANK. (*Reproachful.*) Mollusc!

FEMALE NARRATOR. (*Conciliatory.*) Your chrysalis, the beautiful chrysalis of
your impenetrable privacy, out of which, from time to time, you would
transmit your coded messages to the world.[30]

(*Pause.*)

I quote at length from this scene in order to give some sense of the rich
overlapping of narrative voices. Carter's use of multiple narrators can be
productively read in the light of Stanley's theorisation of an 'auto/
biographical' writing practice (1992) which works to explicitly reinscribe
the authorial voice in the biographical text as politically, historically and
socially grounded. Stanley cites postmodern innovations in feminist
autobiography which insist on 'the formation and perpetuation of
discourses as sets of "voices" speaking referentially to and about each
other' (1992: 15) and Nicholas Pagan (1993) similarly 'rethinks' literary
biography from a postmodern perspective. In just this way Firbank's
reproachful interjection, and the Female Narrator's conciliatory response,
demonstrate the ways in which Firbank is allowed to interact with his
biographers, forcing them to qualify their statements – the biographical
subject refuses to lie down and die gracefully.

Firbank's wilful self-creation, as if from 'shards of ideas' and 'brilliant
fragments', mirrors the renowned collage technique he employed in his
own writing. It also mirrors Carter's method in 'compiling' the artificial
biography of Firbank from the various, often conflicting biographical
sources. Barthes called these fragments 'biographemes' – the resonant
details of a life ([1957] 1993: 30). One such biographeme which Carter
chooses to foreground is Firbank's 'characteristic, wild, nervous laughter;
the laughter with which he advertised his presence' (1996: 130), which
ripples mischievously through the play. Firbank's curious laugh is
described by his contemporaries: Augustus John – 'a long hollow laugh
about nothing in particular' – and Sewell Stokes – 'the most sinister laugh
I had ever heard' (1996: 130). Firbank's laugh acts as his calling card, part
of the creation of his own peculiar legend. As the female narrator points
out, 'the laughter with which he orchestrated his compulsive shyness'
(1996: 130) is not simply a symptom of his social gaucherie, but a

projection, a survival mechanism, a chrysalis. While using the narrators to theorise about his laugh, Carter simultaneously employs Firbank's laughter to disrupt the process of biography itself. His laugh, interpolated ironically at various apposite moments in the narrative, undercuts the authority of the various narrators: objective, critical and partisan alike, mocking those who attempt to capture his shifting identity from beyond the grave.

Barthes' 'biographemes' are akin to 'what Norman Mailer called "factoids": items invented by the publicity department' which Carter cites in her review of movie actresses' memoirs in 'Much, Much Stranger than Fiction' (1992: 358–62). Factoids gives more of a sense of the invented-ness, the artificiality of these biographical fragments. Carter examines the various conflicting 'factoids' which generated around Firbank: 'as with a medieval saint or any other legendary being, fabulous narratives proliferated around his dandified, powdered, occasionally rouged, inimitable figure' (1996: 136). She goes on to examine one such narrative, in which Firbank suggests violets as an accompaniment for steak in an anecdote with two completely different sources, neither source acknowledging the presence of the other. In the play, both versions are dramatised, one immediately after the other. In Nancy Cunard's version, Firbank quips 'try violets!' in response to a loutish young man ordering a steak: 'may all tipsy, bullying, gross "he-men" meet with such a neat little swipe as that dealt by Firbank' (Carter, 1996: 137) she concludes. Carter then dramatises Wyndham Lewis' account of an almost identical incident from his autobiography, *Blasting and Bombardiering* (1937), in which he is dining with a young American friend when Firbank again suggests violets as a garnish. The scene of 'this memorable encounter remains the Eiffel Tower Restaurant but Nancy Cunard is written out of the script' (Carter, 1996: 138). Carter is fascinated by this double 'biographeme' and overtly deconstructs it using the two narrators:

> MALE NARRATOR. Note how Nancy Cunard celebrates her friend in her version of the story, which might be titled: 'Ronald's Triumph over the Boor'; whereas Wyndham Lewis –
> LEWIS. ... 'the fawning and attentive Firbank' –
> MALE NARRATOR. – parodies him.
> LEWIS. ... 'he frothed obsequiously';
> MALE NARRATOR. caricatures him; turns him into an offensive cartoon.
> FEMALE NARRATOR. But perhaps ... Firbank suggested the violet garnish on two quite separate occasions, after all.
> FIRBANK. 'I wonder.' (1996: 138–9)

The intercutting from the Male Narrator's comparison between the two versions of events to Wyndham Lewis' dramatised interjections works to

undermine Lewis' interpretation, deconstructing his attempt to carica-
ture Firbank. As the Female Narrator suggests, it is impossible to arrive at
the objective 'truth' of the incident and Firbank's ironic and enigmatic, 'I
wonder,' gives nothing away. Lord Berners informs us that this refrain
'was constantly on his lips, and uttered in a tone that seemed to evoke all
the unsolved riddles of the universe' (1996: 135). By situating the phrase
in the mouth of Firbank, Carter allows him to comment on the very act of
biographising which she perpetrates herself.

It is useful to return to Gilbert's notion of the 'metabiographer' here,
in order to describe Carter's simultaneous deconstruction and perpetration
of biography (Woolf, [1928] 1993: xxv). Once again, Carter's radical
artificial biography subverts the traditional biographer's claim to render
the final, objective 'version' of a life, and draws attention to the inevitable
cultural and historical bias inherent in all literary acts. In Carter's
multiperspectival version, at least four points of view are proffered in this
brief extract: the two characters' dramatised sketches, the Male and
Female narrators' and Firbank's cryptic analysis, 'I wonder'. As the Male
Narrator warns: 'as with all such narratives, they may be only loosely
based on real events and capable of many different interpretations' (1996:
136).

The sketch demonstrates Firbank's peculiar relationship with food,
which is established as an important theme of the play. Only Firbank
would suggest violets as a garnish, Carter implies. In the play other
characters comment on Firbank's eating habits. Philip Moeller describes
a diet of 'peaches and champagne' and Nancy Cunard reminisces
'perhaps, if you were peckish, a strawberry or two' (Carter, 1996: 134).
Having noted the family propensity for alcoholism – as realised by the
exaggerated sound effects of corks popping and champagne fizzing
(1996: 133–4) – Carter goes on to suggest that Firbank's food fetishism is
part of his dandified, decadent performance:

> MALE NARRATOR. He ate as he lived, as he wrote, exiguously, but with
> tremendous style. A minimalist. Impossibly luxurious little nibbles,
> sketches of meals, vague idealised outlines of meals ... so that
> malnutrition may have helped to hasten his end. (1996: 134)

Carter was aware of how food could be used as a way of controlling one's
physical image, foregrounding the relationship between eating and power
in her writings about food.[31] In an excellent essay, 'The Infernal Appetites
of Angela Carter', Sarah Sceats examines the politics of appetite and
desire in Carter's fiction and journalism, arguing that Carter exposes
appetite to be socially and culturally constructed, rather than 'natural'
(1997: 100–15).[32] Her analysis of Carter's representation of food is

apposite here, revealing as it does the power politics which Carter suggests are implicit in Firbank's minimalist eating habits, representing a public assertion of his individuality and becoming part of his self-creation, part of his own legend, part of his dandyism.

The power politics of Firbank's eating eccentricities might well have drawn Carter's attention because of her own experience of anorexia.[33] In 'Fat is Ugly' Carter describes anorexia as an extreme type of dandyism:

> Woman, regarded as an item of conspicuous consumption (though that is becoming somewhat less true), has traditionally the sole creative function of Dandy; she is tacitly encouraged to sacrifice much for the sake of appearances. Dandyism is the last resort of the impotent, and the pro-tracted attempted suicide by narcissism (which is how my anorexic experience now appears to me), can be regarded as a kind of batty exhibition of heroics, which ironically underlines the impotence it was adopted to combat. (1997: 56–60)

This statement reveals an equivocal response to the phenomenon of anorexia, simultaneously figuring it as both subversive and self-destructive, both an act of heroics and of impotence. Whilst Carter acknowledges the futility of self-starvation as a political strategy, she also recognises the impulse behind anorexia as one of self-assertion in which the 'anorexic uses food as a weapon to establish some kind of autonomy' (1997: 561). Anorexia, therefore, foregrounds food as a point of resistance and agency, albeit a limited one.[34]

Carter demonstrates Firbank's role in the creation of his own identity further in his adoption of a decadent, dandified persona: 'he undoubtedly assisted in the manufacture of his own legend; the legend followed him about like the shadow of his arduously constructed artificial temperament' (1996: 139):

> FEMALE NARRATOR. Clothes, as they say, make the man; and the woman too. The dandy, who creates himself or herself afresh as a work of art each time he or she changes a shirt or a frock, is the perfect 'self-made' person. Yet the dandy's obsession with dress is but a symptom of the disease, not the disease itself. True dandyism is an existential condition.
>
> MALE NARRATOR. Charles Baudelaire, in his essay, 'The Painter of Modern Life':
>
> BAUDELAIRE. (*On speaker. Slight French accent, not too much.*) [...] 'For the perfect dandy, clothes and material elegance are no more than the symbol of the aristocratic superiority of his mind. It is, above all, the burning desire to create a personal form of originality, within the eternal limits of social conventions. It is a kind of cult of the ego ... It is the pleasure of causing surprise in others ...'
>
> CYRIL BEAUMONT. '... we always spoke of him as "the man with red nails"' ...

BAUDELAIRE. '... and the proud satisfaction of never showing any oneself'. (1996: 142–3)

The potential double meaning of 'oneself' is crucial here. The dominant reading – never revealing oneself to anybody else – could also be read as never showing any one (singular) self – proposing dandyism as a strategy which fundamentally disrupts the notion of coherent identity through a refusal to present a united self.[35] Firbank's paradoxical disclosure and disguise, his 'dandified persona' is part of his private chrysalis, his exhibitionism is a way of not showing any *one*self. Gamble reads the figure of the dandy in Carter's early fiction as:

> the self-created being who exists for nothing but display, and in whom all the paradoxes of a constructed subjectivity are incarnated. In playing games with the state of being itself, the dandy raises the spectre of the empty self whose gaudy façade is no eccentric decoration, but perhaps a practice which is vital to his very existence in the world. (1997: 8)

Carter's engagement with Firbank's dandified persona suggests a more equivocal, paradoxical relationship with the figure of the dandy than Gamble allows. In *A Self-Made Man* Carter celebrates Firbank's self-creation as an act of resistance against the dominant ideology of masculine subjectivity. While Gamble's overwhelmingly negative configuration of the dandy in Carter's early fiction is apt, it is necessary to qualify this in relation to Carter's treatment of dandyism as self-creation in her later work.[36] The figure of the dandy operates both as a seductive but empty façade and as the symbol of a positively reconstructed subjectivity. In Carter's fiction the dandy explicitly enacts the subject in process. Carter proposes here, and elsewhere in her writings about dandyism, that this is a subversive although limited strategy, just as the quotation from Baudelaire here foregrounds the 'eternal limits of social conventions'.

In 'The Savage Sideshow' she states, 'everybody's appearance is their symbolic autobiography. I'm a part-time sociologist of fashion – I'm very interested in the iconography of clothes and gestures' (Sage, 1977: 51–7). She comments on Firbank's eye for fashion: 'his heroines he dressed to perfection, with the eye of a fashion journalist attuned to the extremes of the decorative, as if the clothes of those self-entranced women were a primary function of their being, as if they were not fully alive until they were dressed' (Carter, 1996: 141). The aptly named novella, *The Artificial Princess*, revolves around a society garden party the sole function of which is to create a backdrop for descriptions of outrageous, impossible clothes; these are literally fabulous creations (Firbank, [1915] 1934).[37] Carter's fascination with the semiotics of fashion is evidenced in her fiction and journalism.[38] In 'Notes for a Theory of Sixties Style' she argues:

The nature of apparel is very complex. Clothes are so many things at once. Our social shells; the system of signals with which we broadcast our intentions; often the projections of our fantasy selves ... Clothes are our weapons, our challenges, our visible insults. (1997: 105)

Carter reads Firbank's dandyism, his jewelled mollusc, his self-created chrysalis, his social shell, as a weapon, a visible insult.

Although employing a similar formal strategy to that used in *Come Unto These Yellow Sands*, Carter's relationship with her biographical subject, Firbank, is more complicated in *A Self-Made Man*.[39] Where Carter is more overtly critical of Dadd as a product of Victorian repression, she is less critical of both Firbank and the period of the 'naughty noughts' (1996: 131) which produced him. She celebrates his eccentricity as a productive, if limited, space from which he was able to critique his society from the margins.[40] Not only does she formally challenge biography as a genre, but in Firbank she chooses a subject whose manipulation of his own identity unsettled the cultural and social norm in ways which made the establishment uneasy in his own day and which are still resonant today.[41] As Magrs argues, Carter draws on the 'model of shifting, self-reinventing subjectivity' figuring in Butler's and Garber's theories of the 'transvestite as deconstructive figure, one provoking a crisis in categories and culture itself' (1997: 195–6). Like Quentin Crisp, whose autobiography Magrs cites, Firbank 'engaged in open hostilities with the unreconstructed straight world' (Magrs, 1997: 195). Magrs acknowledges both the risks and the rewards of this marginalised position: 'for reconstructed, self-conscious, performing liminal beings, that swinging is an effort, a struggle, and exercise in dogged resilience' (1997: 196). As a biographical subject Firbank pre-empts Carter's deconstructive project, in a sense, because he so explicitly constructs himself. His 'arduously constructed artificial temperament' (1996: 139) is mirrored by, and reflects back, her artificial biography. Carter is more interested in the construction of Firbank's elaborate mask than locating the 'real' man behind the mask. His peculiar style of construing and constructing his public personae already exaggerates, and thus defamiliarises, the very process of identity formation which Carter seeks to destabilise.

## Notes

1 Carter's description of *A Self-Made Man* in a letter to director Glyn Dearman.
2 Shelston offers a useful survey of modern biography, tracing its course from the translation of Plutarch's *Lives of the Most Notable Greeks and Romans* in 1579, via Samuel Johnson's *Lives of the Poets* (1778) and James Boswell's *Life of Samuel Johnson* (1791) and

Elizabeth Gaskell's *Life of Charlotte Brontë* (1857) to Lytton Strachey's iconoclastic *Eminent Victorians* (1918) and beyond. However, whilst he recognises the fictive element of traditional biography, suggesting that 'there has always been a tendency in biography to select in order to interpret – to select and perhaps even to invent' (1977: 13–14), as well as acknowledging its contingency upon socio-historical contexts, Shelston nevertheless appears to endorse the implicit ideological function of the traditional biographer.

3  Significantly, Carter was commissioned to write the libretto for an operatic adaptation of *Orlando* for the Glyndebourne Opera House in 1979, but the project was never realised. Carter's script is published in *The Curious Room* (Carter, 1996). Woolf's *Orlando* is clearly an intertext for *The Passion of New Eve* (Carter, [1977] 1990) in which Eve/lyn undergoes a similar gender transformation.

4  In her critical writings Woolf critiques the formal structures of Victorian biography, not its central project of reaching some essential 'truth' about personality, as also illustrated by her challenge to the Victorian novel for failing to capture the 'the essential thing' in 'Modern Fiction': 'for us at this moment the form of fiction most in vogue more often misses than secures the thing we seek. Whether we call it life or spirit, truth or reality, this, the essential thing, has moved off, or on, and refuses to be contained any longer in such ill-fitting vestments as we provide' (Woolf, 1994: 160).

5  Compare this with Carter's deconstructive treatment of the binary opposition between truth and fiction in *Nights at the Circus* ([1984] 1985), in which Fevvers' slogan, 'Is she fact or is she fiction?' sets up one of the central enigmas of the novel.

6  Writing from within the tradition she critiques, Woolf's parodic engagement with biography stems in part from the fact that she was exposed to the genre from a very young age. As Shelston points out in his bibliography, Woolf's father, Leslie Stephen, was in fact the first editor of *Dictionary of National Biography* (1882), founded the same year she was born. As Gilbert argues (Woolf, [1928] 1993: xxi), Woolf was 'preoccupied with the personal but often "official" genre of biography and its relationship to "official" public historiography from early in her career', and her early biographical writings represent 'a gesture of rebellion against both paternal and patriarchal authority'.

7  Stanley (1992: 16) is similarly sceptical about the 'authority' of those theorists who propose the death of the author, claiming that 'this argument is articulated by a few white middle class male first world elite self-styled "intellectuals"' and suggesting that 'the denial of authorship' disenfranchises marginalised groups – such as the anti-colonialist, feminist, black and gay movements – just at the point at which they are beginning to find a voice for their oppression.

8  See her reviews of Anthony Alpers, *The Life of Katherine Mansfield* (1978) and Michèle Sarde, *Colette: A Biography* (1980), collected in *Nothing Sacred: Selected Writings* (1982d); Phyllis Rose, *Jazz Cleopatra: Josephine Baker in her Time* (1990), collected in *Expletives Deleted: Selected Writings* (1992); Carol Ascher, *Simone de Beauvoir: A Life of Freedom* (1982) and Barry Paris, *Louise Brooks* (1990), collected in Angela Carter, *Shaking a Leg: Collected Journalism and Writings* (1997).

9  In many ways Carter seems equally 'besotted' with Colette, and reveals a similar admiration for Louise Brooks in her review of Barry Paris' biography of the same name.

10  Carter particularly takes issue with his 'gynaecologically exhaustive' approach: 'once Alpers has worked out the code Mansfield used in her journals to indicate her periods, she is allowed no outburst of temper or fit of depression without a reference to pre- or post-menstrual tension. He is so protective of 'Katherine', as he always calls her, that he appears to be conducting a posthumous affair with her. Presumably this is the fate of any attractive, mysterious and sexually experimental woman at the hands of a gallant male biographer' (1982d: 158, 161).

11  Emphasis added to script, although it is there in Carter's voice in the programme.

12  In this respect her writing prefigures Judith Butler's theory of gender as performativity (1990 and 1993), which has since so often been applied to her work (see, for example,

Paulina Palmer, 1997). As Christina Britzolakis suggests (1995: 459), 'the concept of "gender performance" ... has become *de rigueur*' both within contemporary feminist theory and recent critical engagements with Carter's work. As Elaine Jordan points out (1994: 190): 'Butler's *Gender Trouble* has had considerable influence in disseminating theoretical arguments which deconstruct the opposition between what is "natural" and what is "artificial", which is embedded in our language and ways of thought, but not universal. These arguments are already implicit and explored in Carter's writing over three decades.'

13  Note the butterfly as metaphor for self-transformation which Carter found useful for discussing Firbank's artificial persona, as I argue below.

14  Elaine Jordan (1990: 38) also refers to this quotation from Barthes in relation to Carter's demythologising project in *Nights at the Circus*. As observed in my introduction, Carter relates her demythologising practice to that of Barthes in *Mythologies* 'ideas, images, stories that we tend to take on trust without thinking what they really mean' (Katsavos, 1994: 12).

15  I quote from the play in performance, in the script the announcer introduces the play as 'an artificial documentary for radio' (1996: 122).

16  Where Carter acknowledges her debt to Allderidge in the preface of her play anthology (1985), *A Self-Made Man* was published posthumously and so the biographical sources are less explicit. The following are mentioned in the play text: *The Concise Oxford Dictionary of English Literature*, *The Who's Who* and Percy Wyndham Lewis' autobiography, *Blasting and Bombardiering* (1937). Other possible sources include the memoirs of Osbert Sitwell (1949) and biographies by I. K. Fletcher (1930) (which includes personal reminiscences by Lord Berners, V. B. Holland, Augustus John, R. A. and Osbert Sitwell), Miriam Benkovistz (1969) and Brigid Brophy (1973).

17  Undated letter to Glyn Dearman in Mark Bell's archive.

18  As noted in Chapter 2, Carter made specific notes about the character's accents. Augustus John, for example, is 'bluff; upper class', Siegfried Sassoon, 'upper class but less offensively so', even stipulating that the 'upper class characters talk with "Edwardian" accents' and urging Dearman to 'listen to Archive records if you feel you need guidance' (Mark Bell, editor of Carter, *The Curious Room*, has generously given me access to this unpublished archive material).

19  Carter treats Firbank's little-known Catholic conversion and lapse with glee. The play begins with the comic dramatisation of his Protestant funeral and subsequent exhumation and re-burial in 'more appropriately consecrated soil': 'even in death, always on the move' (1996: 121–2). Firbank's profanity got him into trouble with his American publishers who refused to publish the novel on religious and moral grounds, and Carter's enjoyment of his irreverence clearly relates to her own attitudes towards religion as revealed in her controversial television programme, *The Holy Family Album*, discussed in Chapter 8.

20  As mentioned in Chapter 1, it won the Sony Award for Best Drama Documentary in 1979 (see Carter, 1996: 503).

21  This scene foregrounds radio's capacity for portraying the fantastic, the alien and the odd; its ability to play tricks with temporal and spatial awareness; and to conjure up images in the listener's imagination: the play's deconstructive mix of biography, drama, documentary, art history and cultural criticism reflecting Carter's faith in the audience's ability to juggle with multiple strands of sound and meaning. As argued in Chapter 1, Guido Almansi, having not heard the play, has less faith in the listener's imagination: 'I doubt whether a listener, without previous knowledge of Dadd's paintings and of his unhappy life, would make head or tail of these uncanny sounds ... (the other plays are easier to understand)' (1994: 228).

22  Almansi's patronising tone can clearly be heard: 'come off it, Ms Carter ... I wish it were true, because this would mean that this horrible repression belonged to the past, and that

the Freudian revolution has freed us from it. Of the whole ideology of the 1960s, to which we are indebted for the welcome irruption of irrespectability, the polemics against the Establishment, the new immense freedom of subject matter and the healthy scepticism which has been so useful to us in the last decades, the sociological jargon is, on the contrary, the most obnoxious and pernicious heritage' (1994: 228–9).

23 In 'Titillation' she acknowledges 'all the internal contradictions of "permissiveness". After all, who is doing the permitting? Why? What caused all that repression, anyway?' (1982d: 152).

24 Carter had an ambivalent relationship with Shakespeare, she cites *A Midsummer Night's Dream* as her favourite play, but goes on to add: 'I'm completely steeped in the raw language and culture of Shakespeare. Miserable, rotten, reactionary bourgeois, old fuddy-duddy that he is. You know, we were all subsumed to the huge over-arching intellectual glory of Shakespeare, a man who was probably deeply lovable but not, I think, terribly clever' (Evans and Carter, 1992: 29–30). Carter's fiction has engaged extensively with Shakespeare, namely in *Wise Children* (1991) in which she subversively celebrates the great Bard, from the wrong side of the tracks, in her exploration of the Hollywood screen adaptation of *The Dream*.

25 It is worth commenting on the double meaning of 'buy' here – as in 'believing' or buying into the orientalist construction of Egypt via buying souvenirs.

26 Carter's take on orientalism here can be linked to her own experience of alienation as 'the other of the other' in Japan which, she claims, informed the development of her feminist and political consciousness (1982d: 28). Lorna Sage has described this as a 'new-fangled orientalism' (1994: 26). I address this in my unpublished conference paper, '"The Other of the Other": Angela Carter's "New-Fangled" Orientalism' (Crofts, 1999b). Almansi clearly does not 'get' Carter's 'new-fangled' orientalism.

27 Indeed, Said himself continues to revise and extend his theories. See, for example, Said (1995), in which he addresses the alleged anti-Westernism of his original thesis in *Orientalism* (1978). See also Said (1993), *Culture and Imperialism*, in which he extends and updates his original argument.

28 This demonstrates Carter's manipulation of biographical material. Dadd's archivist Patricia Allderidge, whose book Carter acknowledges as a source, writes 'Titania herself perpetuates the ultimate joke, as she crushes a delicate flower together with its fairy occupant beneath her clumsy foot. The joke is very much at the expense of her diminutive forerunner who nestled in a moonbeam in 1841' (Allderidge, 1974: 29). Here the words of the art historian are uttered by the fairy subject of the painting as she compares her depiction in the two paintings.

29 She offers a similar socio-historical analysis in the novels of Firbank's exact contemporary, in 'D. H. Lawrence: Scholarship Boy', arguing that they 'describe the birth of the upper working, lower middle, upwardly-socially-mobile-via-education class as a force to be reckoned with' (1997: 533). In the same article, Carter suggests 'there are few other major English novelists this century; and some of them, like Firbank, would have regarded both "great" and "English" as mild insults' (1997: 532).

30 The chrysalis develops into the butterfly metaphor which Carter uses as a symbol for Firbank's artificial temperament: Firbank later describes himself as 'Pavlova, chasing butterflies' whereas Sassoon is 'Tolstoy, digging for worms', in an anecdote which exists in two distinct versions (1996: 139–40). Carter explicitly acknowledges the difficulty of analysing so fragile and mysteriously beautiful a phenomenon as Firbank and his self-created persona: 'how can one dissect a butterfly?' (1996: 140). The butterfly motif appears again when Firbank quotes from his own novel, *The Prancing Nigger*, in which Charlie Mouth marches into town with nothing to declare except 'butterflies' in a knowing allusion to Oscar Wilde (1996: 149).

31 There is a section entitled 'Food Fetishes' in *Shaking A Leg* (1997), which expands slightly on the food section, 'Tomato Woman', in *Expletives Deleted* (1992).

32 As Sceats points out, this is a similar project to that in *The Sadeian Woman* ([1979] 1992b).

33 As Sage explains, 'at or around eighteen she had anorexia, though it hadn't been fully invented; she got down to six stone something in a classic attempt to postpone womanhood, or whatever' (1977: 54). Carter's brother, Hugh Stalker, recounts 'I came home from holiday once ... and the door was opened by this sylph and she had over a very short period decided that she was going to slim, and she did. I mean most drastically. This caused terrible problems at home because my mother thought she was going to kill herself, starve herself to death and there were terrible scenes' (Evans and Carter, 1992: 12).

34 As Carter asserts, 'emaciation, therefore, equals emancipation; another false equation, but one way that presents itself to the baffled ego as a method of escaping a physical trap' (1997: 561). Carter also stresses the relationship between anorexia and rejection of adult sexuality, particularly associated with the onset of menarche for adolescent girls. In *The Magic Toyshop*, for example, Melanie's avoidance of Mrs Rundle's bread pudding is indicative of her equivocal attitude towards female sexuality: 'Melanie grew to fear bread pudding. She was afraid that if she ate too much of it she would grow fat and nobody would ever love her and she would die virgin'; contrasting with her brother Jonathan, who eats 'like a blind force of nature, clearing through mounds of food like a tank' ([1967] 1981: 3–4). Although she overlooks Carter's anorexic experience, Sceats does address the ways in which food can be used as a form of subversion in her discussion of the power relations of food in *The Magic Toyshop* (see Sceats, 1997: 103–4, 106–8).

35 The homophonic play on 'one self' and 'oneself' has greater impact in performance, again illustrating the need for analysis of the recorded plays in tandem with the printed scripts.

36 Marc O'Day (1994: 56) also recognises the figure of the dandy in Carter's early fiction, reading Honeybuzzard in *Shadow Dance* (1966a) as 'the fictional exemplar of the dandy self as work of art'. As noted above, Magrs (1997) discusses the reconstructed male figures, Walser and Uncle Peregrine, in Carter's later fiction.

37 This title may or may not have been the inspiration for the title of *A Self-Made Man*.

38 As O'Day has pointed out, Carter's early fiction, in particular, reveals an eye for contemporary fashion which extends to her cultural criticism and journalism (1994: 24–58). See 'Notes for a Theory of Sixties Style', 'People as Pictures', 'The Wound in the Face', 'Recession Style' (1980), all collected in *Shaking a Leg* (1997).

39 Carter recognises Firbank as a literary influence in interview with John Haffenden (1985): 'it is to a degree true that, as we used to say in the sixties, you are what you eat, because what I had been reading were people like Isak Dinesen, Cocteau and Firbank – a certain kind of non-naturalistic writing that was very much around but which nobody seemed to be reading. (Earlier this summer, in fact, I did a radio play about Firbank called "A Self-Made Man.") Firbank has a beautiful precision of language, and he's also so very funny and melancholy; his evocation of landscape is as economical and beautiful as *haiku*' (Haffenden, 1985: 80–1).

40 She adds, 'I've always thought that he was a plucky little bantam weight' (Haffenden, 1985: 80–1).

41 Firbank's position is still on the outskirts of the modernist canon, although his experimentation with dialogue arguably prefigures Joyce.

# 'Anything that flickers': the cinema[1]

Angela Carter's love and knowledge of the cinema filters through her work for the written page as much as it informs her involvement in adapting her own work for film. While radio's 'aural hallucinations' enabled her to challenge the dominance of the visual economy from the margins, she was drawn to the cinema because it allowed her to explore and demythologise these structures of looking within the mainstream (Carter, 1985: 7). She wrote extensively about film in her fiction and journalism. An entire section of *Shaking a Leg* is devoted to 'Screen and Dream', including pieces on the iconographic Louise Brooks and Marlene Dietrich, Nagisa Oshima's *Ai No Corrida* and *Gone With The Wind* (Carter, 1997).[2] Many of the concerns expressed in these reviews, articles and essays also materialise in her fiction. An analysis of Carter's engagement with the cinema in these writings reveals a remarkable congruence with recent debates in feminist film theory around the construction of femininity, the gendering of the gaze and the politics of spectatorship. In this chapter I analyse Carter's film criticism and the use of cinematic reference in her poetry and fiction in the light of these developments in feminist film theory, in order to contextualise her film adaptations, *The Company of Wolves* (1984b) and *The Magic Toyshop* (1986a), which form the focus of Chapters 5 and 6.

## The fantastic power of the silver screen

Carter's early fiction is saturated with allusion to cinema, not only in its direct reference to film styles, but also to the experience of watching films or the fantasy of being in them. In her first novel, *Shadow Dance*, the disfigured Ghislaine is described as the Hammer Horror 'bride of Frankenstein': 'now her voice gave the final, unnerving resemblance to a horror-movie woman to her' (Carter, 1996a: 4).[3] In *The Magic Toyshop*

Melanie fantasises about her life in terms of cinema; Uncle Philip becomes a character in a film played by Orson Welles, and she imagines watching herself in a new-wave British film (Carter, [1967] 1981: 76, 106). In *Love*, Lee describes Annabel in terms of 'stills from expressionist films, stark, grotesque and unnatural' and Lee's lover Carolyn finds herself 'cast willy-nilly in the role of the Other Woman and now she had to learn the entire traditional script, no matter how crippling she found it to her self-esteem' (Carter, [1971] 1987: 40, 42). Furthermore, these early novels not only refer to films and film genres but to the technological 'apparatus' of cinema itself (see de Lauretis and Heath (eds), 1980). When Melanie dreams about her younger brother Jonathan, in *The Magic Toyshop*, he begins 'to flicker; as in a faultily projected film' (Carter, [1967] 1981: 175) and similarly, in Carter's third novel, *Several Perceptions*, Kay is described 'as if he were a piece of trick photography' (1968: 152).[4] Carter herself, of course, was not unaware of her debt to film. In a Radio 4 (1989) discussion she states: 'I'm perfectly conscious of using all kinds of narrative technique that I've taken from the cinema. Our experience of watching narrative in the cinema has completely altered the way that we approach narrative on the page, that we even read nineteenth-century novels differently.' David Wheatley, director of *The Magic Toyshop*, was attracted to Carter's writing precisely because of this cinematic quality: 'that's what struck me about her. I thought that her book was influenced by films' (1996: 237).

Carter's later fictions also draw on cinema, as Elaine Jordan asserts, 'exemplified most obviously in the obsessive Amerika of *The Passion of New Eve*, with its allusions to *Metropolis*, Greta Garbo, *Sunset Boulevard*, the swimming pool frozen in tears, and so on' (1994: 204). Cinematic reference even seeps into her non-fiction writings. In 'Tokyo Pastoral' Carter describes the Japanese metropolis in terms of European art-house film: 'It is as though Fellini had decided to remake *Alphaville*' (1982d: 32). And, as Laura Mulvey maintains, 'her books seem to be pervaded by this magic cinematic attribute even when the cinema itself is not present on the page' (1994: 230). However, my project is not to simply catalogue the ways in which film pervades her frame of reference and imagery, but to investigate why the cinema held such an attraction for Carter.

### 'You can put your knickers back on in a minute, dear'

One of Carter's earliest published writings, *Unicorn* (1966b), examines the gender dynamics of looking which were to become so central in her later work.[5] This strange piece, an experimental poem, ostensibly explores the myth of the unicorn and the virgin but becomes an investigation of representation itself – the unicorn and virgin, as it were, in quotation marks. I explore the poem here in some depth, first because it requires some explication owing to its relative obscurity, and secondly because it illuminates Carter's later concerns with demythologising the construction and representation of gender in her fiction, journalism and her work in media. The poem is introduced by a quotation from Sir Thomas Browne on the legendary method of catching unicorns: 'A virgin girl is led to where he lurks and there is sent off by herself into the wood. He soon leaps into her lap when he sees her and hence he gets caught' (1966b: 2). The poem is then divided into three parts, prefaced by the imperative: 'Let us cut out and assemble our pieces.' In section (a) 'The Unicorn' is described in overtly phallic terms: 'Then the horn sprouts, swells, blooms in all its glory./SEE THE HORN/(bend the tab, slit in slot/marked "x")' (1966b: 3). Carter then poses the question: 'Q. What have unicorns and virgins got in common?/A. They are both fabulous beasts' (1966b: 3). In section (b) 'The young girl' is configured as a passive object of desire, 'all white and naked; arrange her/among innocent and fragile leaves' – the object of a voyeuristic male gaze:

(Strip-club agents cramped in cabinet de voyeur
massage their trembling buttocks;
fungus of stubble erupts in jowl and chin before
your very eyes; they dribble down apricot limbs
of the painted undressed ladies on their ties.) (1966b: 4)

The final section, '(c) Lights, action', reinforces the voyeurism of the scene which has been staged for the camera: 'Luminescent, her belly gleams/with a cold, lunar brilliance; the curious plantations/of pubic hair crackle electrically, spark/a magnesium flash' (1966b: 5). The virgin is situated as a character in a pornographic scenario, possibly a film, as suggested by 'Lights, action' and the 'magnesium flash', the object of the camera's fetishising lens. But the young girl celebrates the very cause of her fetishisation – her image as castrating woman, her sinister genital organs:

I have sharp teeth inside my mouth,
Inside dark red lips,
And Lacquer slickly hides the claws
In my red fingertips.

So I conceal my armoury.
Yours is all on view.
You think you are possessing me –
But I've got my teeth in you. (1966b: 6)

The poem ends not with the unicorn nor with the virgin but with the anonymous 'They', sharpening their knives and whispering to the young girl: 'You can put your knickers back on in a minute, dear' (1966b: 6). 'They' are implicated as male by the patronising 'dear'.

Carter's engagement with pornographic representation in this early poem prefigures her later feminist reappropriation of the Marquis de Sade in *The Sadeian Woman*, in which she proposes the concept of the 'moral pornographer' who will put 'pornography in the service of women' ([1979] 1992b: 19, 37).[6] Carter suggests that Sade exposes the power politics of sexuality and so enables women to see the cultural constructed-ness of their own oppression: 'The hole the pornographer Sade leaves in his text is just sufficient for a flaying; for a castration. It is a hole large enough for women to see themselves as if the fringed hole of graffiti were a spyhole into territory that had been forbidden them' ([1979] 1992b: 36). She has Desiderio describe one of the peep-show spectacles in very similar terms in *The Infernal Desire Machines of Doctor Hoffman*: 'The dark red and purple crenelations surrounding the vagina acted as a frame for a perfectly round hole through which the viewer glimpsed the moist, luxuriant landscape of the interior' (Carter, [1972] 1982: 44). This porno-graphic spectacle works to foreground voyeuristic looking via the male protagonist's gaze, but also functions to demystify gendered power relations for the female reader. In *Unicorn*, Carter undertakes a similar project, aiming to draw attention to, and so disrupt, the fetishistic apparatus of pornography, stripping away 'the mystifications of sex ... to reveal the workings of power underneath' (Sage, 1994: 12).

Carter's poem is radical in suggesting that the unicorn (representing phallic masculinity) is a fabulous beast (cultural construction), which can be caught (sustained) only by the virgin (the equally constructed myth of femininity). Rather than simply describing or, worse, reinscribing the patriarchal status quo, the network of looks in *Unicorn* functions to fore-ground the mechanisms by which these gendered identities are culturally constructed. In other words, the poem works to radically challenge notions of gendered identity by drawing attention to the constructedness of both masculinity and femininity. Read in this context it becomes apparent that Carter's primary interest lies, not with pornography, nor with cinema *per se*, but in an examination of culturally inscribed patriarchal structures of looking which are exaggerated in pornographic represen-tation and magnified on the silver screen.

Carter's preoccupation with the apparatus behind the objectification of the female body bears a remarkable similarity to the concerns of early feminist film theory. In her seminal essay, 'Visual Pleasure and Narrative Cinema', Laura Mulvey identifies a gendered structure of looks in operation in classical narrative cinema whereby visual pleasure is split between passive/female 'to-be-looked-at-ness' and an active/male gaze ([1975] 1989: 19–26). Mulvey's hierarchical configuration of 'woman as image, man as bearer of the look' ([1975] 1989: 19) is contingent upon psychoanalytic structures of sexual difference, in which the formation of male subjectivity is said to be founded on the male child's fear of castration on witnessing the woman's visible lack of a penis.[7] In traditional narrative film, Mulvey proposes, the 'male unconscious has two avenues of escape from this castration anxiety': the first, voyeurism, is located in a 'preoccupation with the re-enactment of the original trauma (investigating the woman, demystifying her mystery)'; the second, 'fetishistic scopophilia', signals the 'complete disavowal of castration by the substitution of a fetish object or turning the represented figure itself into a fetish so that it becomes reassuring rather than dangerous (hence overvaluation, the cult of the female star)' ([1975] 1989: 21). As E. Ann Kaplan argues, 'the sexualization and objectification of women'

> is designed to annihilate the threat that woman (as castrated and possessing a sinister genital organ) poses ... the camera (unconsciously) fetishizes the female form, rendering it phallus-like so as to mitigate woman's threat. ([1983] 1993: 31)

Thus Carter's poem plays with the very dynamics of voyeurism, fetishism and disavowal which early feminist film theory identifies as operative in traditional narrative cinema. Although Mulvey acknowledges that 'the woman, as icon, displayed for the gaze and enjoyment of men, the active controllers of the look, always threatens to evoke the anxiety it originally signified', she argues that, in mainstream Hollywood cinema, the mechanisms of voyeurism and fetishism more often work to contain that threat ([1975] 1989: 21). But in Carter's poem, the threat of castration is not so straightforwardly contained. Instead of disavowing the threat of the woman, the poem celebrates an active female sexuality which threatens to overspill the controlling male gaze. The virgin's armoury of 'sharp teeth' and 'claws' threatens to rupture the surface of lacquered femininity which has been designed to conceal them: 'You think you are possessing me/But I've got my teeth in you' (Carter, 1966b: 6). While it could be argued that any threat to patriarchal looking is comically undercut by the last line of the poem, the moment of excess in which the young girl sings of her castrating toothed mouth/vagina is not completely eradicated.

It is germane to turn to Barbara Creed's (1993) analysis of the vagina dentata and the 'monstrous feminine' in the modern horror film in this context. While the 'fear of the castrating female genitals pervades the myths and legends of many cultures', Creed suggests that the notion of the vagina dentata is repressed in Freud's writings on sexuality (1993: 105). Creed argues, convincingly, that Freud fundamentally misreads man's 'generalised dread of the woman' as a fear of the woman's lack of a penis (she has been castrated and by analogy the same may happen to him), instead proposing that this fear stems from the configuration of woman as castrator rather than castrated.[8] As Creed asserts (1993: 110): 'The idea that woman's genitals terrify because they might castrate challenges the Freudian and Lacanian view and its association of the symbolic order with the masculine' which underpins much early feminist film theory. Whilst many feminist theorists have felt it necessary to engage with psychoanalysis in order to deconstruct it, more recently contemporary theorists have questioned the usefulness of psychoanalysis for feminism and feminist film theory.[9] As Sue Thornham argues (1997: xiv), the 'cine-psychoanalysis' of early 1970s theory leaves 'little space for resistance by female spectators to the power of patriarchal structures', concentrating as it does on the dominance of the male gaze. Indeed, theories of the male gaze, and the psychoanalytic framework of sexual difference on which they are based, are increasingly being overtaken by a more complex theorisation of gender and spectatorship (see Creed, 1993; Clover, 1993). Carter's exploration of the moments of excess, the gaps within psychoanalytic discourses in *Unicorn*, needs to be read in the light of these contemporary debates. Indeed, it is remarkable that she was already engaging with these issues in such an early poem.

## Hollywood, the wood that makes you go mad

In her later work Carter became more overtly interested in mainstream cinema. She was fascinated by Hollywood, 'the place where the United States perpetrated itself as a universal dream and put the dream into mass production', and explored it extensively in both her fiction and journalism (Carter, 1992: 137). Reviewing Robert Coover's collection of short stories, *A Night at the Movies*, she claims: 'In the days when Hollywood be-straddled the world like a colossus, its vast, brief, insubstantial empire helped to Americanise us all' (Carter, 1992: 131). She responds to this cultural imperialism with mixed feelings: 'It seemed to me, when I first started going to the cinema intensively in the late Fifties, that Hollywood had colonised the imagination of the entire world and was turning us all into Americans. I resented it, it fascinated me' (Carter, 1992: 5).

Hollywood's grip on the collective imagination is evoked by the city bombarded by mirages in *The Infernal Desire Machines of Doctor Hoffman*:

Dr Hoffman's gigantic generators sent out a series of seismic vibrations which made great cracks in the hitherto immutable surface of the time and space equation we had informally formulated in order to realize our city and, out of these cracks, well – nobody knew what would come next. (Carter, [1972] 1982: 17)

Here, Carter explores in terms of the fantastic the critique of the Americanisation of the Western imagination undertaken in her journalism. Reviewing a book on *Classical Hollywood Cinema*, she contemplates the paradox that Hollywood, 'the capital city of illusion', should also be the place where nothing was real 'except hard work, mass production, the conveyor belt, the tyrants, and madmen running the studios' (Carter, 1992: 135, 137). As Jordan points out (1994: 203), the mad scientist, Dr Hoffman, can also be read in terms of the tyrannical studio boss, 'the Merchant of Shadows, the producer of cultural representations which control desire and perception'. Of course, Hoffman's castle turns out to be just as prosaic and industrial as the Dream Factory itself: 'Here, nothing could possibly be fantastic. That was the source of my bitter disappointment. I had wanted his house to be a palace dedicated only to wonder' (Carter, [1972] 1982: 200). Revealing the everyday, hard-work banality behind the dream demystifies the illusion for Desiderio:

I do not know what I had been expecting – but certainly never this tranquillity [*sic*], this domestic peace, for were we not in the house of the magician himself? However, the transmitters sent out their beams high over its battlements and did not affect the fortress of the enemy itself. Here, everything was safe. Everything was ordered. Everything was secure. (Carter, [1972] 1982: 197)

Carter similarly imagines the labour behind the scenes in 'The Merchant of Shadows' (1993: 75), in which the, now retired, MGM lion pads around in the grounds of a Hollywood mansion, pissing on the garden furniture; a marvellous symbol of the decaying golden age of cinema.[10] The narrator is a male PhD student studying the famous Hollywood director Hank Mann, 'I am a student of Light and Illusion. That is, of cinema' (Carter, 1993: 66). Like Evelyn in *The Passion of New Eve*, he is an innocent abroad, the Englishman at sea in the alien waters of the New World:

My entire European mythology capsized under the crash of waves Britannia never ruled and then I knew that the denizens of these deeps are *sui generis* and belong to no mythology but their weird own. They have the strangest eyes, lenses on stalks that go flicker, flicker, and give you the truth twenty-four times a second. Their torsos luminesce in every shade of technicolor but have no depth, no substance, no dimensionality. Beings from a wholly strange pantheon. Beautiful – but alien. (Carter, [1977] 1990: 67)

The creatures of this New World mythology are hybrids of film-projectors and screens, illustrating cinema's grip on the Western imagination. Indeed, the cinema appears to have taken on almost a religious signi-ficance: 'When first I clapped my eyes on that HOLLYWOOD-LAND sign back in the city now five hours' hard drive distant, I thought I'd glimpsed the Holy Grail' (Carter, 1993: 66). Speaking through Mann's widow, the now geriatric film star, Carter ponders on the nature of cinematic projection and desire:

> 'Now, the priest is he who prints the anagrams of desire upon the stock; but whom does he project upon the universe? Another? Or, himself?'
> 'Is he the one who interprets the spirit or does the spirit speak through him? Or is he only, all the time, nothing but the merchant of shadows?' (1993: 80–1)[11]

Nora and Dora Chance are not quite so star-struck when they journey across the Atlantic to take part in a Hollywood adaptation of *A Midsummer Night's Dream*, taking their patch of Shakespearean soil with them, in a reverse attempt at cultural imperialism. But the forest of Arden cannot hope to compete with 'Hollywood, the wood that makes you go mad' (Evans and Carter, 1992: 32). As Carter comments, 'Dora, the heroine of *Wise Children*, is perfectly aware that when they go to Hollywood they're taking leave of their senses' (Evans and Carter, 1992: 32). As Lorna Sage has pointed out (1994: 57), Nora and Dora have the 'looks of Louise Brooks' in Pabst's *Pandora's Box*, 'though they are a comic variant on the theme, *Femmes Fatales* who merely doubled for the part, laughed, and grew old'.[12]

In an *Omnibus* interview, Carter outlines how her patronage of the National Film Theatre contributed to her fascination with the icono-graphic faces of Louise Brooks, Greta Garbo and Marlene Dietrich: 'I loved these faces, I loved them as faces. I loved them as objects' (Evans and Carter, 1992: 13–14). She takes a similar line to that of Roland Barthes, who conducts a semiotic analysis of Garbo as 'face-object' in 'The Face of Garbo' ([1957] 1993: 56). Referring to early Dietrich, Carter demonstrates how this early love of cinema was also an education in the cultural production of femininity:

> I was able to watch the progression of her lacquering as she becomes more unreal. More and more an object, more and more an object of desire. This is the fascination of it. How that face is created from, you know, from raw material, how it's invented, like a piece of cookery really, a piece of haute cuisine ... And then you have to ask yourself why is it done. How have they made this woman into this, you know, fantasy creation? And why? What do they think they're doing? What's up? Is it for money, is it for status, is it for oppression? (Evans and Carter, 1992: 14–15)

She poses similar questions about the construction of femininity in 'Man-Made Women: Winning the Peroxide Wars', a newspaper article on three icons of the Hollywood studio system, in which she suggests that Harlow, Garbo, Dietrich 'are irresistible both to women and to female impersonators. What does that mean? Does it mean that we all know in our hearts that femininity is one big drag act, all the time?'[13] Carter's take on the construction of femininity, here, recalls feminist film theory's engagement with Joan Riviere's essay 'Womanliness as a Masquerade' ([1929] 1986: 35–44, see also Heath, 1986: 45–61). The idea of gender as masquerade is pursued in *The Passion of New Eve* which, Carter claims, she intended to be 'a careful and elaborate discussion of femininity as a commodity, of Hollywood producing illusions as tangible commodities' (Haffenden, 1985: 86). The novel begins in a movie theatre as Evelyn watches Tristessa in *Wuthering Heights*, whilst being sucked off by a girl whose name he forgets: 'She had been the dream itself made flesh though the flesh I knew her in was not flesh itself but only a moving picture of flesh, real but not substantial' (Carter, [1977] 1990: 8).

Tristessa de St Ange, an amalgamation of Hollywood icons of fetishised femininity, becomes a metaphor for the way in which woman supports the cinematic apparatus. As Mulvey argues:

> Tristessa is an icon of the great movie stars' sublime beauty, but in this short reflection Carter manages to put into a few words something about the cinema that critics and theorists can spread over chapters ... It is hard to think of any more succinct summing-up of the paradox of cinema and its projection of fantasy and illusion on to the female body than the opening of *The Passion of New Eve*. (1994, 231–2)

Carter explores a similar idea in 'The Merchant of Shadows' (1993). In both texts men impersonate ideals of femininity – there never *was* a woman like Tristessa and the 'Spirit of Cinema' (the widow of Hank Mann) turns out to be Mann himself.[14] Drawing attention to the masquerade implicit in classic Hollywood cinema has the effect of disrupting patriarchal structures of looking. Doane emphasises the potential for subversion in the masquerade:

> The masquerade, in flaunting femininity, holds it at a distance. Womanliness is a mask which can be worn or removed. The masquerade's resistance to patriarchal positioning would therefore lie in its denial of the production of femininity as closeness, as presence-to-itself ... By destabilising the image, the masquerade confounds this masculine structure of the look. It effects a defamiliarization of female iconography ... a type of representation which carries a threat, disarticulating male systems of viewing. (1991: 25)

In *Wise Children* the Chance twins continue to apply their 'warpaint' well into old age:

> We're stuck in the period at which we peaked, of course. All women do. We'd feel mutilated if you made us wipe off our Joan Crawford mouths and we always do our hair up in big victory rolls when we go out. We've still got lots of it, thank God, iron grey though it may be and tucked away in scarves turban-style, this very moment, to hide the curlers. We always make an effort. We paint an inch thick. We put on our faces before we come down to breakfast, the Max Factor Pan-Stik, the false eyelashes with the three coats of mascara, everything. (Carter, 1991a: 5–6)

This parody of their youthful self-creation has the effect of drawing attention to their original masquerade and denaturalising the cultural production of gender: 'It took us an age, but we did it; we painted the faces that we always used to have on to the faces we have now' (Carter, 1991a: 192). In a reversal of the transvestite icons of femininity in *The Passion of New Eve* and 'The Merchant of Shadows', Nora comments that 'It's every woman's tragedy ... that, after a certain age, she looks like a female impersonator' (Carter, 1991a: 192).

## A critique of these symbols is a critique of our lives

Carter's film journalism not only shows an extensive knowledge of mainstream Hollywood cinema, but also a scholarly interest in European and World cinema, with reviews on films by Richard Roud Bertolucci, Peter Greenaway, Jean-Luc Godard and Nagisa Oshima. This is not simply a film buff's knowledge, but an informed grasp of both film history and the possibilities of the medium. As John Ellis claims:

> She knew a lot about movies ... she'd read a lot of cinema history, so she knew a lot of the byways. It wasn't kind of a film fad's knowledge, she'd studied it, and knew unexpected stuff. (1995: 250)[15]

She contributed a number of pieces to *Visions*, Channel 4's innovative cinema magazine. Produced by Ellis, *Visions* set itself an 'adventurous brief: to explore the whole world's cinema output, revealing how films give a privileged insight into the societies that produce them':

> Cinema shows other cultures thinking aloud and dreaming in public. It provides an insight that no other form of art or reportage can achieve. It can combine the immediacy and banality of everyday existence with wild passions and extravagant fantasies. In some cultures, cinema becomes an overtly political weapon ... In other cultures, cinema is given over to

fantasies – which themselves have a covert political element, as feminist
critics and film-makers insistently demonstrate. (Ellis, 1985: i)

Carter's involvement right from the beginning of the series illustrates her
ongoing commitment to cinema as cultural practice, as a system of signs
– seeing Hollywood as a purveyor of mass-dreams to be interpreted and
analysed as signs and symbols of the twentieth-century western imagination: 'a critique of the Hollywood movie is a critique of the imagination of
the twentieth century in the West' (Carter, 1992: 131). She explored the
same idea in *The Passion of New Eve*:

> Our external symbols must always express the life within us with absolute
> precision; how could they do otherwise, since that life has generated them.
> Therefore we must not blame our poor symbols if they take forms that
> seem trivial to us, or absurd, for the symbols themselves have no control
> over their own fleshly manifestations, however paltry they may be; the
> nature of our life alone has determined their forms. A critique of these
> symbols is a critique of our lives. (Carter, [1977] 1990: 6)

An analysis of Carter's film criticism demonstrates an informed
knowledge of film history. Her review of Bertolucci's *La Luna* abounds
with references to Buñuel, Fassbinder and Sirk, showing a firm grounding in both mainstream film history and alternative cinematic traditions.
The review reveals an awareness of the uses and abuses of psychoanalysis
in film-making and film theory: 'stock themes and characters of the
Dream Factory' are 'graphically presented in terms of *The Interpretation of
Dreams*' and a 'mirror is propped against the wall in a little homage to
Jacques Lacan' (Carter, 1997: 363–4). She also engages with the concerns
of contemporary feminist film theory, criticising the representation of the
mother/Mother, in Bertolucci's overtly Oedipal film. She argues that the
role of the mother 'is elided with the sterile features of the romantic but
uncomfortable moon', in 'an extraordinary and very beautiful image, a
direct visualisation of the actual process of mystification – the real woman
transposed into metaphor before your very eyes':

> The moon is a dead planet, with no light of its own. Caterina is seen
> externally, always from the outside. Even when she is singing on the stage,
> we watch her, not for her own sake, but because Joe is watching her. Truly
> like the moon, she is visible only because we see her in the light reflected
> by Joe's perceptions of her. (Carter, 1997: 365)

In Bertolucci's topography, this diegetic performance provides an excuse
for the objectification of woman: the gaze of the audience is clearly
aligned with that of the male spectator within the film.[16] As Doane argues
(1991: 101): 'In the structures of seeing which the cinema develops in

order to position its spectator, to ensure its own readability, an image of woman is fixed and held – held for the pleasure and reassurance of the male spectator.' Carter suggests that whilst claiming to be avant-garde, with a nod to Freudian and Lacanian psychoanalysis, Bertolucci merely perpetuates the patriarchal status quo, employing the same voyeuristic and fetishised representation of woman in operation in classical narrative cinema:

> Bertolucci himself may well regard this absence of a sense of self in the character of Caterina as part of the existential characterisation of the New Dramaturgy, of which he claims *La Luna* to be an example. But surely this absence of gravity, in the sense of weight, this depthless yet mysterious quality of Caterina, is no more than the romantic notion of Woman as Other which is characteristic of Bertolucci's treatment of women in all his movies. (Carter, 1997: 365–6)

Carter also reviewed Peter Greenaway's *The Draughtsman's Contract*, a very different kind of film, for the first in the *Visions* series (1982a). Carter's script (1997: 372–7) reveals a precise and thorough approach to film criticism, beginning with an analysis of the film's opening credits and music (extra-diegetic elements often ignored), and interspersed with suggestions for stills and clips. She admires Greenaway's anti-cinematic style ('it's highly self-conscious; it makes few gestures towards naturalism'): 'Oddly enough, although *The Draughtsman's Contract* wouldn't be conceivable in any medium but film, it doesn't really owe much to the movies':

> Because it makes very few concessions to its own status as a movie. Ridley Scott's *Blade Runner*, for example, gains most of its impact from a vast range of cinematic references – from Lang's *Metropolis* to Godard's *Alphaville*. As such, it's a typical contemporary 'commercial' movie – as full of quotations as *Hamlet* and geared to a generation weaned on saturation exposure to old movies. (You can catch five or six on TV now, without going out of the house, after all.) *The Draughtsman's Contract* is not like that. Not at all. It isn't concerned with its own historical relevance to the movies, I think – not a film *about* film, but, perhaps, about the *act of seeing*. (Carter, 1997: 376–7)

As such, *The Draughtsman's Contract* functions in similar terms to Carter's interrogation of the dynamics of looking both in her treatment of the cinema in her fiction and in her later involvement with the film industry. In her contribution to another *Visions* documentary, 'Godard: History: Passion' (1983a), Carter acknowledges Godard's influence on this deconstructive approach: 'Godard's movies are themselves an education in cinema and how to see it … Godard shows how to read movies as … systems of connotations. To see them three-dimensionally, never to take narrative as an end-in-itself' (1997: 381).[17] What this semiotic approach enabled Carter to do was to investigate the dominant ideology of the visible without being beguiled by the illusion, like Desiderio, the 'detached observer' (Jordan, 1994: 203), in *The Infernal Desire Machines of Doctor Hoffman*:

> I survived because I could not surrender to the flux of mirages. I could not merge and blend with them; I could not abnegate my reality and lose myself for ever as others did, blasted to non-being by the ferocious artillery of unreason. I was too sardonic. I was too disaffected. (Carter, [1972] 1982: 11–12)

As we have seen, feminist film theory has criticised traditional narrative cinema for its objectification of woman as the object, but never the subject, of desire. By fetishising woman and making her into the passive object of a male gaze, the classic Hollywood film blasts a female spectatorship into similar 'non-being'. Might not this refusal to surrender to 'the flux of images', therefore, offer a useful template for a feminist politics of vision? Desiderio is immune 'because, out of my discontent, I made my own definitions' (Carter, [1972]1982: 3). But rather than Desiderio's sardonic, disaffected gaze, Carter's engagement with the cinema is one of 'passionate detachment'. The phrase comes from the end of 'Visual Pleasure', in which Mulvey asserts:

> The first blow against the monolithic accumulation of traditional film convention (already undertaken by radical film-makers) is to free the look of the camera into its materiality in time and space and the look of the audience into dialectics and passionate detachment. ([1975] 1989: 26)

Adapting the phrase for the title of her book, Thornham (1997: ix) outlines how Mulvey sought to 'describe the stance which she felt should be adopted by the feminist engaged in a critical reading of cinema – whether as film critic, as film-maker, or as audience member' and how the phrase has also been taken up by postmodern feminist theorist Donna Haraway 'to describe her own ideal of the "critical vision" required of theorists engaged in what she calls "the politics of visual culture"'.

Thornham (1997: xvii) finds the phrase useful because 'it captures the complex positioning of a body of theory which seeks to liberate through explanation and yet which is always *passionately* engaged'. I appropriate it here to describe Carter's paradoxical relationship with the cinema – what Catherine Neale (1996: 102) has identified as her 'simultaneous deconstruction and celebration of Hollywood'.[18] On the one hand she critiques classical Hollywood cinema as an industry, one that creates icons, sells illusions and perpetuates culturally constructed dreams (liberating through explanation). At the same time, she celebrates cinema's capacity as a medium for illusion itself (always remaining passionately engaged). An anti-illusionist critique of Hollywood might seem at odds with such a celebration of cinema's illusive possibilities yet, without denying the inherent contradiction, both are aspects of Carter's interrogation of cinema as 'one of the great mediums for the construction of certain kinds of sexual identity, both for women and for men' (Evans and Carter: 1992: 18).

One of the last things Carter wrote was about the cinema, illustrating its ongoing importance as a creative source and cultural force in her topography. She describes the childhood experience of going to 'The Granada, Tooting' with her father:

> to step through the door of this dream cathedral of voluptuous Thirties wish-fulfilment architecture was to set up a tension within me that was never resolved – the tension between inside and outside, between the unappeasable appetite for the unexpected, the gorgeous, the gimcrack, the fantastic, the free play of the imagination and harmony, order. Abstraction. Classicism. This cinema with its mix of the real and false – real marble hugger-mugger with plaster, so you have to tap everything to see if it sounds hollow or solid – this apotheosis of the fake. There was always the element of surprise. It was like the unconscious itself – like cinema itself – public and private at the same time. I held my breath in the gallery of mirrors – anything might materialise in those velvety depths, monsters, beauties, my own grown self. (Evans and Carter, 1992: 8–9)[19]

This tension between fantasy and reality, between public and private, the gimcrack and Classicism echoes the oscillation between Carter's celebration and critique of the cinema in her fiction and journalism. When she actually came to adapt her own work for the cinema, Carter was overcome with

> the quite unhealthy sense of power with which you feel that you're actually beaming the figments of your imagination across the city, across the country, across the world, is actually quite extraordinary. I hadn't realised it would be like that. It's quite different to a novel which is very much a one to one, you know, blasting all these cinema screens with these images of unrepressed libido is really a very exhilarating thing to do. (Mars-Jones, 1984b)

Carter clearly enjoyed her involvement with the film industry which, as Mulvey asserts, 'gave her the chance to take her fascination with the cinema in to the real world' (1994: 233).[20] Director Neil Jordan similarly recalls that 'she was thrilled with the process, because she loved films, and had never really been involved in one' (Carter, 1996: 506). However,

Neale (1996: 101) argues that Carter's films are ultimately bound to their literary origins, unable to succeed as cinema: 'given Carter's engagement with cinema, and her identification of it as the predominant twentieth-century mode of collective pleasure (with all its inherent equivocations), her own films emerge as curiously downbeat hybrids'. In Chapters 5 and 6 I demonstrate why I disagree with Neale's take on Carter's two screen adaptations, discussing *The Company of Wolves* and *The Magic Toyshop* in the context of theoretical developments which challenge the dominance of the look in film theory, including body horror and animation theory.

## Notes

1  In her Introduction to the posthumously published, *American Ghosts and Old World Wonders*, Susannah Clapp states that 'Angela enjoyed carnival in different forms, as music hall or pantomime and as film – "I like," she said, "anything that flickers"' (Carter, 1993: ix).

2  Uglow borrows the subtitle 'Screen and Dream' from *Nothing Sacred* (Carter, 1982d).

3  The title, *Shadow Dance* itself has connotations of shadows dancing across a cinema screen, or the early shadow shows from which the cinema of illusion developed.

4  *Several Perceptions* takes its title from a quotation from David Hume: 'The mind is a kind of theatre, where several perceptions successively make their appearance, pass, re-pass, glide away and mingle in an infinite variety of postures and situations' which, while obviously referring to traditional theatre, could similarly describe the protohistory of cinema and film itself, the successive images on the screen brought to life by the persistence of vision. Carter's thematic interest in stop-motion photography informs her later work in cinema and television. Both film adaptations employ a variety of animation techniques (see Chapters 5 and 6), as does *The Holy Family Album*, Carter's heretical television programme (discussed in Chapter 8) and her unrealised screenplay, 'Gun for the Devil' (discussed briefly in the Envoi).

5  Like Carter's writing for media, *Unicorn* has been largely ignored. Aidan Day (1998: 1) dismisses Carter's poetry in the same breath as her radio plays, film scripts and journalism and, while mentioning it by name, Linden Peach (1998: 2) similarly lumps the poem, along with the radio plays, in a list of publications in addition to 'the novels', which in both instances are signalled as the primary area of study. Furthermore, *Unicorn* has not since been published in any of the three collected works (Carter, 1995, 1996, 1997).

6  As observed in Chapter 2, Carter's reappropriation of pornography here, like her recasting of fairy tale, has been problematic for a number of feminist critics who argue that she fails to escape the sexist ideology of the genre (see Duncker, 1984: 3–14). Sally Keenan (1997: 143) offers a productive engagement with these debates, asking 'if the pornographer as producer/director of the scene is an inherent element in the repressive and exploitative structures of representation in our culture, of which the pornographic scenario is simply an explicit case, how can pornography be invested with a different ideology, one aimed at exposing its own assumptions and exploitations?'

7  Mulvey draws attention to the failure of psychoanalysis regarding the formation of female subjectivity. Nevertheless, she argues, 'psychoanalytic theory as it now stands can at least advance our understanding of the *status quo*, of the patriarchal order in which we are caught', deliberately setting out to appropriate psychoanalytic theory 'as a political

weapon, demonstrating the way the unconscious of patriarchal society has structured film form' ([1975] 1989: 14–15).

8 Creed's theory of the monstrous feminine also offers a productive way of reading Ghisaline's disfigured face in *Shadow Dance*. Ghisaline's scar, 'all red and raw as if, at the slightest exertion, it might open and bleed; and the flesh was marked with purple imprints from the stitches she had had in it', clearly stands in for her monstrous sex, and Morris's fascinated horror exemplifies the male dread of the castrating, incorporating female genitals: 'the moment she saw him she would snatch him up and absorb him, threshing, into the chasm in her face' (Carter, 1966a: 2, 39).

9 As noted above, Mulvey admits that she finds psychoanalysis a useful tool, but only for describing the existing patriarchal status quo. Lorraine Gamman and Margaret Marshment detect a 'sense of unease about the adequacy of psychoanalysis' (Gamman and Marshment (eds), 1988: 5). See also Luce Irigaray (1985) and Jacqueline Rose (1986).

10 She also mentions 'the MGM lion ("Ars Gratia Artis") who in old age, had to be fitted with dentures' in a review of *Hollywood Anecdotes* (Carter, 1992: 136).

11 Carter states in one of her last interviews, 'I suppose I'm not in the least a religious person, I think that's fairly well known, but there is something sacred about the cinema which is to do with it being public, to do with people going together with the intention of ... experiencing the same experience, having the same revelation' (Evans and Carter, 1992: 7).

12 Carter admired Brooks, writing about her in 'Femmes Fatales' (1982d: 119–23) and 'Brooksie and Faust' (1997: 387–92), a review of Barry Paris' *Louise Brooks*. Carter's adaptation of Wedekind's 'Lulu' plays is discussed briefly in the Envoi (Carter, 1996).

13 Angela Carter, 'Man-Made Women: Winning the Peroxide Wars' (I am afraid I have no place of publication or date for this newspaper article found in the archive at Rogers, Coleridge and White, Carter's literary agents).

14 As Carter asserts in an interview with John Haffenden, 'The promotion slogan for the film *Gilda*, starring Rita Hayworth, was "There was never a woman like Gilda", and that may have been one of the reasons why I made my Hollywood star a transvestite, a man, because only a man could think of femininity in terms of that slogan' (Haffenden, 1985: 86).

15 Owner of Large Door Productions Ltd who produced Carter's controversial television programme, *The Holy Family Album* (1991b), Ellis is himself a respected film and television theorist and is the author of *Visible Fictions: Cinema, Television, Video* (Ellis, 1982).

16 As Susan Hayward claims (1996: 68), the use of a diegetic audience in classical narrative cinema draws attention to the (typically female) star, drawing us, 'as the extra-diegetic audience, into the screen and thereby into the illusion that we too are part of the diegetic audience', citing the musical as a typical example (significantly Caterina plays an opera singer). The enforced spectatorship at the beginning of *The Magic Toyshop* subverts the traditional function of the diegetic audience, as I argue in Chapter 6.

17 Godard's 3-D seeing, here, is reminiscent of radio's 'three-dimensional story-telling' (Carter, 1985: 7), discussed in Chapter 1.

18 Neale emphasises Carter's celebration of cinema's pleasures in *Wise Children*: 'Hollywood comes to represent the twentieth-century admixture of commercialism, exploitation and magic, and cinema signifies not only the film but the place of communal pleasure' (Neale, 1996: 108), at the expense of her materialist critique of Hollywood as an industry, glossing over *The Passion of New Eve*, quoting selectively from Carter's film criticism and completely ignoring 'The Merchant of Shadows'.

19 The published script (Carter, 1997: 400) differs slightly from the programme quoted here. This childhood experience informs the religious invocation of cinema in 'The Merchant of Shadows': 'Night after night prayer wheels ceaselessly turning in the darkened cathedrals, those domed and gilded palaces of the Faith, the Majestics, the

Rialtos, the Alhambras, those grottoes of the miraculous in which the creatures of the dream came out to walk within sight of men. And the wheels spun out those subtle threads of light that wove the liturgies of that reverential age, the last great age of religion. While the wonderful people out there in the dark, the congregation of the faithful, the company of the blessed, they leant forward, they aspired upwards, they imbibed the transmission of divine light' (Carter, 1993: 80).

20 'Everybody always assumes because I'm a writer I don't know what cinema is. I do, I do, I do', Carter insists in a publicity piece for the Australian release of *The Magic Toyshop*, 'I love the movies – I spent the formative years of adolescence at the movies and dreamed of making movies until I realised how laborious it is' (O'Brien, 1987).

# 5

# (Re)animating the body of the text:
## *The Company of Wolves*

Carter's first foray into the film industry was with her film adaptation, *The Company of Wolves* (1984b). According to Mark Bell, editor of Carter's collected dramatic writings, she first approached director Neil Jordan in 1982 with the idea of 'expanding the radio play of *The Company of Wolves* for the screen' (Carter, 1996: 507). Jordan claims that the existing radio adaptation was 'too short for a feature film' and they developed it into a 'Chinese box structure, using the dream of Rosaleen, and the thread of Granny's storytelling as the connecting points, thereby enabling us to integrate other stories and themes of Angela's own' (Carter, 1996: 507). Bell cites these as including other wolf stories from *The Bloody Chamber*, 'Wolf-Alice' and 'The Werewolf', but I would also add 'Peter and the Wolf' from the *Black Venus* collection (Carter, [1985] 1986). According to Bell, Jordan and Carter 'mapped out an outline of proposed scenes, which she then wrote up' throughout the summer of 1983 (Carter, 1996: 507). Jordan recalls, 'once we had agreed on the structure, the writing seemed to flow quite naturally from it, since it gave free rein to Angela's own taste for narrative subversions' (Carter, 1996: 506). It is this 'narrative subversion' which will form the focus for my discussion of the film in this chapter.

The film, *The Company of Wolves*, is an ideal site from which to explore a series of interconnecting discourses around adaptation, animation and abjection, which pivot around the central theme of metamorphosis. The film foregrounds textual and bodily transformation, both in terms of its status as an adaptation of Carter's radio play and the original short stories, and in its explicit depiction of disintegrated and fragmented bodies. The body of the original text is reanimated, or 'brought to back to life', using a variety of animation techniques, from old-fashioned stop-frame photography to high-tech animatronics. However the film's emphasis on graphic special effects has been controversial for some feminist critics who criticise the sexual politics of such a violent film, questioning whether

Carter's feminist project can be successfully translated to mainstream cinema. In this chapter I argue that the film's explicit rendering of violent corporeal transformation can indeed be read in a positive light in the context of contemporary figurations of the body within current feminist, film and animation theory. I also return to the discussion of the female voice and the oral tradition begun in Chapter 2, examining the way in which the film enacts the very feminist reappropriation which Carter undertakes in her reworking of the original fairy tale, in the form of Rosaleen's active story-telling.

## Standard horror

Although highly praised by the British press, *The Company of Wolves* has elicited an equivocal academic response.[1] The film has been criticised from both sides of the film/ fiction divide – either taken to task for failing to live up to the original short story, or seen as unfilmic and unable to transcend its literary roots. In her essay 'Lolita Meets the Werewolf' Maggie Anwell criticises the film for an overemphasis on expensive animatronics in concession to market forces (1988: 76–85). She argues that the film's violent werewolf transformations detract from the feminist power and imaginative subtlety of the original tale. Although she acknowledges the imperative of the medium to find alternative ways of dealing with narrative, Anwell ultimately finds the film too filmic – exploiting cinema's potential for illusion at the expense of the literary quality of the original. Conversely, Catherine Neale (1996: 101) argues that the film remains first and foremost an adaptation trapped in its literary origins, failing to utilise the distinctive possibilities of cinema, and emerging as a 'curiously downbeat hybri[d]'. For Anwell *The Company of Wolves* ultimately fails as an adaptation because it is not literary enough, whereas for Neale it fails as a film because it is too literary. For both critics the film falls down because of its relation to the literary text. Between them Anwell and Neale are trapped in an impossible double bind. The filmic and the literary are set up in an eternal opposition in which screen adaptation can never come out on top

Anwell's critique is part of her wider concern with the question of whether feminist fiction in general can survive the transposition to mainstream cinema without being, in her words, 'reduced, manipulated – even travestied – by the underlying market forces' (1988: 72).[2] These two issues – the tension between the literary original and its adaptation and the concomitant tension between feminism and mainstream popular culture – form an underlying basis for my exploration of textual and corporeal transformation in this chapter.

My dissatisfaction with the available criticism, and my disagreement with Anwell's thesis in particular, drive me to defend the film from a feminist perspective. Focusing on the articulation of female subjectivity and desire, I offer an alternative reading which resists those which construe the film as failing to uphold Carter's feminist message. My intention is not to offer a totalising feminist interpretation of the film, but to open up the debate across the feminist sisterhood (see Crofts, 1998a: 48–63). Furthermore, my analysis seeks to challenge the dominant conception of the relationship between feminism and popular culture as necessarily antagonistic. I address and extend the existing critique, recasting the film both as a radical retelling of Carter's short story and a productive engagement between feminism and the mainstream.

Anwell criticises the film for what she sees as its failure to uphold Carter's radical feminist message. Of course, Carter's feminist project cannot be taken as read and, as established in Chapter 2, her treatment of violence in her fiction has been by no means unproblematic for some feminist critics. However, while she remains somewhat equivocal about the treatment of male aggression in the story 'The Company of Wolves', Anwell argues that the sensitivity with which Carter renders the interior psychic world of the central female protagonist engenders a radical feminist retelling of the original tale. Where Anwell's reading of the sexual politics in the short story is apt, her refusal to see the film as offering a positive space for female subjectivity remains unsatisfactory. Where she sees the short story as successful in its portrayal of female subjectivity, Anwell maintains that the screen adaptation is unable to handle this crucial image of the confident female protagonist. She asserts that: 'the reluctance to allow a positive image of the girl's sexuality in such a violent film is what is most fundamentally at variance with the impact and meaning of the story' (Anwell, 1988: 85). One of her main criticisms is what she perceives to be the film's overemphasis on violent werewolf metamorphoses:

> The blood and violence of the transformations are linked to sexuality in a way that recalls the standard horror movie, in which the girl is seen as victim – no room for the confident folk heroine successfully expressing her desire. (Anwell, 1988: 84)

Although the film's visceral werewolf metamorphoses initially appear to support Anwell's argument, I disagree with her particular take on this film and the politics of 'standard horror' in general, as I go on to demonstrate.

It is fruitful to compare the handling of werewolf metamorphosis in the short story and the film by comparing a scene which appears in both texts, such as the episode in which the bridegroom disappears on his wedding night to answer the 'call of nature'. In the short story, the husband returns years later to find his wife preparing supper for the children of her second marriage. The werewolf metamorphosis is, significantly, precipitated by anxiety over the wife's adultery and reproductive function. When he

> saw she'd slept with another man and, worse, clapped his red eyes on her little children ... he shouted: 'I wish I were a wolf again, to teach this whore a lesson!' So a wolf he instantly became and tore off the eldest boy's left foot before he was chopped up with the hatchet they used for chopping logs. But when the wolf lay bleeding and gasping its last, the pelt peeled off again and he was just as he had been, years ago, when he ran away from his marriage bed, so that she wept and her second husband beat her. (Carter, [1979] 1981: 112–13)

When the wife weeps to see the face of her long lost husband once again, her second husband beats her, with the implication that the threat of violence is firmly situated in the domestic, as much as the supernatural. The second husband's abuse, like the werewolf transformation, is also prompted by fears over female sexuality, the wife's attraction for her first husband threatening the masculinity of the second.

In the film, this scene occurs in the dramatic realisation of one of Granny's werewolf tales. Where the transformation happens in an instant in the short story, the film substitutes a lengthy transformation sequence. While co-producer Chris Brown claims that they had not intended to throw 'buckets of blood' at the audience (McAsh, 1984: 5), the scene ostensibly seems to uphold Anwell's accusation of gratuitous violence. The moment of metamorphosis is rendered in minute and loving detail, using the, then, latest animatronic technology. Stephen Rea peels off the skin on his face, revealing the flesh and musculature beneath. This is realised so vividly that it resembles a medical autopsy. Once pared to the flesh, the head and hands of the long lost bridegroom, grotesque, but recognisably human, begin to metamorphosise into the horrific shape of a wolf. These graphic shots are juxtaposed with reaction shots of sheer terror from the wife, the traditional image of the wide-eyed, screaming female victim. Thus, the scene appears to support Anwell's argument about the polarised gender dynamics of male aggressivity and female victimhood in the film. For Anwell, the werewolf transformations are inherently connected to aggressive, masculine sexuality – reinscribing the patriarchal power structures of the original fairy tale, rather than subverting them as in Carter's original story.

However, there are a number of reasons why I disagree with this somewhat reductive reading. Firstly, it is important to remember that

Granny is narrating this tale of violence in order to teach Rosaleen to fear men: 'Oh they're nice as pie until they've had their way with you. But once the bloom is gone, the beast comes out' (Carter, 1996: 201). Here, just as in the radio play, Granny functions as 'prohibitive mentor' (Jordan, 1990: 28), speaking with the voice of patriarchal interdiction. Read in this context this graphic werewolf transformation and the violence of the scene can be seen as part of Granny's collusion in patriarchal accounts of gender relationships. She supports the patriarchal oppression of female sexuality by perpetuating tales of male sexual aggression. It is also important to remind ourselves of Rosaleen's reaction to Granny's tale in the film: 'I'd never let a man strike me' (Carter, 1996: 201). By contextualising this violent tale in the mouth of Granny, and allowing Rosaleen to comment, the film could in fact be seen to offer an overt critique of the violence it evinces. This contradicts Anwell's reading of the power relations involved in the film. By ignoring the context of the violent transformation, Anwell interprets the film as upholding Granny's patriarchal collusion.

Equally misplaced is Anwell's insistence on the gratuitous violence of the film's graphic werewolf transformations. Taking the film's most visceral transformations as her benchmark, Anwell argues that the film surrenders to the commercial pressures of mainstream cinema in its use of expensive, state-of-the-art animatronics to effect the werewolf metamorphoses. But, Anwell's contention that the film's emphasis on graphic special effects is due to pressure from market forces to utilise the latest technology is not entirely accurate. It is important to note that the screen adaptation is also mediated through another version: according to Neil Jordan (Carter, 1996: 507), the film treatment actually developed out of the radio play, not the short story.[3] Writing about the radio play in the preface to her play anthology, *Come Unto These Yellow Sands: Four Radio Plays*, Carter notes that in the process of reformulating the short story '"The Company of Wolves" took on more of the characteristics of the pure horror story, became almost an exercise in genre' (1985: 10). If we return to the Hunter scene examined in Chapter 2, it becomes clear that a dramatic shift in emphasis in the handling of the transformation from wolf into man has already occurred in the reformulation of the short story for radio:

> NARRATOR. (*Centre. Close.*) The desperate claws retract, refine themselves as if attacked by an invisible emery board, until suddenly they become fingernails and could never have been anything but fingernails, or so it would seem. The leather pads soften and shrink until you could take fingerprints from them, until they have turned into fingertips. The clubbed tendons stretch, the foreshortened phalanges extend and flesh out, the bristling hair sinks backwards into the skin without leaving a trace of stubble behind it. (Carter, 1985: 63)

In the short story the metamorphosis is handled obliquely without a description of the actual transformation: 'and then no wolf at all lay in front of the hunter but the bloody trunk of a man, headless, footless, dying, dead' (Carter, [1979] 1981: 111). The short story concentrates on the fact of transformation, which just 'occurs' in an instant like the magical metamorphoses of fairy tale. Conversely, in the radio play the transformation is narrated in minute, juicy detail, objectifying a specific bodily part – the paw/hand – down to the individual pores of the skin, the fingernails and fingertips. The radio play's treatment of the werewolf transformation has more in common with the graphic transmogrification scenes of pure horror, placing more emphasis on the specific details of the transformation and foregrounding the process of metamorphosis itself. The film's origination in the radio adaptation goes some way towards explaining the shift in emphasis towards horror in the film – which Anwell puts down to market forces.

## Adaptation, reanimation and the remake

The film's history of generic transformation foregrounds the problematics of screen adaptation, and its hybrid status within literary and film studies. Indeed, the central figure of the werewolf can be seen as an extended metaphor for the generic transformation performed by the screen adaptation of Carter's story. As Paul Sutton and Anne White argue, the film is 'an articulation of not only the kinds of transformations suggested by the device of the werewolf, but also an enactment of the very process of adaptation' (1997: 27), further suggesting that it is 'rather fitting that the werewolf should be read as symbolising the cultural hybrid which is literary adaptation' (Sutton and White, 1997: 32).

John O. Thompson suggests that 'there is *something* generically eerie about adaptation' which defies analysis from both sides of the film/fiction divide (1996: 11–12). He identifies a disturbing tension between the literary original and its adaptation which, he argues, has its locus in modernist questions of 'authenticity', 'fidelity' and 'art-form specificity'. With all the implications of cultural elitism and the continued privileging of literary texts over electronic media, screen adaptation seemingly cannot win – on the one hand indicted as the uncanny 'simulacrum' of the authentic original – while, on the other, condemned as a generic hybrid which fails to emerge as either film or fiction. Adaptation is not only a cultural and generic hybrid, but also straddles a theoretical divide, which Lisa Trahair suggests might be cast in terms of an opposition between the pejorative treatment of a would-be remake as merely a copy by modernist literary criticism and an affirmative proclamation of it as embodying a dionysian or simulacral power by a certain postmodernism that is also at times informed by post-structuralism. (1991: 184)

And as Thompson points out, although modernist concerns with textual authority might seem 'unfashionable' in the context of post-structuralist notions of the death of the author, they continue to dominate discourses around adaptation (1996: 11–12).

In order to break this impasse, it is necessary to formulate an alternative way in which to discuss adaptation. The horror film is a particularly productive model through which to explore adaptation because, as an essentially formulaic genre, it has no reverence for modernist concepts of originality and individuality. As Trahair argues, horror is a 'privileged site for the consideration of the remake':

> Not only does it seem to have a more obvious predilection for the remake than other genres ... it takes remaking as one of its most popular themes and by so doing raises questions concerned with identity, monstrosity, doubling and the uncanny. (1991: 183)

Philip Brophy's work on contemporary horror foregrounds the self-referential, intertextual, parodic tendencies of the genre, which he suggests, result from 'an historical over-exposure' to generic conventions (1986: 3, 5). Trahair argues that contemporary horror film inherently takes on the properties of the postmodern, self-reflexive remake:

> the self-conscious film manifests its consciousness of its precursors by allusion, by the practices of quotation and appropriation. Thus, we can see already a certain complicity between the horror film and the postmodern remake. (1991: 184)

Trahair attempts to unravel various theorists' attempts to define and differentiate between postmodern concepts such as 'appropriation', 'quotation', 'allusion', 'parody' and 'pastiche', arguing that apart from their distinction from 'modernism's attitude to imitation as derivative and parasitical', these terms remain 'undertheorized' (1991: 185).[4] She argues against Noël Carroll's umbrella usage of 'allusion' (1982: 52) and his 'tendency to privilege canonisation over other practices of quotation such as pastiche, parody and irony' and similarly takes issue with Frederic Jameson's rejection of the term 'parody', as descriptive of postmodernism, in favour of 'pastiche': 'a neutral practice of imitation, without parody's "ulterior motives"' (1984: 65).

Instead, Trahair posits a form of irony in which the dead styles to which Jameson refers can be reanimated and revivified by the practice of quotation in the remake, 'not the inversion of parody, not a turning upside down, but a subtle twisting of the direction of the original film, a taking up of lost potentialities' (1991: 186). This 'taking up of lost potentialities' seems particularly apposite in any consideration of *The Company of Wolves*. As Trahair suggests:

> the contemporary remake does not intend to erase its predecessors but depends on audience awareness of other 'versions', which become a constitutive part of the film's structure. (1991: 184)

Not only does the film remake Carter's text(s) and the original Red Riding Hood fairy tale, it also refers intertextually to the classic werewolf movie and the stock conventions of horror genre.[5]

Trahair goes on to extend her thesis about the remake to a discussion of (re)animation. Formally and thematically connected with the uncanny, she argues, 'the remake is animated, engendered, vivified, regenerated; and all of these are morphologically complicit with metamorphosis' (1991: 183), elucidating her argument with an analysis of David Cronenberg's remake of *The Fly*:

> Cronenberg's film tropes reanimation, reanimating reanimation as its subject by reanimating (remaking) Kurt Neumann's film. Metamorphosis, remaking, reproducing and rebirthing are splattered metonymically and metaphorically over its whole surface. (1991: 192)

As Trahair points out, *genetic* metamorphosis within the diegesis foregrounds the *generic* metamorphosis performed in the remake of the film.[6]

Trahair's argument is clearly useful for a discussion of textual and lycanthropic transformation in *The Company of Wolves*. Rather than focusing on authenticity and fidelity the paradigm of the reanimated text allows us to explore the abject borderline between the original and its adaptation. The transformation of a text from one medium to another can be seen as a process of revivifying the body of the original text. As we have seen, the textual history of *The Company of Wolves* comprises a series of such reanimations. Not only does the film refer to texts outside itself – the original fairy tale, Carter's adapted story and the werewolf genre as noted above – but the act of transformation is literally and repeatedly animated within the film, mirroring the act of adaptation itself and foregrounding the multiplicity of potentialities in any one text. The trope of reanimation makes explicit this link between the process of transforming a text (itself intimately connected with the metamorphic potential inherent in the abject figure of the werewolf) and the use of actual film animation in the realisation of the werewolf transformations. Furthermore, reanimation is particularly apposite in a discussion of *The Company of Wolves*, because of the variety of animation techniques with which the different werewolf transformations are executed. Adaptation is repeatedly performed on the body of the werewolf, 'reanimating animation' and exploiting the full range of cinema's technical properties from hi-tech animatronics to old-fashioned stop-frame animation.

## Body horror

The third problem with Anwell's reading of the gender dynamics of 'standard horror' is that she relies on theories of 'the male gaze' which, as we have seen, are becoming increasingly inadequate for describing the complex processes of identification at work in horror (and arguably most other forms of cinema). Anwell's essay appears in Lorraine Gamman and Margaret Marshment's collection, *The Female Gaze* (1988), which focuses on 'women as viewers of popular culture', explicitly reappropriating Laura Mulvey's concept of 'the male gaze' ([1975] 1989: 14–26) for the female spectator. The collection as a whole sets out to interrogate the dominant discourse of feminist film theory: the emphasis on 'the look' and its basis in psychoanalytical accounts of gender difference. Gamman and Marshment question the orthodox 'notion of a "male gaze" as dominant in all mainstream genres' (1988: 5), attempting instead to carve out an alternative space for feminism within the mainstream.[7] It is this space which Anwell ironically overlooks in her reluctance to abandon the trope of the male gaze and her consequent insistence on the film's voyeuristic portrayal of the central female figure. In reducing the gender dynamics of the film to the binary opposition between male aggressivity and female victimhood, Anwell fails to recognise any positive representation of female subjectivity and misses much of the film's radical potential.

Contemporary film theory has shifted its focus from this preoccupation with theories of the male gaze to a more complex and productive rendering of the relation between gender and spectatorship. In particular, as Duncan Petrie argues (Petrie (ed.), 1993: 2), 'recent considerations of fantasy and horror films' have opened up 'more sophisticated and challenging insights into such questions as the nature of cinematic spectacle, the construction of gendered subjects in the text and the psychic processes of identification'. Indeed, the sexual politics of 'standard horror' can no longer be taken as read in the context of feminist theories of the fantastic, from Ellen Moers' tracing of a female gothic tradition in *Literary Women* (1977), to Rosemary Jackson's *Fantasy: the Literature of*

*Subversion* (1981). More specifically, film theory's recent engagement with horror film has desimplified the gender dynamics of spectatorship. I am thinking here of theorists such as Barbara Creed on *The Monstrous-Feminine* (1993) and Carol Clover's extensive work on cross-gender identification in the slasher movie, in *Men, Women and Chainsaws* (1993). These theories of the fantastic offer a fruitful point of departure for a feminist reclamation of the film adaptation of *The Company of Wolves*, and a productive counterbalance to Anwell's reading of the film in terms of theories of the male gaze. In order to move beyond Anwell's account of the gender politics in the film, I now want to take a more detailed look at the graphic werewolf transformations in the light of these contemporary developments in film theory.

The film's graphic transformation scenes could be interpreted in terms of 'body horror', an area of fantasy film theory which looks at theories of abjection and fragmentation in relation to depictions of the body in horror film. Mark Jancovich defines body horror as a 'subgenre' emerging in the 1970s, dealing with a contemporary 'crisis of identity through a concentration on processes of bodily disintegration and transformation ... Within these films, bodies erupt and mutate before the eyes of the audience, and it is these processes which are the central preoccupation of their narratives and visual styles' (1992: 112). Jancovich argues that body horror explores contemporary cultural anxieties around the body and its relation to private and public domains:

> With the emergence of bourgeois individualism, the body was defined as a private space, an inalienable private property which guaranteed the sense of self; but with the rational control of society, the body increasingly became an object of regulation ... It becomes increasingly clear that, rather than being a private space, the body itself is penetrated and tied into a whole series of processes, and these developments blur the distinctions necessary for a stable sense of self. (1992: 112–13)

According to Linda Ruth Williams (1994) body horror embodies (if you will excuse the pun) fantasies of interiority: boundaries between inside and outside are transgressed, insides are rendered visible, the body within ceases to be a private space. Body horror is intimately connected with the abject. In *The Powers of Horror* (1982), Julia Kristeva defines the abject as those elements which remind us of the origin or end of identity – bodily functions, decay, death. The rejection of the abject can be interpreted as a conservative act, one of shoring up identity, inserting oneself in the 'phallic' symbolic order as opposed to the pre-symbolic, maternal 'chora'.[8] Kristeva argues that 'defilement rituals' are needed in order to 'mark the boundary between clean and proper symbolic order and abyssal, impure abject' (Vice (ed.), 1996: 153). Judith Butler recognises the ambiguous role of the abject in the construction of identity:

> The 'abject' designates that which has been expelled from the body, discharged as excrement, literally rendered 'Other'. This appears as an expulsion of alien elements, but the alien is effectively established through this expulsion. The construction of the 'not-me' as the abject establishes the boundaries of the body which are also the first contours of the subject. (1990: 133)

Thus, while the abject is necessary in order to define the subject, it is also a constant threat to the subject. Indeed, it is as much the self, as the alien, which is established through this process of expulsion. Creed sees the horror film as a modern-day equivalent of Kristevan rites of defilement. She argues that the central activity of the popular horror film is the 'purification of the abject':

> The horror film attempts to bring about a confrontation with the abject (the corpse, bodily wastes, the monstrous-feminine) in order to eject the abject and redraw the boundaries between the human and non-human. As a form of modern defilement rite, the horror film attempts to separate out the symbolic order from all that threatens its stability. (1993: 14)

This 'purification of the abject' is inherently gendered because of the abject's association with the oozing of bodily fluids and therefore with menstruation, childbirth and the feminine. Creed recognises the monstrous-feminine as a patriarchal construct (just as she would argue masculine, phallic monsters are constructed), but then asserts that 'her representation in popular discourses as monstrous is a function of the ideological project of the horror film – a project designed to perpetuate the belief that woman's monstrous nature is inextricably bound up with her difference as man's sexual other' (1993: 83). But, the abject is not as straightforwardly contained nor is the horror film necessarily as conservative or reactionary as Creed seems to imply. On the contrary, the abject can be the site of a more sustained resistance to the symbolic order. In marking the boundary between subject and abject it is impossible to avoid also foregrounding the necessary relationship between them. Modern horror plays with this ambiguity between demarcation, distinction, exclusion and recognition, just as it plays with the dynamics of repulsion and fascination which have also been related to the abject.

To return to the film, the violent corporeal transformation discussed earlier situates the werewolf as abject, collapsing boundaries between animal and human, and challenging the constitution of the human body itself.[9] As the long-lost husband tears the skin from his own face, distinctions between inside and outside are transgressed. We are presented with a flayed human head with all the working musculature beneath, flesh, sinews, tendons, veins. Before the actual cross-over from man to wolf occurs, the human body is quite literally deconstructed, pared to the very working mechanism and then reconstituted in the form of a wolf.[10] As Alan Cholodenko argues (Cholodenko (ed.), 1991: 14), animation has a 'special association with the "abject", the double, the "uncanny, the sublime, seduction, *différance*, disappearance and death – all those improper, unseemly things"'. The scene is further implicated in the abject when the werewolf's decapitated head lands in a pail of milk, recalling Kristeva's 'food loathing' – the skin of the milk (1984: 2).[11] The decapitated head (abject in its very status as werewolf, and as corpse, decay, waste) penetrates the smooth, white surface of the milk (clean, nourishing, the opposite of abject), staining it with blood, and resurfacing as a human head, in a further metamorphosis back into a state of youthful beauty.

Neither the subject positions portrayed within the film nor those available to the spectator, fit into the male/female binaries which Anwell refuses to abandon. As Clover argues in relation to the victim/aggressor subject positions in the slasher horror genre, (coincidentally invoking the archetype of Red Riding Hood):

> just as attacker and attacked are expressions of the same self in night-mares, so they are expressions of the same viewer in horror film. We are both Red Riding Hood *and* the Wolf; the force of the experience, in horror, comes from 'knowing' both sides of the story. (1993: 12)

This ambiguity is played out in the film, *The Company of Wolves*. The werewolf is at once victim and aggressor, painfully ripping off his own skin and giving birth to the animal within. The wife is at once masochistic viewer and sadistic voyeur. In another visceral transformation, which occurs towards the end of the film, the wolf erupts fully formed from the mouth of the Hunter. The image of the wolf emerging out of the mouth of a man directly evokes childbirth, with the mouth standing in for the vagina, implicating him in the feminine. As Jancovich points out, a central theme in body horror is the 'body as womb which gives birth to a new life-form which discards the original body and the original self; although it comes from within' (1992: 13).

These violent werewolf transformations position the male as a feminised figure, with the abject connection between blood as vital fluid, menstrual flow and after-birth. They may be horrific, but they are not gratuitous. Far from reinscribing the 'phallic aggressivity' of the original Red Riding Hood tale, they offer a much more complicated exploration of gender dynamics than has hitherto been acknowledged. The only characters in the film to undergo such visceral transformations are male – subjected to pain, abjection, penetration, expulsion, they are implicated in the feminine. Breaking down gender differences, these violent transformation scenes can therefore be read in a feminist light. The film's project is to foreground the fragility of culturally constructed gender roles as opposed to essentialist accounts of gender. This is obviously a transformative project.

As Jancovich argues, 'concentrating on the process of bodily fragmentation and transformation is a way of representing and examining the crisis of identity within contemporary society' (1992: 13). But body horror offers not merely a reflection of our postmodern condition, it also posits the radical possibility of cultural and social change. In its destabilisation, deconstruction and decentring of essentialist notions of identity as unified and whole, body horror creates a productive space for marginalised subjectivities. As Jackson suggests:

> The many partial, dual, multiple and dismembered selves scattered throughout literary fantasies violate the most cherished of all human unities: the unity of character ... fantasies provide very different images of identity from the solid bodies found in 'realistic' fiction. (1981: 82–3)

As discussed in Chapter 3, the violation of the unity of character forms one of fantasy's most radical operations. In body horror, this violation is enacted on the screen. As Jancovich suggests, 'these physical processes of transformation ... not only threaten engulfment and assimilation, but they also offer the possibility of liberation and power from the conventional limits of the body and the self' (1992: 115). Read in this light, the film's graphic werewolf metamorphoses can be seen to offer a more radical interrogation of gender and identity than Anwell suggests in her reading of 'standard' horror. But while it is important to desimplify readings of horror which situate it as necessarily reactionary, it is equally crucial not to go to the other extreme and suggest that horror is always inherently subversive. Also central to this debate is the issue of whether body horror can indeed offer a feminist challenge to essentialist notions of identity. There is always the implied risk of psychosis and nonsignification in privileging the decentred subject. But, while acknowledging the dangers of upholding body horror as an inherently radical feminist textual strategy, I would argue for its usefulness as a theoretical paradigm for opening up alternative configurations of subjectivity and desire, and breaking down traditional gender binaries. *The Company of Wolves* consciously plays with bodily and textual transformation, in order to challenge the dominant ideology of the unified self via the fragmentation of both the body *within* the text and the body *of* the text.

## Speaking female desire

One of the main ways in which the film creates space for female subjectivity is in the use of a modern-day dream framework. Dream is evoked both overtly within the frame of the dreaming girl and more subtly in the use of filmic techniques, lighting, editing and music to create the mise-en-scène of fantasy. The dream frame, added, according to Neil Jordan (Carter, 1996: 507), because the radio play on which the film is based was not long enough for an extended feature film, acts on a number of levels to enrich the film beyond this practical consideration . As Laura Mulvey argues, the narrative space of the film 'emanates unquestionably from the heroine's imagination' offering an unusually strong point of insertion for the female spectator and foregrounding the subjectivity of the central protagonist and her developing awareness of her own sexuality (1994: 238).[12]

Anwell asserts, however, that the portrayal of the dreaming girl is voyeuristic, 'our first view of her is, indeed, an image of adolescence firmly fixed as object of the male gaze, the successor to Pretty Baby and Lolita' (1988: 82), quoting at length from the pre-publicity synopsis and a film review from the *Daily Telegraph* (Castell, 1984), both describing the opening sequence. But by relying on these sources to identify the reception of the film, Anwell fails to address the issue of female subjectivity in relation to the image of the dreaming girl, or the possibility of a male audience identifying with the the female protagonist.[13] Anwell disavows the possibility that mainstream cinema might effectively configure female desire because it does not fit with her overall thesis that feminism cannot engage with popular culture without being somehow diluted or exploited. She argues that 'the use of the dreamer as an introductory image offers the viewer an object to gaze at, rather than to identify with. We remain fixed spectators, viewing the violence of her adolescent fantasies' (1988: 82). Although the opening scene ostensibly upholds her analysis – we are invited to identify with the camera's eye, admitted into the privacy of the young girl's bedroom to anonymously watch her as she sleeps – the way in which the dream frame works throughout the film undermines Anwell's argument. In fact, as I have suggested above, the dream frame offers unique access to female subjectivity, which is constantly reaffirmed through flash backs to the 'reality' of the bedroom of the dreaming girl.

The context of the dream introduces the fact of the girl's adolescence. She is going through a 'difficult' stage, she has tummy ache, she is sulking, she has been trying on clothes and lipstick. Oscillating between childhood and adulthood, the ambivalent figure of the adolescent girl is intimately connected with that of the werewolf. Both are linked to the cycle of the moon which triggers bodily transformation.[14] This is reinforced by Rosaleen's identification with the adolescent boy who meets the Devil in the forest, in a dramatisation of Granny's old wives' tales. When the boy rubs the Devil's ointment on his chest he rapidly begins to sprout hairs and vines creep up suggestively around his legs. As the camera zooms out from a close-up on the boy's screaming face it becomes framed by the mirror in Rosaleen's bedroom. We have suddenly been transposed from the fantasy world of the story, to the reality of the dream frame. At the same moment, Rosaleen sits up abruptly and turns to face mirror but instead of her own reflection she sees the image of the adolescent boy. That Rosaleen identifies with, as well as fears, the image of the boy in the mirror is demonstrated by her reaction to Granny's tale: 'That's a horrid story. I didn't like it at all' (Carter, 1996: 208).[15] Rather than reinscribing the equation 'wolf equals aggressive male sexuality', the film effectively overturns the violent rhetoric of fairy tale by explicitly linking the were-wolf with female sexuality.[16]

In the short story the theme of the girl's puberty is explored through the third-person narrator. She exhibits the visible signs of puberty, 'her breasts have just begun to swell' and she has just started her menses, 'the clock inside her that will strike, henceforward, once a month' (Carter, [1979] 1981: 113–14). In a similar scene in the radio play Red Riding Hood describes herself, speaking directly to the audience. As discussed in Chapter 2, this description occurs in the middle of Granny's old wives' tale about a werewolf who attacks a little girl, 'just as old as you are' (Carter, 1985: 61). Red Riding Hood mentally rejects Granny's identification and the narrative is interrupted while she describes her own burgeoning sexuality. As argued previously, rather than being described objectively by an omnipresent, anonymous narrator (situating the girl as the passive object of a masculine gaze), the radio play gives us access to Red Riding Hood's subjectivity, she is given an active voice with which to negotiate an independent path through Granny's narrative.

The film deals with this theme of the girl's developing sexuality in a magical sequence in which she suddenly breaks out of the topography of the dream world and climbs a tree in the middle of the forest. At the top of the tree she finds an abandoned stork's nest containing eggs and a hand mirror. She paints her lips and admires herself in the mirror, referring back to the sleeping girl of the dream framework, the mirror in her bedroom and her lips smudged with lipstick. The eggs, the visual mani-festation of the 'unbroken egg' of the short story, crack open to reveal figurines of babies representing the girl's passage into womanhood, her sexual potential. The juxtaposition of the mirror, lipstick and eggs symbolises the socially and biologically determined aspects of femininity.[17]

This episode serves a dual purpose, not only depicting the girl's adolescent state through an economic use of symbols taken directly from the literary text, but also reinforcing female subjectivity via visual reference to the dream framework. Thus it can be seen that the film consistently foregrounds female desire, and not, as Anwell asserts, male fantasies about girlish adolescence.

I particularly take issue with Anwell's contention that the film leaves 'no room for the confident folk heroine successfully expressing her desire' (1988: 84). On the contrary, Rosaleen's desire is quite literally articulated in the film in two sequences in which she tells stories. In the first of these – which I call the wedding feast – Rosaleen tells her mother a story while they sit in front of the hearth – a domestic setting which highlights the warmth of their mother/daughter relationship. Based on a brief passage in the short story, Rosaleen relates a tale of a pregnant woman who turns 'an entire wedding party into wolves because the groom had settled on another girl' (Carter, [1979] 1981: 111).[18] Rosaleen's story is realised in some detail with elaborate set and period dress, elevating it from just another bit of werewolf lore into a magnificent set piece. The transformation of the wedding guests into wolves is precipitated by the woman's look into a mirror which magically cracks from side to side.[19] This sequence is in stark contrast to the visceral transformations narrated by Granny elsewhere in the film – no rending flesh or muscle being ripped apart here. Old-fashioned special effects replace the complex animatronics of the almost medical transformation in the earlier scene. In homage to classic werewolf cinema paws erupt comically from the ends of elegant shoes and an elaborately dressed lady develops a hairy chest and hands. The use of circus music and sweeping camera movements create a Carnivalesque atmosphere, reinforcing the appearance of kitsch intertextuality. Neale suggests that this is an intentional alienation technique which ultimately fails, arguing that 'in the decision to sacrifice the illusion of transformation at this point in the film, presumably in order to force the viewer to appraise what they are seeing, elements of bathos and banality cannot be controlled' (Neale, 1996: 105).

However, offering as it does a frame of reference with which to compare the other werewolf transformations, this scene is pivotal to the meaning of the film, the key point being the radically different narrative contexts of the tales: the most violent transformations are narrated by Granny, while Rosaleen's story portrays the woman as having agency over the transformation of the guests. It is telling to compare the use of the reaction shot in the two scenes. In the earlier scene, the wife is portrayed as the typical wide-eyed victim. In the wedding feast scene, the woman's laughter enacts Cixous' 'The Laugh of the Medusa', working 'to smash everything, to shatter the framework of institutions, to blow up the law, to break up the "truth" with laughter' ([1976] 1980: 264). Indeed, the image of the powerful woman proactively expressing her desire, is just such a 'confident folk heroine' as the one whose absence Anwell laments.

Rosaleen's second story, told to the wolf, is a tale about an injured wolf-girl who receives succour from the compassionate village priest. Once again rejecting Granny's religious superstition, the girl concocts her own tale of reconciliation between the animal and human world. But this is also a story of reconciliation between the sexes and a repudiation of the psychology of male aggressivity and female victimhood promoted by Granny. Appropriating Granny's werewolf lore 'for her interior psychic needs' (Mulvey, 1994: 239), Rosaleen finds a voice with which to articulate her developing sexuality and with it the power to break free from the damaging patriarchal formulae of fairy tale. Rosaleen's story-telling undermines Anwell's thesis about the violence of the film, which, far from being gratuitous, is clearly contained in the mouth of Granny. In addition, by allowing Rosaleen to comment on Granny's tales the film not only foregrounds the act of story-telling, but also invites us to examine the complex interactions involved in the transaction between narrator and listener, extending the project of the radio play.

While the short story has been the subject of numerous critiques from a variety of different feminist perspectives, in the case of the film, *The Company of Wolves*, Anwell's critique remains unanswered and consequently the debate is rather one-sided. Although she offers a sensitive reading of Carter's sexual politics in the story, by refusing to abandon the logic of the gaze, Anwell mistakenly interprets the film as reinscribing the patriarchal victim/aggressor mentality of the original fairy tale. Highlighting 'the struggle to speak female desire', she then ignores the pivotal role of the female voice and story-telling in her enthusiasm to criticise the film for a voyeuristic portrayal of the central female protagonist (Anwell, 1988: 85).

As we have seen, the theories of the male gaze upon which Anwell relies have come under scrutiny for effacing the female spectator and constructing 'woman' as universal object of masculine desire. It is therefore necessary to reconsider the film in the context of feminist film theory which challenges the privileging of the visible in the hierarchy of the senses.[20] Shifting from the paradigm of the male gaze to that of the female voice engenders a more positive feminist interpretation. This is not to suggest that the female voice itself offers a utopian space for a feminist reclamation of the film. As previously argued in Chapter 2, it is important to problematise the feminist 'politics of the voice' (Doane, 1980: 344). As Mary Ann Doane warns, 'to mark the voice as an isolated haven within patriarchy, or as having an essential relation to the woman, is to invoke the specter of feminine specificity, always recuperable as another form of "otherness"' (1980: 346). But it is equally vital to include the role of the voice in a discussion of the film which has so far been dominated by the look.

Just as in the radio play, the film's foregrounding of story-telling serves a double function, first by contextualising the violent tales of male aggressivity in the mouth of Granny, the 'prohibitive mentor', and secondly by allowing Rosaleen to speak for herself. In fact, by giving the main female protagonist a more vocal role, the film could be seen to offer a greater space for the articulation of female subjectivity and desire than is available in the short story. Locked in the very masculine economy of looking which she attempts to critique, Anwell is ironically blind to this successful enunciation of female identity. Furthermore, her reliance on masculine structures of looking denies the agency of the female spectator. Where, in her interpretation of the short story, she finds the female reader able to negotiate Carter's oscillating narrative strategy, the film's audience is constructed as being predominantly male and the meaning of the film fixed. Anwell's overarching thesis that feminism will inevitably be 'reduced, manipulated – even travestied' in any encounter with mass culture echoes Woolf's characterisation of screen adaptation as a violent assault on the literary text. It becomes clear, then, that Anwell's critique stems from a modernist rejection of popular culture and a privileging of the literary original, as much as a specifically feminist agenda, and she is consequently unable to see the film as the successful engagement between feminism and popular culture which it undoubtedly is.

## Notes

1 See as a representative selection, Ackroyd (1984: 33–4), French (1984: 9), Malcolm (1984: 11), Parente (1984: 6), Pym (1984: 23) and *The Economist* (1984: 100).

2 As argued in my Introduction, Anwell's antipathy to media is indicative of a wider suspicion of the mainstream from within the feminist sisterhood.

3 The film's relationship to the radio adaptation is highly significant in the context of this debate because it reveals that Carter had already reworked the original material to suit another medium and that the screenplay originates from an existing dramatic script, not a literary narrative. It also explains some of the textual changes, the conflation of the original story with elements of 'The Werewolf', another radical retelling of 'Little Red Riding Hood' which precedes 'The Company of Wolves' in *The Bloody Chamber* ([1979] 1981), and other wolf stories, which had already taken place in the adaptation for radio.

4 For just such a modernist account of film adaptation, see Virginia Woolf's essay, 'The Cinema', in which she imagines film adaptation in terms of a vampiric exchange: 'the cinema fell upon its prey with immense rapacity, and for the moment largely subsists upon the body of its unfortunate victim' (1994: 350).

5　The most obvious example of this is the wedding feast scene, which Catherine Neale has identified as a reference to Dr Jekyll and Mr Hyde, but others include the 'slasher' reaction shots in first transformation scene and the casting of David Warner, the journalist from *The Omen* (1976) as Rosaleen's father (1996: 105).

6　Trahair makes a point of footnoting the fact that she focuses specifically on the film remake, not the issue of the adaptation from the original short story, saying that 'the question of film as literary adaptation is too large to broach here'. Despite the fact that I am dealing with a literary adaptation (and its very literariness is one of the things that has caused so much controversy on both sides of the film/fiction interface), much of Trahair's thesis about the film remake is relevant to my argument (1991: 207, n.17).

7　Gamman and Marshment problematise both feminism's and film theory's engagement with psychoanalysis, identifying the difficulties in moving beyond the parameters of psychoanalytic theory (Gamman and Marshment (eds), 1988: 5).

8　One of the problems with abjection is its basis in psychoanalytic theory. Both Creed (1993) and Clover (1993) have challenged Freudian accounts of sexual difference and their dominance in much contemporary psychoanalytic, feminist and film theory. Creed interrogates Freud's notion of woman as 'castrated' other, positing the monstrous-feminine as constructed upon men's fears of woman as 'castrator' not castra*ted*. Clover connects formulaic horror film with a pre-modern, oral narrative tradition with 'one-sex' theory, questioning dominant binary accounts of sexual difference. More work needs to be done in this area.

9　The dual persona of the werewolf can usefully stand in for the abject border between the original and its adaptation, between literature and film which I outlined earlier.

10　Screening this scene at lecturers and conferences elicits various reactions, such as turning away from the screen, or being somehow repulsed by the scene: as Creed asserts (1993: 10): 'when we say such-and-such a horror film "made me sick" or "scared the shit out of me", we are actually foregrounding that specific horror film as a "work of abjection" or "abjection at work" – almost in a literal sense. Viewing the horror film signifies a desire not only for perverse pleasure (confronting sickening, horrific images/being filled with terror/desire for the undifferentiated) but also a desire, once having been filled with perversity, taken pleasure in perversity, to throw up, throw out, eject the abject (from the safety of the spectator's seat).'

11　Kristeva suggests that 'Food loathing is perhaps the most elementary and most archaic form of abjection. When the eyes see or the lips touch that skin on the surface of the milk – harmless, thin as a sheet of cigarette paper, pitiful as a nail paring – I experience a gagging sensation and, still further down, spasms in the stomach, the belly' (1982: 2).

12　It is ironic that while Anwell (1988) invokes Mulvey's theory of 'the male gaze' to critique the film, Mulvey herself offers a positive feminist reading, although, sadly, she does not engage with Anwell's article.

13　See, for example, Clover (1993) on cross-gender identification.

14　Carter describes *The Company of Wolves* as a '*menstrual* film' (Romney, 1985: 31). Suzy McKee Charnas also links menstruation and 'werewolfery' in her short story, 'Boobs' (1990).

15　Again, Rosaleen's reaction to Granny's tale demonstrates the interactive nature of story-telling, and her rejection of Granny's ideology.

16　Carter asserts that the wolves 'stand for the girl's own sexuality, rather than rough, hairy male sexuality – perhaps they stand for rough hairy female sexuality' (Johnstone, 1984: 55).

17　Significantly, Rosaleen leaves the mirror behind once she meets the werewolf in the forest.

18　Interestingly, this episode does not appear in the radio play.

19　Note the allusion to Tennyson's 'The Lady of Shalott' (1833), l. 115. I return to the issue of the active female gaze in Chapter 6.

20　I am thinking particularly of work on sound and the voice referred to in Chapter 2, such as Doane ([1980] 1986: 33–50, 47–60) and Silverman (1990: 309–27).

# Looking askance: *The Magic Toyshop*

# 6

Angela Carter's second novel, *The Magic Toyshop* ([1967] 1981), opens with Melanie's narcissistic gaze as she examines herself distractedly in front of the mirror, introducing looking as one of its central themes. Carter's concern with the act of looking, and what happens in particular when women look, is part of a wider feminist concern with the visible. In *Sexuality in the Field of Vision*, for example, Jacqueline Rose calls for a 'feminism concerned with the question of looking' which works to 'trouble, break up, or rupture the visual field before our eyes ... by blurring the field of representation where our normal forms of self-recognition take place' (1986: 227–8, 231). As we have already seen, such a political engagement with the gaze has also been the specific project of much feminist film theory.

Given this emphasis on looking, it is important to examine what happens to Carter's politics of vision when her novel is transposed to the screen. For some feminist critics the screen adaptation of feminist texts is inherently problematic (see the discussion of Anwell, 1988, in Chapter 5). It could be argued that Carter's discursive portrayal of female sexuality in the novel is inevitably 'travestied' (Anwell, 1988: 72) by its visual representation, reinscribing Mulvey's well-known binary: 'woman as image, man as bearer of the look' ([1975] 1989: 19). However, far from compromising the novel's feminist critique of looking, the film adaptation of *The Magic Toyshop* in fact works to disrupt the visual field from within using the very medium which has traditionally been said to fix women as object of the male gaze.[1] This chapter examines how the novel's feminist preoccupation with looking, watching and being seen is taken up and amplified by the film adaptation (1986a).

## Decentred screens

Before going on to discuss these themes, it is important to address some textual issues. There is some argument about whether *The Magic Toyshop* should be discussed as film or television. Susannah Clapp, in her introduction to *The Curious Room*, opts for television (1996: ix), while Laura Mulvey states that the novel was 'turned into a film by [producer] Stephen Morrison in 1988' (1994: 233). The date of the film is directly linked to these formal questions. Lorna Sage cites the year as 1987 in her bibliography (1994: 66). Mark Bell correctly notes that the adaptation 'was first broadcast on ITV on 5 November 1988', but does not mention any cinema release (Carter, 1996: 508). In fact, according to director David Wheatley (1996: 234), *The Magic Toyshop* was originally shot on 16mm film for television. According to their press release publicising the first television broadcast (1988: 12), Granada Television then decided to blow up the negative to 35mm, the size of a feature film, and *The Magic Toyshop* became 'the first Granada production to be shown in the commercial cinema in the UK. It was premiered during the London Film Festival in 1986 and went into theatrical distribution in July 1987.' The film was later broadcast on ITV on Guy Fawkes night, 1988.[2]

While the film was initially conceived for television, in many ways it was an unlikely film to have been produced by a commercial television company. Wheatley himself expresses disbelief that Granada were willing to back such an unusual project:

> I'll never believe to this day that they commissioned it, because it was such a kind of way out piece of work. I mean you've got a commercial, ITV television company ... it's the most esoteric piece that Granada Television have ever made. (1996: 232)

Furthermore what is unusual about the production was the fact that Carter was included in the adaptation process. This collaborative relationship with an original author is unusual in television. As Wheatley suggests, a third party is usually 'commissioned to actually come in and do the job' (1996: 233).[3] The fact that *The Magic Toyshop* was produced by an independent television company clearly affected the production values of the film, both on a financial and an aesthetic level.[4] However, while originating as a television drama, *The Magic Toyshop* was released as a feature film and toured film festivals in Britain, Japan, Australia and Canada, actually winning The Grand Prix du Jury for Best Foreign Film in the Features section at the Balfort Film Festival which showcases directors' first films (Granada Television, 1988: 12). The film had modest box-office success as an arthouse film, won critical acclaim at home and abroad and injected new life into the British film industry.

This confusion surrounding the textual status of the film foregrounds the problematics of postmodern media culture. How does one describe a text that was both released as a feature film and transmitted on television? Is it still possible to theorise the spectator in the context of such disparate contexts of textual consumption? As Sue Thornham suggests, it has been necessary for contemporary feminist film theory to adjust in the face of changing postmodern viewing practices and their implications in the theorisation of spectatorship. Film theory has tended to privilege cinema – both in terms of the filmic text and the engaged spectator – above other visual media in order to justify its existence as a discrete discipline. But, as Thornham argues 'in the 1990s world of mass media apparatuses ... this abstraction – and its bracketing out of the empirical, historically situated spectator – becomes more and more difficult to maintain' (1997: 160). Thornham illustrates the expanding network of viewing practices now available:

> I may watch a film in the cinema; I may watch (or re-watch) it on video; I may watch it on large-screen TV. I may watch in all three contexts in a concentrated fashion; alternatively, I may accord it only ... 'TV's delegated look and distracted glance' ... The film itself may have been produced for screening on television (or video) as well as, or instead of, in the cinema. (1997: 160–1)[5]

It is necessary for film theory to acknowledge these shifting apparatuses of contemporary visual culture in which the contexts of production and consumption are no longer fixed.

I am conscious, therefore, of appearing to privilege film in my choice to include *The Magic Toyshop* for discussion in the Film section of this book, perpetuating a certain intellectual snobbery surrounding the perceived relationship between television and film, where television is seen as the feature film's poor relation.[6] This is certainly not my intention. Wheatley, himself, finds this distinction confusing, 'it was the content I was interested in, the shape of the screen is obviously important, but primarily you are interested in the world you are trying to create ... I think you aspire to the best quality, the best shots to tell the story as most interestingly as you possibly can, then it is a film ... I think it's to do with what you aspire to' (1996: 234). For this reason, and because of Wheatley's and Carter's conscious aspiration to the silver screen, I examine the film as cinema rather than television.

Of course, these issues are further complicated by the film's hybrid status as an adaptation. Wheatley claims he was immediately attracted by the novel's cinematic quality:

> I felt the book was filmic, I felt there were images that were referred to in the book, and when she told me that she was a film reviewer and also

fascinated by film, I just became fascinated by the notion of what films she might have been looking at when she wrote the book and if they'd had any influence. (1996: 243)

At the beginning of the collaborative process Wheatley explains that he and Carter sat down and watched the films she had been watching when she wrote the novel. These were to include *Valerie and Her Week of Wonders*, *Goto: Island of Love* and *The Tales of Hoffmann*.[7] Wheatley claims that he and Carter shared a particular love for the work of Powell and Pressburger: 'fantastic film makers, but she adored that, *The Red Shoes*, *A Matter of Life and Death*, *Black Narcissus*, all these films, which I adore as well' (1996: 236).

The adaptation process was clearly facilitated by this shared frame of cinematic reference. Like much of Carter's writing, the novel is saturated with cinematic allusion, both in terms of direct filmic reference and in the vivid nature of the writing itself. There is extensive explicit allusion to a range of film genres, from the Western, British new-wave, Hammer horror and the Hollywood woman's film to home movies and documentary footage of concentration camp victims (Carter, [1967] 1981: 12, 106, 122, 189, 76, 132). Melanie imagines Uncle Philip 'as a character in a film':

> possibly played by Orson Welles. She was sitting in a cinema watching a film. Soon a girl in white would come round selling ice-cream, salted nuts and popcorn ... And Melanie had spied on them through a keyhole, and would never get closer to them than the keyhole in the door behind which they lived. Watching a film was like being a voyeur, living vicariously. (Carter, [1967] 1981: 76)

Cinema forms part of the topography of the novel. Wheatley attributes this to the more general cultural influence of film on the collective imagination:

> If you look at García Márquez or you look at Borges, or you look at other Latin American writers, I think you find the magical realism they talk about (I think that phrase is overused, 'Magical Realism', but Angela's in that tradition as well), the magic somehow has transcended itself, it's gone from books into films and then come back again, and I think it's actually percolated into the way that people think about story-telling. (1996: 237)

In an interview with Saskia Baron (1987: 26), Carter asserts: 'I've always written with visual images first and no adaptor could crack it.' As Baron explains:

> there have been some 15 attempts to turn it into a successful film script. But Carter's second novel proved tricky ... The Eighties have seen a

willingness in both cinema and television to break with social realist conventions and dabble in something a little more shadowy, a little fantastic. (1987: 26)

But how far the film indeed breaks with the dominant, social realist conventions is open to question. In an interview with Australian journalist Stephanie Bunbury, Carter claims:

> One of the really difficult things about making a script out of *The Magic Toyshop* is when I read it again I realised it didn't have a plot. It had a vague beginning and an end but not much middle. And one of the things this particular kind of film needed was a coherent narrative structure, so one had to reassemble the novel in that form. (1987: 38)

Carter's language is telling here. 'This particular kind of film' suggests some friction between her vision of the film and the pressures to conform to the production values of a commercial television company. As Bunbury explains, 'something had to crystallise the menace of the story into concrete images':

> She is humble in the face of the demands of the medium. The story itself was full of holes which gaped once the novel's language was stripped away. 'The holes can't be left empty for the reader to imagine what's going on, because that's not how the cinema works,' she says, then adds 'It could be how the cinema worked, but it would be cinema of a different kind, operating at a different level. This is a straightforward narrative movie.' There were certain pressures from the Granada producers, who insisted everything should be explained. (1987: 37)

Rather than being 'humble in the face of the demands of the medium', as Bunbury suggests, Carter seems all too aware of alternative cinematic traditions which might have been able to accommodate those elements of the novel which do not readily fit into classical narrative cinema. It is important, however, not to overlook the film's achievement by simply dismissing it for not being avant-garde or experimental enough. Although the film largely adheres to the conventions of narrative cinema, *The Magic Toyshop* remains a magical and enigmatic film, offering a productive feminist adaptation of Carter's novel. This is largely achieved via the employment of an active female gaze and the use of cinematic illusion, puppetry and old-fashioned special-effects, all of which work to disrupt the established structure of looks at work in mainstream narrative cinema from within.

## When the woman looks

If female looking is one of the central themes of the novel, how does the film deal with the representation of female subjectivity and desire? In particular, how does the film handle Melanie's gaze at her nude self in the mirror without falling into the trap of fetishising femininity as spectacle? In the novel, Melanie's nudity is couched in highly wrought, discursive language. Her adolescent self-discovery is described in terms of colonial exploration of virgin territory:

> O, my America, my new found land. She embarked on a tranced voyage, exploring the whole of herself, clambering her own mountain ranges, penetrating the moist richness of her secret valleys, a physiological Cortez, da Gama or Mungo Park. (Carter, [1967] 1981: 1)

Alongside literary allusion embedded within the narration such as this, there is direct allusion to the texts and paintings from which Melanie takes her female role models, significantly all male representations of women. She tries on the various cultural alternatives available to her as a woman in the context of a patriarchal society: pre-Raphaelite virgin, Lautrec tart, Cranach Venus, bride for a 'phantom bridegroom' (Carter, [1967] 1981: 1–2). These patriarchal fantasies of female sexuality are taken to their logical extreme in Uncle Philip's attempts to coerce Melanie into the role of victim, forcing her to play puppet to his puppetmaster, Leda to his swan. As Elaine Jordan points out (1990: 28): 'Melanie's initial narcissism – the ready-made poses she adopts before her mirror, in her pubertal fantasies – is ready-made to collude with the scenarios her Uncle Philip, the cultural puppet-master, wants to play out.' Indeed, the novel explicitly links Uncle Philip's fantasy of her, with Melanie's earlier experimentation with male images of women: 'Melanie would be a nymph crowned with daisies once again; he saw her as once she had seen herself. In spite of everything, she was flattered' (Carter, [1967] 1981: 141).[8]

Melanie's narcissism is a product of patriarchal structures of looking, in which women are inculcated to see themselves as objects of masculine desire. As Sigrid Weigel suggests:

> This means for woman's self-awareness that she sees herself by seeing *that* and *how* she is seen. She sees the world through male spectacle. (The metaphor 'spectacles' implies the utopia of a liberated, unhindered gaze.) She is fixated on self-observation refracted in the critical gaze of man ... Thus her self-portrait originates in the distorting patriarchal mirror. In order to find her own image she must liberate the mirror from the *images of woman* painted on it by a male hand. (1985: 61)

But, as Sarah Gamble argues (1997: 69), while Melanie's narcissistic self-regard stems from 'a male-identified perspective', it is accompanied by 'a wonderfully self-absorbed auto-eroticism [which] keeps breaking through her reveries, showing that the real object of her desire is, in fact, herself'. The novel thus avoids fetishising the female body, as Linden Peach concurs (1998: 75). But what happens when the scene unfolds in front of the camera? In the transition to film there is a danger of Melanie's body becoming a fetishised object of audience's desire, not her own pleasure. Does the film manage to represent Melanie's erotic exploration without reinscribing patriarchal structures of looking?

Where the novel opens with Melanie's voyage of self-discovery, this scene is preceded in the film with a brief title sequence. I examine this opening sequence in detail here, because it usefully sets up some of the central themes of both the film and this chapter. The film begins with the figure of Francie smoking under a lamp-post. We register the tension in his face as he takes one last drag on his cigarette, drops it onto the glistening wet pavement and heads towards the shop. The shop-front lights up as he approaches, silhouetting the figure of Aunt Margaret as she opens the door to him. The film cuts to a close-up of the shop window. One of the toys, a merry-go-round, is spinning. The camera then pans down, through the ground, tracking through a window into the basement workshop at just the moment at which Francie and Aunt Margaret enter. According to Wheatley, this impossible pan through the pavement and the closed window, which appears to happen in one continuous take, is an allusion to the elaborate opening shot of Orson Welles' *Citizen Kane* (Jeffrey, 1987). Finn urges Francie to 'get a move on', and they take their places as Uncle Philip emerges menacingly from between the closed curtains of the puppet theatre, snapping at Francie, 'now you've deigned to arrive, Mr Fiddler, we can begin' (Carter, 1996: 246–7). He disappears and the curtains glide back to reveal a marionette dressed as Coppelia, occupying centre stage. The marionette begins to dance *en pointe* to Francie's fiddle. Stiff, but life-like, 'spinning like a top', her 'unstoppable pirouette' cuts to Melanie 'pirouetting ferociously to music she hears in her mind' (Carter, 1996: 247). As Laura Mulvey argues, 'the sequence allows the film to shift, with a beautiful cut-on action, from the marionettes' wooden dance to Melanie, in her own fifteen-year-old flesh and blood, as she dances for herself in front of her mirror' (1994: 234).

At the most basic level, this title sequence functions to establish the eponymous toyshop and its inhabitants in the topography of the film world, setting up a tension between the strange, seedy toyshop and the cozy, middle-class household of Melanie's parental home. But, more importantly, this opening sequence draws attention to our own position as spectators, portraying, as it does, the viewing of a theatrical spectacle in a darkened room. The use of diegetic audiences has traditionally served to emphasise femininity as spectacle in classical narrative cinema, inviting the cinema audience to collude in the objectification of the female star (Hayward, 1996: 68). But here, Aunt Margaret's enforced spectatorship deneutralises this activity, problematising the act of spectatorship itself, and drawing attention to the relationship between private and public looking. Both the life-size marionette and Melanie's adolescent role-play imitate femininity, foregrounding the constructedness of the object of the cinematic gaze. In this sense, our 'reading' of Melanie's self-absorbed gaze in the film is mediated by the structures of looking that have already been put into question in this opening sequence.

Furthermore, although the film has been accused of a gratuitous use of flesh by the British tabloid press, *The Magic Toyshop* in fact finds ways of successfully annunciating female subjectivity and desire without fetishising Melanie.[9] Although there is more nudity in the film than in the script, the nudity in the film is in fact closer to the spirit of the novel, which is unequivocal about it: 'for hours she stared at herself, naked, in the mirror of her wardrobe' (Carter, [1967] 1981: 1).[10] We can only speculate about the absence of nudity in the screenplay. It may have been some form of self-censorship, bearing in mind the film's intended audience (the film was given a 15 certificate). Alternatively, perhaps, Carter was wary that Melanie's auto-eroticism might be misinterpreted as straightforwardly replicating the structures of voyeuristic looking inherent in classic narrative cinema, given the history of femininity as cinematic spectacle.

Nicola Shaughnessy (1996: 53) identifies a similar dilemma in the representation of the gender transformation in Sally Potter's 1992 adaptation of Virginia Woolf's *Orlando*: 'How are we to read this moment? At one level, the exposure of Orlando via the spectacle of the female body seems to endorse Laura Mulvey's well-known theorisation of the dominant cinematic apparatus in terms of "woman as image, man as bearer of the look"'. She goes on to argue, however, that Potter avoids this voyeuristic structure of looks by aligning the spectator with Orlando's own point of view in the mirror:

> quite clearly and emphatically, it is the female subject who has ownership of the gaze at this crucial moment ... It is this calm, confident act of looking that re-appropriates the image from the domain of male sexual fantasy and offers the possibility of an empowering, pleasurable and non-masochistic identification for the female spectator. (Shaughnessy, 1996: 53–4)

A similar positioning of the camera operates in *The Magic Toyshop*, circumventing an objectifying 'male gaze' by inviting the spectator to identify with, rather than to fetishise, Melanie. The novel's dense literary style gives us access to Melanie's fantasy life which undercuts the potential for physical objectification. While the film picks up on some of the visual references (the camera panning over open art history books as Melanie poses), it is impossible for traditional narrative film to fully capture the metaphorical tone of the novel.[11] However, the film does allow access to Melanie's internal thought processes via the device of voiceover, 'physically, I've reached my peak. From now on, I can only deteriorate' (Carter, 1996: 247).

Furthermore, as Joanne Hill argues (1987: 12): 'the film successfully avoids an overly voyeuristic portrayal of Melanie's sexual explorations', through the use of Melanie's active gaze. Caroline Milmoe, the actress who plays Melanie, claims she attempted to engage with the camera in order to challenge the voyeuristic gaze of the camera lens/ spectator:

> I was keen for Melanie not to be passive – I wanted to catch the camera with my eye and make the audience conscious of her voyeurism of them. I don't know how much of that is visible 'cause a lot of it is cut. (Hill, 1987: 12)

Milmoe's portrayal of Melanie's active gaze is not entirely cut from the film, however. At one point in the sequence Melanie's eyes, wandering over her own image in the mirror, momentarily shift to look directly into the camera. This appropriation of the look is reinforced by the fact that she is partially obscured by the black lace shawl through which she looks. The veil mimics the anonymity of the voyeur, partially blocking the return of the spectator's gaze. In 'Veiling Over Desire: Close-Ups of the Woman', Doane suggests that the image of the veiled woman has the potential to unsettle epistemological structures of looking: 'a site where the classical film acknowledges the precariousness of vision and simultaneously seeks to isolate and hence contain it is the close-up of the woman, more particularly, the *veiled* woman' (1991: 46). The veil represents this 'precariousness of vision' because it foregrounds the subtext of epistemological 'seeing is believing', that appearances can also be deceiving. While Doane argues that this threat is generally contained in classical Hollywood cinema by using the veil to further fetishise the woman's face as surface, screen, texture, she ends her article by asking what the woman's return look might be like, from behind the veil: 'usually, the placement of a veil over a woman's face works to localize and hence contain dissimulation, to keep her from contaminating the male subject. But how can we imagine, conceive her look back?' (Doane, 1991: 75).

Carter was aware of the power of an active female gaze to disturb and denaturalise the relationship between the image and the viewer.

Describing the direct gaze of silent film icon, Louise Brooks, Carter argues:

> That straightforward look of hers is what makes these sixty-year-old photographs of Louise Brooks so provocative, so disturbing, so unchanged by time ... she is directly challenging the person who is looking at her; she is piercing right through the camera with her questing gaze to give your look back, with interest. (1997: 387)

But as Linda Williams argues, in 'When the Woman Looks' (1984: 83), in classical narrative cinema the female protagonist more often 'fails to look, to return the gaze of the male who desires her'. Drawing on Laura Mulvey's seminal theory of the male gaze (see [1975] 1989: 6–8, 1989: 14–26), Williams argues that this is a result of the dominance of the 'male look at the woman that leaves no place for woman's own pleasure in seeing; she exists only to be looked at' (Williams, 1984: 83). But, in addition to the three looks which Mulvey identifies in 'Visual Pleasure' (those of the camera, the audience and the characters within the film), Paul Willemen identifies a 'fourth look', 'the look at the viewer' (1994: 107):[12]

> It must be stressed that the fourth look is not of the same order as the other three, precisely because the subject of the look is an imaginary other, but this does not make the presence of that look any less real. However, although it is continuously present in all filmic experiences, the over-whelming majority of films, as well as the other aspects of the cinematic institution, such as theatres, projection conditions and so on, conspire to minimise its effects, with the aim of trying to erase it altogether. (Willemen, 1994: 108)

Willemen is particularly interested in those moments when the fourth look, implicit in all cinema, becomes explicit. This scene in *The Magic Toyshop* constitutes just such a moment. Both Melanie's self-regarding gaze into the mirror and Milmoe's self-conscious look into the camera draw attention to, and so disrupt, these dominant structures of looking. Like Louise Brooks' 'straightforward look', Melanie's direct gaze momen-tarily reflects back the voyeuristic gaze of the audience, reappropriating the look for a female spectatorship.

The theme of female looking is further explored when Melanie spies on the Jowles through the kitchen keyhole. In the novel, Melanie's point of view is already described almost in terms of film language, Melanie's shifting gaze corresponding with the angles and focus of a camera:

> She knelt down and put her eye to the keyhole, to see what she could see ... Melanie shifted her position a little and Aunt Margaret moved into the

focus of the keyhole ... Melanie moved again and saw Francie, like a statue
of a fiddler, with only his hands alive ... And this was how the red people
passed their time and amused themselves when they thought nobody was
watching. (Carter, [1967] 1981: 50–2)

In the film, this scene is rendered via a simple edit between a shot of
Melanie kneeling at the keyhole and a point of view shot through the
keyhole, framing the three figures.[13] Melanie's secret viewing, here,
duplicates what Linda Williams identifies (with reference to Mulvey,
[1975] 1989, and Christian Metz, [1975] 1986: 244–78) as 'the voyeuristic
pleasure of the cinematic apparatus itself ... the impression of looking in
on a private world unaware of the spectator's own existence' (Williams,
1984: 83).[14] The use of the keyhole mask to frame the shot works as a
visual metaphor for the look, recalling early film practice in which visual
cues, such as the magnifying glass, telescope and keyhole, were used to
establish the point of view shot and direct the gaze of the viewer (Cox,
1995).[15] As Judith Mayne argues, 'voyeurism has become so institution-
alized a feature of the cinema that we tend to take it for granted',
suggesting that 'early films are enormously instructive in this respect'
because they explicitly frame the camera's look, which has since become
'naturalized' (1984: 54). In alluding to early film, then, the use of the
keyhole mask draws attention to and denaturalises voyeuristic structures
of looking.

Melanie learns that she is not the only one doing the looking when she
notices the peephole in the dividing wall between her and Finn's bedroom.
In both the film and the novel Melanie's discovery of the peephole occurs
immediately after Finn has kissed her in the pleasure gardens:

> One rose, two roses, three roses ... and, at the heart of the third rose, a
> gleam of light. A round gleam. She looked at it idly at first and then with
> increasing curiosity. A hole in the wall, through which light shone from
> the next room. A neat, round hole.
>
> Finally, she got up and knelt by the hole, which was the size of a penny.
> Remembering the first night, when she watched the Jowles through the
> kitchen key-hole, she thought that she was always spying on them. Now
> she saw the terra incognita of the brothers' bedroom, lit by an unshaded
> central lamp. (Carter, [1967] 1981: 108)

Melanie's ambivalent initiation into adult (hetero)sexuality, signalled by
her mingled desire and horror at Finn's wet kiss, is concurrent with her
initiation into the structures of patriarchal looking:

> The spy-hole was neat, round and entirely premeditated. Someone had
> made the spy-hole. Why? Presumably to watch her. So she was not only
> watching but being watched when she thought she was by herself, when

she was taking her clothes off and putting them on and so on. All the time, someone was watching her. (Carter, [1967] 1981: 109)

But, in discovering the peephole, Melanie is able to appropriate it for her own viewing pleasure, and, as Gamble points out (1997: 73), 'she's annoyed enough to turn tables and use the peephole to spy on him, catching him walking on his hands across the room; a grotesque spectacle that accurately encapsulates the topsy-turvy situation in which both protagonists find themselves'. As Paulina Palmer similarly suggests , the peephole functions to foreground 'the power exerted by the male gaze':

> The gaze is a practical means for men to impose control on women, as well as a symbol of sexual domination. However, the fact that Melanie responds with indignation to the intrusion on her privacy and retaliates by using the peephole to spy on Finn back ... complicates the meaning of the image. On peering in it, she catches sight of him walking on his hands. This results in a momentary instance of role-reversal. She becomes the observer and he the observed. She represents the norm, while he, in his odd position, becomes the freak and 'spectacle'. These are roles which, in a patriarchal society, are generally reserved for women. Thus, in her treatment of both motifs Carter indirectly reveals that, despite appearances to the contrary, the roles adopted by men and women are, in fact, flexible. They are open to change. (1987: 185)

The role-reversal becomes even more explicit in the film where the traditional structures of looking are turned on their head. In classic narrative cinema, as Doane suggests (1984: 72) 'the woman's exercise of an active investigating gaze can only be simultaneous with her own victimisation'. As Williams argues, when the woman looks, her gaze is punished 'by narrative processes that transform curiosity and desire into masochistic fantasy' (1984: 85). In *The Magic Toyshop*, however, while the threat of male violence is always implicit (hence the multiple references to the ultimate punisher of female curiosity, Bluebeard, in the novel, see Carter, [1967] 1981: 82–3, 118, 146, 198), Melanie is not punished for her curious gaze. Consciously revising her earlier theory, Mulvey suggests that 'the drive of curiosity can be a critical response to the lure of voyeurism' (1996: 62):

> My interest in the Pandora myth stemmed originally from a wish to consider the aesthetics of curiosity, in order to give greater complexity to the argument in my article 'Visual Pleasure and Narrative Cinema'. An active, investigative look, that one that was also associated with the feminine, suggested a way out of the rather too neat binary opposition between the masculine and the female image on the screen, passive and exhibitionist. (Mulvey, 1996: 80)

Unlike the 'unmistakably male voyeuristic' peep-show scenarios in *The Infernal Desire Machines of Doctor Hoffman* , the peephole operates here to articulate female desire, reclaiming woman's pleasure in looking (Sage (ed.), 1994: 114). Indeed, as Gamble contends, 'perversely, it is through the practice of Finn's voyeurism that she is enabled to see out' (1997: 73). As well as appropriating the peephole for her own active gaze, Melanie also literally takes control of Finn's access to the peephole, physically blocking the view by placing a chair in the way.

The novel's subversion of patriarchal structures of looking is made more explicit when it is adapted for the screen because the politics of vision are enacted right before our eyes. As Mayne argues, 'many women filmmakers have turned around the voyeuristic gaze in order to critique the convention from within' (1984: 55). This is clearly what Carter is attempting to achieve in her exploration of female curiosity in *The Magic Toyshop*. But what else does Melanie see? In the novel, the first thing she focuses on is a painting of Aunt Margaret. In the film she is immediately confronted with an image of herself, not Aunt Margaret. 'That's me!', she exclaims out loud at the moment of self-recognition. This is the painting of Melanie which later turns up in Finn's cupboard in the novel: 'then she saw herself, and was touched ... He did not see her precisely as she saw herself but it could have been very much worse' (Carter, [1967] 1981: 153–4).[16] Thus, there is a doubly complex structure of looks in the film as we watch Melanie spying through the peephole at an image of herself.

In the film, there is an additional scene in which Melanie looks through the spy-hole. This occurs after Finn gets thrown down onto the stage by Uncle Philip for manhandling one of his precious puppets. This time we see a shot of Melanie's eye looking though the peephole from the other side. Her eye, framed by the hole, looks directly into the camera. Once again, this 'fourth look' at the viewer (Willemen, 1994) unsettles the experience of spectatorship. As in the earlier shot when Melanie gazes through the black lace shawl, her face is obscured, making it impossible for the spectator to return a voyeuristic gaze. A strange sequence unfolds before her eyes. Finn is lying lifeless on the bed, according to the script, 'looking like "The Death of Chatterton"' (Carter, 1996: 274). Francie begins to play the fiddle and Finn's limp body springs to life in a horizontal gig. In the script Finn 'shudders convulsively jerking and twisting. The candle flames shiver, creating grotesque shadows' (Carter, 1996: 274). This disturbing effect is realised in the film by editing the footage of Finn backwards, so that when it is projected his muscles do not move in the expected manner. This subtle effect creates an uncanny sensation – without knowing precisely why, something looks slightly awry – which brings me on to the second strand of my argument.

## Out of the corner of one's eye

While the film explicitly challenges patriarchal looking via the portrayal of an active female gaze, it also works to disrupt the dominant ideology of the visible on another level. In addition to reappropriating the 'male gaze' for the female spectator, the film works to unsettle the very epistemological basis of patriarchal discourse in the visual economy via the use of old-fashioned animation techniques and trick photography – 'fluctuating optical effects that make us question the veracity of our vision' (Carter, [1974] 1987: 34). Seeing is believing, but appearances can also be deceiving, as Doane argues:

> an investigation of these moments of slippage between vision and epistemological certitude in the cinema can illuminate something of the complexity of the relations between truth, vision and the woman sustained by patriarchy. For the subtextual theme recurrent in filmic texts, which resists the dominant theme whereby vision is constantly ratified, is that appearances can be deceiving. (1991: 45–6)

If, as Doane asserts, 'the epistemological cornerstone of the classical text is the dictum, "the image does not lie"' (Doane, 1991: 103), what happens in those moments when the epistemological 'truth' of the image is open to question? As I demonstrate, the use of optical effects in *The Magic Toyshop* troubles the field of vision by drawing attention to those elements which occur on the margins of vision, those things which move out of the corner of one's eye.

Duncan Petrie notes the 'fundamental aesthetic duality which generated, at the very birth of the medium, two opposing tendencies' in film history (Petrie (ed.), 1993: 2): on the one hand the realist tradition growing from the camera's ability to capture photographic 'truth', the faithful moving image (pioneered by Louis Lumière); the fantastic tradition, on the other, developing from the camera's capacity for photographic illusion, the ability to deceive the eye with optical tricks (innovated by Méliès). But, while these two traditions have been seen as opposing poles representing radically different schools of film, this dichotomy is misleading because even the realist tradition is founded on the illusion of the moving image: what we in fact see is only a series of still images, brought to life by the persistence of vision. In this sense all cinema can be seen as a form of animation, an optical illusion which animates the frozen image (see Cholodenko (ed.), 1991). As Steve Cox suggests (1995), 'cinema itself is a kind of trick. The eye is deceived into thinking there is actual movement. The element of illusion is there right from the word go.'[17]

While the camera supposedly never lies, the illusion of reality is in fact a fiction, a con trick, an elaborate trompe l'oeil. As Doane maintains

(1991: 196), 'classical cinema diminishes and controls the threat of the trompe l'oeil by making the image central to its reality, by constituting itself on a large scale as a trick of the eye with a deeper, more profound truth which justifies the trick'. As Peter Wollen similarly suggests, the apparatus of 'illusionist' cinema seeks to hide its materiality in order to uphold the illusion of reality, striving for 'the recreation of the world in its own direct image' (1982: 190). In contrast, Wollen maintains, avant-garde film makers deliberately foreground the material properties of film as a medium in order to defamiliarise and denaturalise the cinematic illusion (1982: 189–223).[18] As Doane concurs, 'avant-garde film explores the extent of the image's deception … the task is to interrogate the integrity of the image rather than to preserve it. Far from feeling threatened by the trompe l'oeil, the independent avant-garde film explores its multiple ramifications' (1991: 196).[19]

*The Magic Toyshop* is clearly not an independent, avant-garde film, but the product of a mainstream television company. Yet, despite Carter's contention that it is a 'straightforward narrative movie', the film's use of animation techniques works to interrogate the 'integrity of the image' and challenge epistemological looking. If all film recreates the illusion of life, animation makes this disturbingly explicit. As Alan Cholodenko argues, 'animation is never only a benign activity. It troubles, and its troubling includes troubling thought' (Cholodenko (ed.), 1991: 10). The use of optical illusions, trick photography and old-fashioned animation techniques disrupts epistemological looking because we are unable to trust our eyes. Animation – both in terms of animation film and in terms of vivification – is closely connected with Freud's notion of the uncanny, 'that class of the frightening which leads back to what is known of old and long familiar … the name for everything that ought to have remained … secret and hidden but has come to light' (1955: 220, 224). The notion of the uncanny is slippery and hard to put your finger on. As Robyn Ferrell suggests, it occurs in the 'moment between the repressed and its repression, there but not quite there. Out of the corner of your eye you glimpse it; but when you turn to face it, it is gone' (1991: 131). As Ferrell goes on to argue, 'in unsettling your distinction between animate and inanimate, the uncanny unsettles distinction itself' (1991: 138).

Significantly, as Cholodenko attests, animation is one of the 'least theorized' areas of film (Cholodenko (ed.), 1991: 9). This is ironic precisely because, as established in Chapter 5, all cinema can be seen as a form of animation, as Cholodenko concurs: 'animation film not only preceded the advent of cinema, it engendered it' (Cholodenko (ed.), 1991: 9). Cinema has its historical roots in magic and optical tricks. As Duncan Petrie explains, 'the on-screen magic tricks of Georges Méliès and other pioneers' developed both from 'a vaudeville tradition of conjuring' and 'the realm of the fantastic in pre-cinema optical entertainments such as the phantasmagoria, shadow plays and magic lantern shows' (1993: 3).[20] Carter loved this old-fashioned film trickery and enjoyed the magical possibilities of stop-frame animation.[21] She particularly admired the Czech animator, Jan Svankmayer, who uses a frenetic mix of puppets and stop-frame photography in his films, writing in praise of his work in 'Alice in Prague or The Curious Room' (1993).[22] Carter shared this affinity for old-fashioned animation techniques with Wheatley, who had already revealed an early preoccupation with the deliberate use of special effects to deceive the eye in an art school film, *Sleight of Hand*.[23]

The uncanny pervades *The Magic Toyshop* right from the beginning of the film with the automated toys in the shop window in the opening sequence. But the magic is not contained in the seedy London toyshop, but also infiltrates Melanie's middle-class world when she ventures into the garden in the middle of the night. Wheatley celebrates the work of camera-man Ken Morgan in recreating the heightened experience of the novel:

> Always shoot against the light, that was Ken's experience and he's right as well ... if you shoot with the light it's flat, if you shoot against the light it makes it magical, and the water's beautiful, and that garden at that time of year, for some weird reason, the garden was just about to explode into life, I think it almost had that quality about the scene, that everything was going to go, it was almost moving, you could feel the undergrowth starting to twitch. (1996: 242–3)

Just as in the novel, this reverie of magic and harmony is shattered when the night garden suddenly conspires against Melanie, bringing on the ruin of the wedding dress, and by some weird extension, the death of her parents. In the novel: 'the garden turned against Melanie when she became afraid of it' ([1967] 1981: 18). In the film, this is signalled by a sudden gust of wind which catches her veil and slams the front door shut. The transformation from the magical moonlit garden to threatening night-time world is achieved by the use of a number of subtle special effects. The door appears to slam in slow motion with the use of stop-frame animation. As Melanie struggles to climb the tree one of the branches comes to life, physically grasping her wrist, in a concrete realisation of the menacing branches in the novel, which 'tore her hair and thrashed her face' ([1967: 1981: 18).[24] When she flings herself in through the bedroom window she actually flies with the aid of a harness.

In another magical sequence Melanie wakes up in a rose forest, in the literal realisation of a passage in the novel in which she momentarily mistakes the roses on her new wallpaper for real roses:

Now, who has planted this thick hedge of crimson roses in all this dark, green, luxuriant foliage with, oh, what cruel thorns? Melanie opened her eyes and saw thorns among roses, as if she woke from a hundred years' night, la belle au bois dormante, imprisoned in a century's steadily burgeoning garden. But it was only her new wallpaper, which was printed with roses, though she had not before noticed the thorns. ([1967] 1981: 53)

In the film she awakes to a magnificent outdoor scene, her bed overhung with a bower of roses which magically transform into the roses on the wallpaper: 'close-up Melanie's face as she wakes up, opens her eyes. She sits up; the roses retreat, flattening out and becoming two-dimensional. She rubs her eyes. The roses are back on the wallpaper, again' ([1967: 1981: 259). Wheatley explains that the process of realising this transformation involved a mixture of old-fashioned animation techniques (1996: 240). The effect of a decomposing rose is created by filming a live rose being flattened under a piece of glass. The design for the rose wallpaper is then traced around the squashed rose. The final effect is created via a dissolve between the footage of the live rose and the wallpaper. All these effects create an uncanny atmosphere without overly drawing attention to themselves or becoming contrived. They work more on the level of the unconscious, unsettling epistemological looking and creating a sense of not quite believing your eyes.

The fact that Carter particularly liked old-fashioned animation techniques suggests a certain willingness to explore illusion as illusion – being able to see how it is done. As Doane suggests, 'in the trompe l'oeil in art, the eye is "taken in" or deceived only momentarily, the entire aesthetic effect being dependent upon the eventual recognition that the painting is, in fact, a painting' (1991: 194). The recognition of the trompe l'oeil, then, creates a defamiliarising effect. Animation's trick photography similarly draws attention to the materiality of the medium, revealing the illusionism of realist cinema. The use of these old-fashioned animation techniques in *The Magic Toyshop* functions as a foregrounding device, drawing attention to the illusive nature of film as a medium and challenging the visual field.

In parallel with this love of animated film, Carter was fascinated with animation in its more literal sense – animation as in bringing something to life, the movement of inanimate objects, imitation human beings. Animation's potential for the uncanny appealed to Carter because it enabled her to question what it is to be human: 'are they animate or not, these beings that jerk and shudder into such a semblance of life?' (1993: 135). Commenting on the toys in *The Magic Toyshop* she states, 'I had a passion for automata at one stage; I think it's the simulations of human beings that I'm interested in' (Bunbury, 1987: 37). And, again in a late interview, she states:

> I'm very interested in the idea of simulacra, of invented people, of imitation human beings, because, you know, the big question that we have to ask ourselves is how do we know we're not imitation human beings? (Evans and Carter, 1992: 24)

Populated with life-imitating figures, the concept of animation is explored extensively in Carter's fiction. In 'The Tiger's Bride', the girl compares her own status within patriarchal society with that of her 'clockwork twin':

> how I had been bought and sold, passed from hand to hand. That clock-work girl who powdered my cheeks for me; had I not been allotted only the same kind of imitative life amongst men that the doll-maker had given? ([1979] 1981: 63)

She allows her automated maid to take her place in society, thus liberating herself to pursue her animal nature: 'I will dress her in my own clothes, wind her up, send her back to perform the part of my father's daughter' ([1979] 1981: 65). Dolls and mannequins have often been used by women writers in this way, to symbolise women's lack of status in patriarchal society. Sylvia Plath's poem 'The Applicant', for example, describes the role of a wife in terms of a sinister female automaton:

> A living doll, everywhere you look.
> It can sew, it can cook,
> It can talk, talk,talk.
>
> It works, there is nothing wrong with it.
> You have a hole, it's a poultice.
> You have an eye, it's an image.
> My boy, it's your last resort.
> Will you marry it, marry it, marry it. (1965: 14–15)

Carter similarly concocts an automated geisha girl in her article 'Poor Butterfly', 'a computerised playmate' for the busy Japanese businessman:

> It would be easy to construct a blueprint for an ideal hostess. Indeed, if the Japanese economy ever needs a boost, Sony might contemplate putting them into mass production. The blueprint would provide for: a large pair of breasts, with which to comfort and delight the client; one dexterous, well-manicured hand for pouring their drinks, lighting their cigarettes and popping forkfuls of food into their mouths; a concealed tape-recording of cheerful laughter, to sustain the illusion that the girls themselves are having a good time; and a single, enormous, very sensitive ear for the clients to talk at. (1982d: 46)

In 'The Loves of Lady Purple', Carter becomes interested in the puppet-master manipulating these inanimate beings:

> the more lifelike his marionettes, the more godlike his manipulations and the more radical the symbiosis between inarticulate doll and articulating fingers. The puppeteer speculates in a no-man's-limbo between the real and that which, although we know very well it is not, nevertheless seems to be real. He is the intermediary between us, his audience, the living, and they, the dolls, the undead, who cannot live at all and yet who mimic the living in every detail since, though they cannot speak or weep, still they project those signals of signification we instantly recognise as language. ([1974] 1987: 23)

Lady Purple, the terrible, beautiful marionette, occupies an uncom-fortably liminal position between the living and the inanimate. Hanging lifeless while the Professor dutifully mends a rent in her dress, she retains the appearance of life even when he is not pulling her strings: 'the ends of her hair flickered with her random movements, creating upon the white blackboard of her back one of those fluctuating optical effects which make us question the veracity of our vision' ([1974] 1987: 34).

The Asiatic Professor prefigures Uncle Philip in *The Magic Toyshop*, whose Marionette Microcosm allows Carter to further explore the link between humans and puppets. As Gina Wisker argues the central conceit of 'the living doll [blurs] the boundaries of performance and experience, of effect and affect' (1997: 121). In the novel Uncle Philip resents Melanie 'because she was not a puppet' ([1967] 1981: 144), nevertheless putting her to work in his production of Leda and the Swan. Uncle Philip gets Finn to help Melanie rehearse her role, attempting to cast him in the role of rapist. But Finn sees through his machinations: 'He's pulled our strings as if we were his puppets' ([1967] 1981: 152). I agree with Aidan Day when he suggests, rather tentatively, that 'it is possible to pay insufficient attention to the way in which Finn is presented as actively rejecting patriarchy and reinventing himself' (1998: 31). As we have seen in Chapter 3, part of Carter's feminist project has been to suggest that masculinity is just as culturally inscribed, and therefore just as open to reconstruction, as femininity. Finn's oblique gaze enables him to see differently, suggesting that it is both necessary and possible for men, as well as women, to challenge patriarchal structures of looking. The result of a bee sting, Finn's 'slanting eyes' disturb the usual processes of patriarchal looking: 'there was a slight cast in the right eye, so that his glance was disturbing and oblique' ([1967] 1981: 33). 'I wouldn't know myself without it' he claims ([1967] 1981: 179). As Day suggests (1998: 28), Finn is equally the object of Uncle Philip's objectifying gaze, but resists this 'dehumanisation'.[25] And as Sage argues (1992: 170), both Finn and Melanie are 'toys who rebel, objects who insist on being subjects', refusing to play to the puppetmaster's tune.

In the film the relationship between puppets and people is even more blurred. When these beings are brought to life on the cinema screen, like Lady Purple, they make us question the 'veracity of our vision'. As Robyn Ferrell suggests, 'animated figures are capable of seeming uncanny ... the sly turn of a doll's head, the imperceptible flicker of a statue's eyelids, the animals whose expression is for a moment almost human' (1991: 132). And, as Mulvey argues, these animated beings could be seen as analogous to cinema itself which, if seen in terms of the materiality of film, projects simulated human beings onto the screen, creating the illusion of life:

> The beautiful automaton, the inanimate object that seems to come to life and entrances its audience, has sometimes been cited as an analogy for the cinema. The cinema, too, is inanimate, consisting of still frames which the projector's movement brings to life. (1994: 233)

In the film, the uncanny effect of the puppets being brought to life is achieved with the subtle editing of three-quarter life-sized marionettes with footage of dancers imitating puppets. The almost seamless transition between marionette and human is accomplished with the use of elaborate make-up. The dancers' faces are so lacquered that they look like painted wood, fixed in one expression (see Figure 9). Body make-up is used on the arms to create the effect of wooden joints, as demonstrated in the photograph of the female dancer in full costume (see Figure 10). The dancers are suspended, just like the "real" puppets, as demonstrated by the male dancer in harness imitating the walk of the marionette (Figure 11). The dancers themselves create the ultimate effect. Their near perfect imitation of the gauche movement of puppets makes the line between reality and fantasy almost imperceptible. Wheatley notes the difficulty faced by the dancers having to move ungracefully like puppets, contradicting years of classical ballet training as illustrated by the photograph of the dancers with the choreographer (see Figure 12).

This use of complex intercutting between puppets and dancers blurs the line between the inanimate and the human. It is a testimony to the effectiveness of this technique that Mulvey mistakenly asserts that 'while the artist is portrayed only by the marionette, the film uses an actress to perform the uncanny moment of Galatea's animation' (1994: 235). In fact, both the artist and his creation are portrayed by marionettes and dancers, with skilful editing between human and doll. For example, when the nymph marionette is accidentally destroyed by Finn's out-of-control puppetry, a wooden marionette arm falls in slow motion from the body of

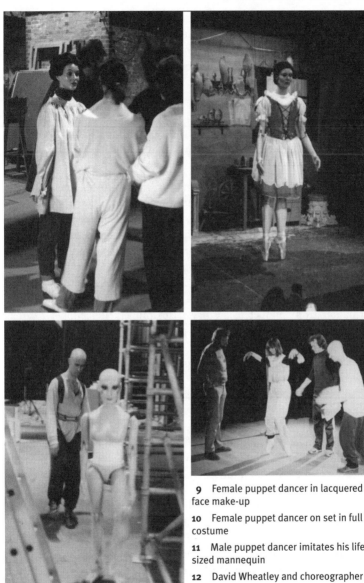

**9** Female puppet dancer in lacquered face make-up

**10** Female puppet dancer on set in full costume

**11** Male puppet dancer imitates his life-sized mannequin

**12** David Wheatley and choreographer with puppet dancers

the real dancer. Not quite knowing whether the puppets are human or not creates an uncanny atmosphere and gives the sense of puppets as doubles for human characters. This is reinforced both by the film's opening sequence (outlined above) in which the pirouetting marionette cuts to

Melanie spinning in front of the mirror in her bedroom and, in turn, Melanie's later enforced performance in Uncle Philip's puppet theatre.

The uncanny effect of the more than life-like puppets was so successful that Carter was disappointed that the same effect could not be achieved with the swan. As Wheatley states:

> That was the one criticism that she had to make about the film, she actually said, 'Where was the real swan?' I said, 'We just couldn't have that', she wanted the animated, the puppet swan to turn into the real swan at a certain point. Have you worked with swans? I've seen a few, I haven't worked with them! (1996: 239)

However, the portrayal of the swan in the film is disturbing nevertheless. It is worth comparing the treatment of the scene in the two texts. The transformation from puppet to real swan is only suggested in the novel: 'she was hallucinated; she felt herself not herself, wrenched from her own personality, watching this whole fantasy from another place; and, in this staged fantasy, anything was possible. Even that the swan, the mocked up swan, might assume reality itself and rape this girl in a blizzard of white feathers' (Carter, [1967] 1981: 166). In the screenplay an actual transformation from puppet to swan is also implied: the puppet swan is described as 'an egg-shaped sphere, painted white, coated with glued-on feathers. The neck lolls comically. The wings are like those of model aeroplanes, again coated with glued-on feathers. Its black, rubber legs are tucked up underneath it' (Carter, 1996: 282). But Melanie's mimed horror at the 'ingenuity and vaguely suggestive ugliness of the swan' becomes genuine terror when 'the screen is filled with the image of the great, beating wings' (Carter, 1996: 282). In the film, however, the puppet remains as a puppet, although the simulated rape of Melanie by the mechanical swan is perhaps even more menacing because of the very unreality of the swan, reinforcing the fact that it is Uncle Philip who is controlling the strings.

Furthermore, when Finn later destroys the swan, subtle animation techniques are used to create the uncanny impression that the swan actually has a life of its own beyond Uncle Philip's manipulations. In the novel the swan's demise is only described after the event in dialogue between Finn and Melanie ([1967] 1981: 171). In the film the event is actually re-enacted in a flashback in which Finn violently attacks the swan with an axe. Decapitated, its body jerks on its strings, its wings flapping furiously. Blood seeps from the stump of its phallic neck, which writhes suggestively on the floor. The swan appears to be indestructible, until it finally expires with a hiss. In the film, then, the actual realisation of this scene, which is only reported in the novel, concretises a pivotal moment in the narrative when Finn rises up from his patriarchal oppression.

Surprisingly the severed hand, one of the most striking images in the novel and one which would have lent itself to being animated, did not survive the process of adaptation. In the novel the severed hand is the embodiment of Melanie's feelings of alienation at being transposed from her middle-class home to Uncle Philip's toyshop: 'an amputee, she could not yet accustom herself to what was lost and gone' ([1967] 1981: 31). Invoking the spectre of Bluebeard, the severed hand also serves to foreground the exaggerated patriarchal power relations in Uncle Philip's household:

> She opened the dresser drawer to put away the knives and spoons. In the dresser drawer was a freshly severed hand, all bloody at the roots ... It was the hand of a child who goes to dancing class and wears frilled petticoats with knickers to match. From the raggedness of the flesh at the wrist, it appeared that the hand had been hewn from its arm with a knife or axe that was very blunt. Melanie heard blood fall plop in the drawer.
> 'I am going out of my mind,' she said aloud. 'Bluebeard was here'.
> ([1967] 1981: 118)

No explanation is given for the severed hand in the novel. We do not know whose hand it is, why it is there, or whether it is real or imagined. It is an element of pure horror: 'the moment she closed her eyes, the severed hand flashed onto her eyelids like a still from a Hammer film' ([1967] 1981: 122). Here the severed hand reminds us of the 'Walpurgisnacht of carved and severed limbs' ([1967] 1981: 66), hanging in the basement workshop. These are faithfully represented in the film, echoing the lifeless limbs of the mannequins in Stanley Kubrick's *Killer's Kiss* (1955). There is something innately eerie about the way mannequins simulate human beings at the best of times, but dismembered, they move from the uncanny to the downright disturbing.[26]

The issue of whether to include the scene in the film was discussed at length between the producer Steve Morrison, Carter and Wheatley. Although the severed hand could be read as a particularly cinematic element of the novel, as illustrated by the reference to Hammer film quoted above, it was omitted from the film for this very reason, being considered too Gothic for the film's magical *mise-en-scène*. While the novel was able to sustain the unexplained severed hand, it was felt that the film could not. Wheatley argues that 'there's a different kind of logic in film':

> It didn't make sense in the book, which was alright, but in terms of television it made less sense. I think in the end we rejected it because it was

an interesting dramatic moment in the novel, but in the film, it seemed to sort of need some explanation or be so obtuse a dramatic vehicle that it couldn't justify itself. (1996; 244)

Another major difference between the novel and the film is the ending, which Wheatley encouraged Carter to change, feeling that the existing ending would be impossible to realise in visual terms:

> we had to rebuild the end of the story, because she got bored with the characters and burnt the lot of them, and when I said, 'Well, what happened? What happened, where did Aunt Margaret go?' and she said, 'Oh, she's in the spirit world'. I said, 'Angela, but how do I visualise that? How do I kind of make that real for our audience?' (1996: 238)

In the novel, we are left to wonder what happens to the other characters as Finn and Melanie escape the burning house:

> 'Do you think they are all burnt up?' Melanie said to Finn.
>     'I think Francie and Maggie and the baby are safe. And the dog is an old dog and knows many tricks'.
>     'You don't think so. You only hope so'. ([1967] 1981: 200)

Finn and Melanie voice the concerns of the reader, but no consoling answers are offered in the novel. We do not know what has 'really' happened to Francie, Margaret and Victoria, we can only hope. But, Wheatley argues, in order for the film to have a satisfying resolution the audience needs to know:

> In terms of an audience, we need to know what happens to all the people involved in this ... some notion of where they go, what, are they safe, are they hurt, are they in trouble? You need to know where they are emotionally, for an audience, emotionally you need to know what's happened to them. (1996: 238)

Wheatley, then, felt compelled to adhere to the formal conventions of traditional narrative cinema, providing a sense of explication, resolution and closure.

It is worth examining the differences between the two endings in more detail. In the novel Melanie dreams that she is Jonathan sailing away to sea ([1967] 1981: 174–8). In the film the dream is realised in a magic sequence in which, as Laura Mulvey explains (1994: 237), 'the sea sweeps onto the puppet stage and Jonathan rows away, out of the story, in a little boat'. In the novel Aunt Margaret runs into Melanie's bedroom in a 'red veil of dishevelled hair' taking Victoria with her ([1967] 1981: 196).[27] In the film this becomes another magnificent set piece with the use of a number of special-effects. Aunt Margaret appears to float into the room, giving the scene a particularly dream-like quality.[28] She takes leave of Finn and Melanie and, taking Victoria with her, disappears in a whirlwind of red hair which takes over the entire screen – huge hair extensions blown about by a wind machine – a striking visual metaphor for the end of her oppression.[29] Her disappearance is then effected with stop-motion photography, recalling the trick photography of early cinema. Again, these special-effects and old-fashioned animation techniques create a sense of heightened reality which disrupts the certainties of epistemological looking.

It is not clear what happens to Francie in the novel. In the film he plays a crucial part in Uncle Philip's downfall which constitutes one of the major differences between the endings of the two texts. In the book we assume that Uncle Philip goes up in flames with the house. In the film Francie lures him into the puppet theatre where he discovers the dismembered swan. There is rapid intercutting between Uncle Philip's enraged face and the various toys in the workshop which whirr into uncanny life. As Robyn Ferrell argues, 'the flickerings of life in the wooden toys and puppets warn that the excluded category may not play dead but could spring at any moment into life-threatening life' (1991: 139). As Francie strikes up a tune on his fiddle, the life-sized marionettes become animated. The puppets clap and dance to Francie's jig, menacingly crowding in on Uncle Philip, who 'looks up at the circle of wooden faces, all of which he has created himself' (Carter, 1996: 292). He starts spinning centre stage: 'the music goes faster and faster. The surrounding, clapping puppets whirl into a blur' (Carter, 1996: 292). The scene cuts to exterior, night, as the neighbourhood children jostle excitedly around the bonfire. Finn lights a match and says 'Me brother's fetching the guy' (Carter, 1996: 293). The film ends with fireworks exploding out of the toyshop window. The last frame, held as the credits roll, is a shot of an effigy of Uncle Philip burning on the bonfire.[30]

In many ways the fact that Philip is overcome by his own puppets in the film is more satisfying than merely implying that he is left to burn with the house. Destroyed by his own creations, hoist by his own petard, Uncle Philip gets his just deserts and the puppets turn on the puppetmaster, just as Lady Purple overcomes her Asiatic Professor. As Wheatley suggests, the film's ending is more gratifying, because it fulfils a sense of dramatic irony:

> I thought it was more ironical, I thought that the notion that someone, because of his control, because he's dictated their lives, I just thought the notion that the things he's created and controlled turn against him was a more satisfying solution, than him just burning. The people all escape from him their own different ways, but the notion that his own creations turn against him is somehow ironic, I just found that more satisfying. (1996: 238–9)

Wheatley felt that the film could not sustain elements of the unexplained and, like the omission of the severed hand, the need to change the ending poses interesting questions about the differences between what the novel and film can sustain. As already observed, Carter described the film as 'a straightforward narrative movie' in which the 'holes can't be left empty for the reader to imagine what's going on, because that's not how the cinema works ... It could be how the cinema worked, but it would be cinema of a different kind, operating at a different level' (Bunbury, 1987: 37).[31] Carter was undoubtedly aware of alternative cinematic traditions, such as the surrealism of Louis Buñuel and the animation of Jan Svankmayer. However, although the film aspires towards the production values of mainstream cinema on one level, the extensive use of old-fashioned animation techniques operates on another level to unravel some of the ideological operations implicit in dominant narrative cinema. Despite the fact that the severed hand was omitted and the ending more clearly resolved, there are numerous other elements which disrupt the traditional narrative pattern of the film, such as the magical night garden, the living wallpaper, self-activating toys and the sinister marionettes which come to uncanny life. These defamiliarising animation techniques, combined with the representation of an active female gaze, work to undermine the logic of the 'straightforward narrative movie'. Thus, despite the tension between the production values of Granada Television and Carter's original vision, *The Magic Toyshop* remains a powerful feminist critique of patriarchal structures of looking – all the more effective, perhaps, because that critique is situated within the mainstream.

## Notes

1  Mulvey's notion of the 'male gaze', while useful for describing the patriarchal status quo, is not a monolithically fixed structure of vision, but one which can, and has been, challenged. As Jacqueline Rose suggests, 'history is not a petrified block of a singular visual space since, looked at obliquely, it can always be seen to contain its moments of unease' (1986: 232–3).

2  While none of the above citations are effectively wrong, it seems clear that the film's date should rest on its original premiere at the London Film Festival. I therefore take the film's date to be 1986.

3  According to Wheatley the fact that the programme was commissioned is largely owing to the persuasive powers of producer Steve Morrison, who he also acknowledges as a key player in convincing Granada to pay him to work with Carter on the adaptation.

4  Wheatley had what he calls 'a television budget', with a mere £8,000 for the special effects. Compare this with the budget for *The Company of Wolves* which, although by no means large compared to contemporaneous Hollywood budgets, was considerably more at £2,000,000 for the whole film (McAsh, 1984: 4). The televised programme includes

intertitles indicating the advertising breaks, suggesting that the programme was structurally conceived for commercial television.

5  Upholding Thornham's argument about postmodern viewing practices and the redundant notion of a discrete cinematic text, I have never seen *The Magic Toyshop* on the big screen, having watched and re-watched, paused, freeze-framed an off-air video recording.

6  This is a distinction which, as Mulvey points out (1994: 230), Carter herself makes in 'Acting it up on the Small Screen', criticising, as the title implies, the reduced visual space of the television screen (Carter, 1982d: 124–9). See Chapter 7 for a detailed discussion of Carter's writing about television.

7  Carter describes *Valerie and Her Week of Wonders* as a 'menstrual film' in a discussion of *The Company of Wolves* (Romney, 1985: 31). Wheatley claims 'if you look at *Valerie and Her Week of Wonders* I think you'll find it quite amazing the similarities between that film and *The Magic Toyshop*' (1996: 243).

8  The film makes a visual connection between Melanie's early narcissistic role-play and her enforced performance as Leda in Uncle Philip's puppet theatre. Preparing for her role, Melanie holds up a ream of sheer white fabric. Aunt Margaret throws a handful of daisies over her head. As she spins around in slow motion, the image shifts to Melanie pirouetting in the finished dress. This cut-on edit is obviously an allusion to the opening of the film, and Melanie's costume is, significantly, remarkably similar to the ominous wedding dress and bridal veil in the earlier scene in the night garden.

9  The *Sun* headlined with: 'Prancing naked in front of mirrors' (9 November 1988). Similarly the *Daily Star* headlined with: 'Full Frontal Nude Scene in Front of a Mirror in this "Adult" Fairy Tale' (5 November 1988).

10  The closest we get to a state of undress in the screenplay is Melanie's simulation of Botticelli's Venus, which if not fully clothed, is certainly not nude: 'She irritably shrugs off the bedspread, to reveal the liberty bodice and petticoat business underneath' (Carter, 1996: 248).

11  A specific example is the passage quoted above which alludes directly to Donne's *Elegy: To his Mistris going to Bed*, appropriating the traditional geographical metaphor of the colonised female body, to describe Melanie's discovery of her own body. Where the novel can sustain such heightened language without spilling into the ridiculous, narrative film language tends to be more economical with its symbolism: although it might be possible to approximate this in film (complex intercutting between images of mountain ranges and Melanie's flesh, with a detached and ironic voice-over of Donne's poem, perhaps), this would result in pure surrealism which is not compatible with the production values of Granada's 'straightforward narrative movie' (Bunbury, 1987: 37).

12  Mulvey ([1975] 1989: 25) posits that there are 'three different looks associated with the cinema': 'that of the camera as it records the pro-filmic event, that of the audience as it watches the final product, and that of the characters at each other within the screen illusion. The conventions of narrative film deny the first two and subordinate them to the third, the conscious aim being always to eliminate intrusive camera presence and prevent a distancing awareness in the audience.'

13  Judith Mayne (1994: 54) explores the use of the keyhole shot in *A Search for Evidence* (1903) which uses a similar alternation between 'person looking and object of the look'.

14  The audience's voyeurism is reinforced when the keyhole mask continues to frame the shot even after Melanie takes her eye from the keyhole.

15  The novel uses the language of looks in early cinema to describe narrative point of view again when Melanie visualises the body of her mother as 'seen through the wrong end of a telescope' (Carter, [1967] 1981: 78).

16  In the film, Finn's paintings were painted by Corrina Sargood, Carter's friend, who also did the artwork for both of the Virago collections of fairy tales and worked with the art departments in the production of *The Holy Family Album* (1991b) and *Angela Carter's Curious Room* (Evans (dir.), 1992).

17  As Cox points out, even 'realist' Lumière played with film's capacity for illusion, citing 'The Wall', in which the demolition of a wall was projected backwards, making the wall magically re-erect itself.

18  Hayward (1996: 67) cites Carter's hero Godard as a 'famed practitioner' of these deconstructive, 'counter-cinematic' strategies which, she argues, were intended to 'draw the spectator's attention to the fact that she or he is watching a film'.

19  While Doane examines the use of trompe l'oeil in avant-garde cinema, she does not extend her argument to include animation film.

20  As Cox (1995) also outlines, before the advent of the cinema, fairly sophisticated narratives were created using light slides, dissolving from one slide to another to create special effects. The nineteenth-century diorama consisted of landscapes viewed through an aperture which would alter depending on the amount and movement of light, creating atmospheric effects such as the illusion of dusk.

21  Jo Ann Kaplan, director of *The Holy Family Album*, talks about Carter's working knowledge of magic tricks and their shared love of old-fashioned film animation (1995: 263). Carter's friend, Corinna Sargood, who had a creative role as designer in the film of *The Magic Toyshop*, *The Holy Family Album* and *Angela Carter's Curious Room*, also speaks of their frequent trips to the ICA to watch animation (in personal conversation, 29 March 1996).

22  A note in the text states: 'this piece was written in praise of Jan Svankmayer, the animator of Prague, and his film of *Alice*' (1993: 212).

23  Wheatley explains how he saw *The Magic Toyshop* as 'a vehicle for those moments that are extraordinary, that somehow are surprising and exceptional, which I thought that I had an affinity for and that I found attractive in her. The extraordinary, the extraordinary moments that make life surprising, startling' (1996: 240).

24  It is interesting to compare this sequence with the parallel scene in the film, *The Company of Wolves* in which Rosaleen climbs a tall tree and finds the stork's nest. Both scenes have an intense magical quality about them, and signal an adolescent girl's first encounter with female sexuality, but in *The Magic Toyshop* the experience is a negative one, in *The Company of Wolves* it is somehow liberating.

25  A similar case might also be made around Melanie's younger brother Jonathan who abandons his glasses in the film in the magical scene in which he rows out to sea. As Robyn Ferrell suggests (1991: 136), the 'shortsighted Jonathan' might be 'blind to the Oedipal complex and so able to sail away'.

26  Testimony to this fact is the controversial Chapmanworld exhibition at the ICA. The 'mutated figures' of Tragic Anatomies are comprised of subtly disfigured child mannequins in sexual attitudes (Jake and Dinos Chapman, *Tragic Anatomies*, Chapmanworld, Institute of Contemporary Arts, 11 May–14 July 1996, information from July–August 1996 ICA Bulletin).

27  Significantly, it is at this point in the novel that Aunt Margaret finds her voice: 'With her voice, she had found her strength, a frail but constant courage like spun silk. Struck dumb on her wedding day, she found her old voice again the day she was freed' ([1967] 1981: 197). In the film this moment is precipitated by her laughter in an earlier scene in the kitchen. Containing resonances with Cixous' 'The Laugh of the Medusa' ([1976] 1980): 'Margaret slowly smiles. Then chuckles. Then we hear a musical sound, cymbelum or celesta. It is her laughter' (Carter, 1996: 287). Speaking for the first time, she asks Victoria to fetch her silver necklace which she throws through the window, breaking the glass and literally throwing away the bonds of her slavery, the choker given to her by Uncle Philip on their wedding day.

28  As Wheatley attests, there is 'something extraordinary' about this gliding motion: 'it's just chilling that someone can drift across a room and not walk, they move at the same pace, but the fact that you don't see any bodily movement of walking is terrifying, it's nightmares, it's what you fear' (1996: 237).

29 Wheatley describes the mayhem of filming this scene: 'we had a hell of a lot of bloody trouble trying to blow that hair around a bit. Because she was being dragged across the floor on a platform with little wheels on, so she was standing there and we tried to direct wind machines to keep the hair up and it wouldn't, it kept going all over, oh it was just ridiculous!' (1996: 237).

30 ITV contrived to broadcast the programme on bonfire night, 5 November 1988, which foregrounds the transposition of the novel to Guy Fawkes night. Uncle Philip is reduced to the guy in an exaggerated realisation of the scene in the novel when Francie and Finn torture a voodoo doll of Uncle Philip with matches ([1967] 1981: 156).

31 I quote this passage again because it is particularly pertinent to the question of the possibilities of the medium addressed here.

# 7

# 'The box does furnish a room': television

'She despised the small screen', claims Laura Mulvey (1994: 242) in a throw-away comment at the end of an otherwise illuminating essay, 'Cinema Magic and the Old Monsters', in which she celebrates Carter's love of the magical silver screen. While Carter is better known for her film adaptations than her involvement in the television industry, and her writings about Hollywood are more familiar than her television criticism, Mulvey's assumption of Carter's blanket condemnation of television as a medium demands further analysis. In this chapter I outline Carter's writings about television and briefly contextualise these in relation to British broadcasting history, refuting Mulvey's claim through a close reading of the article on which she bases her comment, 'Acting it Up on the Small Screen' (Carter, 1982d: 124–9).

## Contextualising Carter's work in television

Carter's writing about television has a certain defamiliarising freshness, the quality of an innocent abroad in a new medium, in its deconstructive approach to a variety of television genres, from soap ads to detective series.[1] She came late to the medium, her television criticism coinciding with the acquisition of a television set in 1978: 'I got my own television set, last year', she writes in 1979 (Carter, 1997: 410). In 'The Theatre of the Absurd' (1978) she undertakes a semiotic analysis of the 'art' of television commercials which, she argues, have the 'kind of built-in alienation effect' that 'would make a surrealist weep for joy' (Carter, 1997: 401, 403). She celebrates their ability to inadvertently disrupt the 'fictive reality' of television viewing, acting as 'constant reminders that the medium itself is artificial' (Carter, 1997: 402–3). She pursued the same theme in 'The Box Does Furnish a Room' (1979):

Television as a medium is not 'for' showing the disjunction between different kinds of reality, but it cannot help do so because of the disjunction between the kinds of life shown on the screen and the one which the viewer knows to be real. And since one cannot fool all the people all of the time, television may be implicitly radical all the time, in spite of itself. (Carter, 1997: 410)[2]

The article begins with what appears to be a rejection of the medium, 'The more I watch television the more I wonder what it's *for*' (Carter, 1997: 409). But what at first seems to be a pessimistic commentary on television as inherently unworthy and threatening to other, more established cultural forms ('it has replaced the story book') turns out to be more of a cultural critique of the medium, a search for its social use: 'never mind what's on it, look instead at what it does' (Carter, 1997: 410, 411–12). Indeed, Carter mocks the sneering 'British intelligentsia' (herself included) who privilege books and radio but 'sneak off to friends when there's something they really want to watch, like *Fawlty Towers* or *Days of Hope*', and she goes on to suggest that television fulfils a crucial social function as 'electronic companion and nanny' making 'family life possible in a high-rise flat on a wet day' (1997: 411).[3]

While always remaining critically objective, Carter appears to have warmed to the medium in her later television journalism. In 'Monkey Business' (1980) she raves about the surreal Japanese series, *Monkey*, 'by far the oddest thing on television at the moment, and also the most engaging' (Carter, 1997: 413). 'The Wonderful World of Cops' (1982) is an indictment of the naturalisation of violence and the erosion of justice in American 'cop-operas', such as *Hill Street Blues*, and she offers an ambivalent analysis of the feminisation of the genre in *Cagney and Lacey* (1997: 416–19).

Carter's perspective on television in these articles is, of course, prescribed by the context and period in which she writes. Published in *New Society*, between 1978 and 1982, they were aimed at the very intelligentsia she pokes fun at in 'The Box Does Furnish a Room'. Her initial recalcitrance at having to confront the medium reflects and engages with the bourgeois left's prevalent fear and loathing of modern media. But these pieces also demonstrate a shift towards a critical engagement with the social and cultural impact of the medium, reflecting a growing awareness of mass media and communications theory.[4]

It is also important to contextualise these articles in terms of the rapidly expanding history of television broadcasting. They predate a number of significant cultural and technological developments: Channel 4 had not yet been realised; the video age was in its infancy; the Broadcasting Audience Research Board (BARB) had only just been set up, as had the new unified television ratings system, all of which went on to significantly change the face of television (particularly the latter with its emphasis on audience ratings which has had a marked impact on arts programming).[5] As Barrie MacDonald writes in 1988: 'the first half of the 1980s were to see rapid acceleration in the development of broadcasting, with the expansion of the existing public service broadcasting systems, and the emergence of new cable and satellite television services' (MacDonald, 1988: 23). This is not to mention the ongoing developments in broadcasting since 1988: satellite and cable TV, the birth of Channel 5, developments in widescreen television and the rapidly developing digital technologies which have made interactive television, television-on-demand and teleshopping possible.

Carter's journalistic writings about television dwindle as she becomes actively involved in the industry itself from the early 1980s onwards, first contributing to arts programming and later writing directly for the medium. John Ellis records her involvement in the early days of Channel 4 (1995: 249), reviewing *The Draughtsman's Contract* for the first of his world cinema series, *Visions*, which was transmitted during the second week of the channel's broadcasting history in November 1982 (Carter, 1982a). In the programme Carter directly addresses the camera using highly wrought sentences and stylised language not unlike that used in the film itself. But this is obviously not just an essay with pictures; the music and film clips were specified by Carter herself, and her narration, full of suspenseful pauses, interacts with the chosen visuals to dramatic effect, already revealing an awareness of the requirements of the medium.[6] She went on to contribute to programmes on Jean-Luc Godard (Carter, 1983a) and the making of *The Company of Wolves* (Carter, 1984b).

### Acting it up on the small screen

The quotation from 'Acting it Up on the Small Screen' (1979), which Mulvey uses to justify Carter's sweeping contempt for television, certainly seems to offer a damning view of the medium:

> Television has extraordinary limitations as a medium for the presentation of imaginative drama of any kind. It has an inbuilt ability to cut people down to size, to reduce them to gesticulating heads or, in long shot, to friezes of capering dwarfs. (1982d: 124)

But, read in the context of her other writings on television, it becomes clear that Carter's was a more complex critical engagement with the medium than Mulvey allows. It is also worth remembering that 'Acting it

'Up on the Small Screen' is a piece of journalism, not an academic article. I do not wish to denigrate Mulvey's article, which is excellent on Carter's cinema, but I do think it important to defend television from such an entire dismissal. Mulvey quotes this passage without acknowledging either the inherent contradictions of the article or Carter's journalistic style, which is humorous, discursive, conversational; the argument often contrary and paradoxical.[7] In her Introduction to Carter's collected journalism Joan Smith identifies this as 'a quality I don't want to describe as feminine precisely, but which struck me ... as aeons away from the bombastic, know-it-all style of much male discourse':

> One of the many things I like about *Shaking a Leg*, in fact, is the way in which the articles and reviews show Angela Carter's mind working, coming at a subject from different angles, changing its focus, trying out a thought and seeing where it goes. The result isn't tentative, far from it – few authors have been so passionately engaged – but it's a kind of writing which invites the reader to think, to argue back, to accost its creator with sentences beginning: 'yes, but what about ...?' (1997: xii)[8]

Like her fiction, then, Carter's journalism leaves space for the active involvement of the reader: we share in the development of her arguments; we witness her ideas in process.[9] The quotation which Mulvey cites is just such an example of Carter's wayward mode of discourse, baldly dismissing 'imaginative drama of any kind' (Carter, 1982d: 124), whereas the article goes on to identify itself as dealing specifically with classical adaptation. This statement is further qualified at the end of the article by Carter's concession to 'pseudo-documentary social realism' (1982d: 129). Far from despising television, Carter frames the case for the development of a distinct television language which recognises the unique aesthetic of the medium.

In order to illustrate why Mulvey's assertion is unfounded it is necessary to outline the caprices of Carter's argument in detail. The article begins with the argument that television drama is at a disadvantage because it is in direct competition with old movies in the broadcasting schedule. In the next sentence there is an abrupt change of emphasis from film to theatre, with particular reference to classic British television drama, which becomes the main focus of the article. British theatre-trained actors 'come into their own' on television, Carter maintains: 'that dreadful spectacle of painted loons', who 'have inherited the small screen and are inescapable, they spread themselves across all three channels, mopping and mowing and rolling their eyes and scattering cut-glass vowels everywhere' (1982d: 124).[10]

Already there are a series of juxtapositions between television drama and both film and the theatre. On the one hand television drama cannot compete with old movies, even when they are broadcast on the reduced medium of television; and on the other, it is a magnification of the very worst aspects of 'live' theatre which, Carter feels, are bad enough on stage, but cannot be sustained in the immediacy of the living room. In the next twist of the argument television drama 'is more like movies than it is like the theatre, obviously, but it is like the movies through the wrong end of a telescope' (1982d: 124). Although movies are inevitably reduced by the medium, she argues that one of the main reasons to own a set is to catch up on the film seasons. In her attempt to define television as a medium Carter hops from film to theatre as a measure of television's inadequacy and these two elements jostle for supremacy throughout the article.

She juxtaposes the experience of cinema, where 'we accept the convention that the images on the screen are much larger than life without even thinking about it', with the inadequacy of the small screen:

> Take the famous close-up of Barbara Stanwyck's high heels [in Billy Wilder's *Double Indemnity*, (1944)], with the teasing anklet, as she walks down the staircase in order to lure Fred MacMurray to his doom. What this shot means, of course, is that MacMurray's whole attention is focused, not on the woman but on the erotic potential he, she and we know she is exploiting. On television the whole point is lost. The image of Stanwyck's lower limbs is simply no longer large enough to sustain a metaphor. (Carter, 1982d: 125)

Something happens to the system of looks which operate in classic film noir when the object of the gaze is transmitted on television, rather than projected onto the silver screen. The metaphor is literally reduced, made small, by the smallness of the television screen. The power of the metaphor is lost in translation, precisely because there is no translation from one medium to another, just a different means of screening the same object. Carter argues that the cinema can take on a 'higher degree of expressionism than television could ever tolerate on its own terms', while 'in television drama itself, there is not sufficient artistic space to contain this kind of device', without becoming 'phony and contrived' (1982d: 125).

Carter points out that we do not 'look up' to television as a medium, either metaphorically, as an art-form, or literally, as a physical object: as she suggests in 'The Box Does Furnish a Room', it has become part of the furniture (1997: 412). Carter consistently foregrounds the smallness of the screen – faces in close-up are mirror-images of ourselves, not giant icons on the silver screen and long shots dwarf the characters:

> A close-up on television is about the size of one's own face in a mirror. Two is a crowd; scenes involving three or more people involve abrupt changes

of the focus of attention. In three-quarter shot, the actors are already receding rapidly backwards, turning into wee folk before our very eyes. (1982d: 125)

But it is not simply the difference in the size of the screen that differentiates television from the cinema, it is also the context of consumption. In a piece on Godard, she lamented the fact that 'the most public of art forms has been transformed by technological change into the most intimate':

> The communal rituals in the dark became a thing of the past. Cinema became privatised. Movies have turned into things you watched on TV in the privacy of your own home. The little box to which we scornfully left our parents glued all those years ago gobbled up the dream factory and the reality factory, too. (Carter, 1997: 381)

For Carter, the communal experience of cinema is lost in the domestic sphere of home. She states, 'there is something sacred about the cinema which is to do with it being public, to do with people going together with the intention of experiencing the same experience, having the same revelation' (Evans and Carter, 1992: 7).

So far, it seems, the article supports Mulvey's view that she 'despised the small screen' (1997: 242). However, Carter's apparent dismissal of the medium is only half the picture. She goes on to suggest that television needs to find a distinct vocabulary in order to be able to compete with cinema, rather than simply adopting the language of film style, arguing that 'television drama has not yet found its Lilliputian D. W. Griffiths [sic]' (1982d: 125). 'The father of film language', Griffith played a key part in the development of narrative techniques which are still in use today, claiming to have invented the close-up, which has since 'become crucial in the organization of cinematic narrative' (Doane, 1991: 46). Television has not *yet* found its equivalent to film language but, Carter implies, there is potential for television to find its own native tongue. Rather than a damning indictment of television, which Mulvey takes it to be, the article, in fact, calls for the development of a distinct television style which recognises the aesthetic of the medium.

Taking the concept of the artistic possibilities being dictated by the medium to its logical extreme, Carter argues that if television drama is good television then, presumably, it would not look better on the big screen: 'if it would, then it's lousy television. I would have thought this stood to reason, due to the limitations of the form creating the aesthetic of the form' (1982d: 125). But on the contrary, Carter argues, sometimes television drama seems to have been produced for the 'preview theatres rather than transmission' (1982d: 125).[11] Similarly, Carter suggests, television should learn from Hollywood that 'it is a well-known fact that good novels make bad movies. Obviously, what makes a novel good are just those qualities that make it difficult to translate it out of fiction into anything else' (1982d: 126). This statement is interesting in the light of the fact that Carter adapted her own work both for radio and later for film, and in the context of my own arguments about media adaptation. Carter seems to contradict her own practice, paradoxically arguing for the impossibility of transferring from one medium to another. What it does reveal, however, is Carter's awareness of the necessity of respecting the language of the medium, not the impossibility of adaptation. As we have seen in her preface to her radio play anthology, *Come Unto These Yellow Sands*, she preferred the term 'reformulation' to adaptation (Carter, 1985: 10), suggesting that the process of translating a work from one medium to another requires not simply modification, but a complete transformation, taking the aesthetic of the new medium into account.

If good books do make bad movies, Carter continues, 'why, then, should it be accepted as a self-evident fact that great novels make great television?' (1982d: 126). She wonders why the BBC continues to produce its versions of the literary classics and concludes that their main purpose seems to be as an outlet for the overacting of British theatre actors, referring to the 'just-ended *Crime and Punishment* on BBC2' which, she feels, 'really brings out the worst in them':

> They love to get their tongues round those lilting patronymics, they seem grotesquely liberated by personating groovy Slavs, it's an excuse to act your head off. (Carter, 1982d: 126)

It becomes apparent that Carter's attitude towards television in this article should be seen specifically in the context of this adaptation of Dostoievsky's *Crime and Punishment*, which she critiques at length throughout the rest of the article.[12] Rather than embodying Carter's dissatisfaction with adaptation itself, or with television as a medium, the article generalises about good books making bad television in order to endorse and naturalise her personal dislike of a recent adaptation of one of her 'male literary heroes' (Carter, 1983d: 75).

Carter's main problem is not with adaptation, nor television, nor necessarily with British theatre acting *per se*, but the fact that while 'acting it up' is OK on stage, it does not translate to the small screen:

> what looks, if not good, then at least lifelike in a parodic kind of way on a stage, looks like the theatrical equivalent of S. J. Perelman's pastiches of Dostoievsky when it is virtually delivered into your lap, which is what television does. (1982d: 126)

The point Carter makes about the type of acting that classic adaptation tends to produce is still resonant today in the light of the ongoing television revival of the classics, after a brief period out of fashion in the 1980s: 'all at once the BBC remembered its unimpeachable mission to bring classics to the people', and after the success of the BBC's *Middlemarch*, a spate of period-costume dramas poured out of our sets, including *Martin Chuzzlewit*, *The Buccaneers* and *Pride and Prejudice* (Bennett, 1995: 2–4). According to director Ken Loach, famed for his improvisational directing, the tendency to over-act remains a problem for this type of costume drama today:

> The difficulty ... is that it produces a whole style of acting and direction which is rather pickled in the past, and actors lapse into all kinds of thespian tricks that they wouldn't get away with if they were wearing contemporary clothes. Fat men huff and puff, people descend into Dickensian caricatures when they put the costumes on. (Bennett, 1995: 4)

Carter contrasts this style of period acting and directing with that of the classic Hollywood costume drama, citing the understated performance of Greta Garbo in the final scene of *Queen Christina*. The director Reuben Mamoulian, she recounts, 'told her to keep her face a perfect blank, so that the audience could read into her features whatever they felt should be the appropriate response. It works too. Triumph of reticence; her face has the weary immobility of the obsessed' (1982d: 126).[13] In contrast, she argues, 'John Hurt feels it necessary to contort every single facial muscle, until the very hairs within his nostrils seem to rhumba, in a baulked effort to convey spiritual turmoil' in *Crime and Punishment* (1982d: 126). This, she argues, is not the fault of Hurt, but simply the fact that Hurt's style of British theatre acting does not translate to television.[14] Because of the size of the television screen, Carter notes, much television drama is conducted in close-up which conflicts with the British actors' training to 'project emotion, rather than embody it', incidentally making them 'very good at television commercials' (1982d: 127). Carter does give a concession to the BBC in its role as educator, but undercuts it almost immediately: 'after all, as somebody pompously opined about *Crime and Punishment*, if it makes one person who had never heard of Dostoievsky pick up the book and start to read, it will have served its purpose ... and also have the rather self-defeating result of, presumably, making him switch the telly off' (1982d: 128).

Another major hurdle for classic drama, for Carter, is television's slavery to a naturalistic style which, paradoxically, 'is designed to evade truth and celebrate simulation' (1982d: 127). Carter rejects this preoccupation with 'the fictive reality of naturalism, which necessitates the creation of an illusion as an end in itself':

But 'naturalism' as a mode which deals with the recreation of reality as a credible illusion is quite a different thing from the mode of realism itself, which is a representation of what things actually *are* like and must, therefore, bear an intimate relation to truth or else, well, it isn't any good. (And, of course, it doesn't have to *look* real.) (1982d: 127)

She argues that *Crime and Punishment* might have been more successful if it had been directed by someone as 'vulgarly Dostoievskian as Douglas Sirk', director of classic Hollywood melodramas such as *All That Heaven Allows* (1955) and *The Imitation of Life* (1959): 'I doubt if it would occur to a BBC2 classic serial television director to watch Sirk to pick up tips, though I hope I'm wrong' (1982d: 128).

Finally Carter argues for a different approach to these classic serials, one which takes the demands of the medium on board and utilises the specific syntax of television. 'Maybe they could have thrown it open to the school of television social realism – Garnett–Loach–Allen *et al*.', she suggests of *Crime and Punishment*, 'let the cast make up their lines as they went along, shot it in Bradford which really does look like a Russian city, instead of what a Russian city is supposed to look like' (1982d: 128).[15] The article ends not with the wholesale rejection of television as a medium, therefore, but the call for a distinct television language:

> Television pseudo-documentary social realism, after all this time, remains the only genre of television drama in this country that has the marks of a coherent style in which form and content fuse so that the actors appear to believe in what they are doing rather than trying to put one over on you. (1982d: 128–9)

Writing over a decade after Loach's innovatory 'television social realism', Carter laments the fact that television has yet to discover an autonomous style 'after all this time'. A similar plea was being made well into the 1990s:

> if classic adaptations are to amount to anything more than a dignified, time-hallowed form of national escapism, viewers will have to abandon their expectations that old-fashioned books should be shot in old-fashioned ways. In *The Age of Innocence*, Scorsese showed that the most restrained classic adaptation could also be visually thrilling – the camera masterfully contributing more to the film's style than the period whatnots. 'I wanted to find a modern way to tell a period story', Scorsese said. Shouldn't the BBC do the same? (Bennett, 1995: 2–4)

'Acting it Up on the Small Screen' tells us a number of things about Carter's relationship with television. Most obviously, it tells us that she rejected a particular type of dramatic production, the classic adaptation (we could go far as to say that she rejected a specific production, *Crime and Punishment*). Her main criticism of classic television drama seems to be not the attendant problems of overacting and stilted directing, nor even its slavery to naturalism, but its excessive explicitness: its lack of artistic subtlety and imaginative space. This is in stark contrast to her attraction to radio as a medium for dramatic representation, as we have already seen in Chapter 1. The article also tells us that Carter distinguished between classical adaptations and other types of television drama and that she saw potential for different, more challenging ways of adapting the great literary classics: ways that create space for the viewer's imagination and that recognise television as a distinct medium.

The article clearly reveals Carter's awareness of some of television's possible limitations as a medium: its small scale; the consequent distancing of narrative and the tendency to adopt the language of cinema rather than creating a language of its own. But, most significantly, it tells us that, for Carter, television's 'limitations' might actually be the basis of a coherent television style; that we should recognise these limitations as the aesthetic of the medium and attempt to work with them, not against them. She mentions Dennis Potter and Howard Schuman as examples of television writers and practitioners who were beginning to discover and use a distinct language for television. Indeed, she celebrates Potter's *Pennies from Heaven* and Schuman's *Rock Follies* for consciously utilising television's 'diminished reality effect in various sprightly ways' (1982d: 124).[16] Director Jo Ann Kaplan notes Carter's affinity with Schuman, asserting that 'she respected his work enormously because he wrote for the medium' (1995: 288). This is the crux of Carter's relationship with television, not the Luddite condemnation which Mulvey quite understandably implies. On the contrary, Carter actively embraced new technologies, seeing such 'video-gadgetry' as an extension, not the death, of narrative (Carter (ed.), 1990: xxi). She did not despise the small screen, rather she despised the misuse and abuse of a medium that had not yet found its own voice, and perhaps is yet to find it.

When she came to write for television she preferred to use the medium as a tool for disseminating ideas in the form of documentaries, rather than stories.[17] It seems only natural that Carter would gravitate towards documentary and arts programming given her strong background in cultural criticism. Throughout her literary career she produced copious articles for *New Society*, among other journals, ranging from book and film reviews to writing about food fads, fashion and fine art. She edited collections of traditional fairy stories and world folk tales, wrote introductions to volumes by such diverse figures as Charlotte Brontë, Frida Kahlo, Walter de la Mare and Christina Stead, deconstructed the lives of Richard Dadd and Ronald Firbank in her radio drama-documentaries, looked back on the 1960s, and analysed her own writing practice for a collection on women's writing (see Carter, 1982d, 1992, 1997). Her non-fiction writings reveal the same moral curiosity and intellectual dissidence as her fiction, sometimes getting her into trouble, as in the case of her polemical essay *The Sadeian Woman* (Carter, [1979] 1992b). Her documentary on the representation of Christ in Western art, *The Holy Family Album* (1991b) follows in this vein of irreverent cultural criticism. It seems appropriate that the programme was broadcast on Channel 4, given the station's government remit 'to provide programmes calculated to appeal to tastes not generally catered for by ITV, and to encourage innovation and experimentation in the form and content of programmes' (MacDonald, 1988: 24). But even within this 'liberal' context *The Holy Family Album* caused controversy, earning a complaint to the Broadcasting Standards Council and a mention on *Right to Reply*. The programme and its reception are discussed in Chapter 8, together with *Angela Carter's Curious Room*, a BBC *Omnibus* programme on her own life and work (Evans (dir.), 1992), on which she collaborated.

## Notes

1 Indeed, she states, 'its presence is something that continually bewilders me. I grew up without it. I'm not *used* to it as kids today are. I resent having to pay attention to it' (Carter, 1997: 410).

2 Carter's take on the unconsciously defamiliarising nature of television, which functions to disrupt the very 'fictive reality' it tries to create, throws interesting light on her own writing for television which is discussed in Chapter 8.

3 'And who am I to sneer? A television-less childhood I might have had, but it was *Saturday Night Theatre, Monday Night at Eight, ITMA, Take it From Here*', she writes, listing the radio shows of her youth (Carter, 1997: 411). It would have been interesting if Carter had written more about the differences between television and radio, but as she did not, we can only speculate. She does not mention radio at all in 'Acting it Up on the Small Screen', in which she offers an extensive comparison with both theatre and film – even though *Vampirella* had already been broadcast at the time of writing and *Come Unto These Yellow Sands* was transmitted early in the same year. Neither is television mentioned in Carter's Preface to the play anthology *Come Unto These Yellow Sands: Four Radio Plays*, apart from to assert, once again, that she was a child of the radio age, 'as present-day children are the children of television' (Carter, 1985: 9).

4 In 'The Box Does Furnish a Room' she quotes John McGrath in *Sight and Sound*, and Hans Magnus Enzensberger: 'Potentially the new media do away with all educational privileges and thereby with the cultural monopoly of the bourgeois intelligentsia. This is one of the reasons for the intelligentsia's resentment of the new industry' (1997: 410). I have not been able to source this reference from Carter's article, but it might be from Hans Magnus Enzensberger, *The Consciousness Industry: On Literature, Politics and the Media* (1974), quoted in Esslin (1980: 215–20).

5 Note that her last *New Society* article on television, 'The Wonderful World of Cops' was published 23 September 1982, over a month before the inception of Channel 4 on 2 November 1982.

6 The specified film clips are not included in the published script (Carter, 1997: 372–7). See Chapter 4 for further discussion of the programme.

7 Sarah Gamble similarly notes the 'chatty, colloquial tone' of Carter's autobiographical writings as 'deceptive, conning you into thinking you're getting to know her' (Gamble, 1997: 13).

8 Smith deals with similar themes to those of Carter in her own journalism, in pieces such as 'Gentlemen Prefer Dead Blondes' which documents the victimhood of Marilyn Monroe and 'Holocaust Girls' in which she invokes Carter's description of Justine as the image of female suffering, in *The Sadeian Woman* (both collected in Smith, 1989).

9 In this sense it shares the 'open-endedness' of her writing for radio, as discussed in Chapter 1.

10 Carter mentions only three channels, reminding us that the article was written before the advent of Channel 4, which originally had as its remit a more experimental and avant-garde agenda, a point I will return to later in relation to *The Holy Family Album* in Chapter 8.

11 This is pertinent in the context of the hybrid textual status of *The Magic Toyshop*, which was shot as a 16mm television film and then blown up to 35mm and given a theatrical release (see my discussion of decentred screens in Chapter 6).

12 *Crime and Punishment* (BBC, 1979), Jack Pulman (screenplay), Michael Darlow (dir.) and Jonathan Powell (prod.).

13 Garbo's blank face is reminiscent of the blind medium of radio with its potential for leaving interpretation up to the audience. As argued in Chapter 1, Carter saw radio as creating an imaginative space for the listener precisely because of its lack of visual images.

14 Carter obviously respected radio as a medium for imaginative drama, despite the fact that the same classically trained British actors work in radio. Presumably radio can sustain them when television cannot. Perhaps their ability to project which, Carter argues, is too much for television, is more suited to the 'blind' medium of radio?

15 Ken Loach's *Cathy Come Home* (1966), is a prime example of this type of 'television social realism', using outdoor filming, real locations, hand-held camera work, naturalistic sound, semi-documentary style combined with fictional devices such as voice-over.

16 *Pennies From Heaven* (BBC, 1978), Dennis Potter (screenplay), Piers Haggard (dir.) and Kenneth Trodd (prod.); and *Rock Follies* (Thames, 1976) and *Rock Follies of '77* (Thames, 1977), Howard Schuman (screenplay), Andrew Brown (prod.).

17 Although one of her short stories, 'The Kitchen Child' was adapted for television, directed by Joy Perino (Perino (dir.), 1990), Carter was not involved in its production.

# Acting up on the small screen:
*The Holy Family Album*

**8**

As the Channel 4 announcer warns, *The Holy Family Album* is 'a highly personal and provocative look at how some Western artists have portrayed the story of Christ' (Carter, 1991b). As in her 'Polemical Preface' to *The Sadeian Woman*, Carter deliberately sets out to disturb received opinion in this disconcerting and incongruous programme. As Lorna Sage maintains:

> One of the last things she wrote, *The Holy Family Album* (1991) for television, got her into trouble of a characteristic kind. It attacked God the Father for the tortures inflicted on His son in the name of Love, but in the cause of Power, a piece of deliberate blasphemy against the Almighty Author. (1994: 59)

Among the audience Carter intends to disturb is the very media, literary and academic establishment who were to reconstruct her as 'a mythical fairy-tale figure' after her death (Makinen, 1992: 2).[1] It is no accident that *The Holy Family Album* is rarely mentioned in Carter criticism because the script has never been published, nor has the programme ever been retransmitted since its original and controversial broadcast. The programme has, in effect, been edited from the Carter canon. In choosing not to include *The Holy Family Album* in Carter's collected dramatic writings (1996) or her collected journalism (1997), Carter's literary executors speak volumes about the programme's problematic status in relation to the rest of her work.[2] In this chapter I attempt both to revive critical interest in the programme and to reinstate it as an important manifestation of Carter's self-professed 'demythologising' practice of writing. Because the programme is still relatively unknown, I offer a detailed textual analysis later in the chapter, but before doing so it is necessary to contextualise Carter's political project.

## Nothing sacred

While the programme initially appears to be out of keeping with the rest of Carter's work, on closer examination it becomes clear that *The Holy Family Album* represents the most outspoken manifestation of an atheism and materialism which underpins Carter's oeuvre as a whole. That Carter saw herself as a committed materialist is well-known. In 'Notes From the Front Line', she asserts that her demythologising practice is the product of:

> an absolute and committed materialism – i.e., that this world is all that there is, and in order to question the nature of reality one must move from a strongly grounded base in what constitutes material reality. (1983d: 70)

Explaining the paradox of this committed materialism in the context of her engagement with fantasy, carnival and fairy tale in her fiction, Carter states: 'I do like to reduce everything to its material base', but that 'another way of magicking or making everything strange is to take metaphor literally' (Haffenden, 1985: 92). This is precisely what she does in *The Holy Family Album*, applying the metaphor of the family photograph album to the representation of Christ in Western art.

Carter's materialism can be keenly observed in her extensive journalism. As director Jo Ann Kaplan attests, Carter was 'an unbelievably incisive essay writer, which is also an aspect of *Holy Family Album*' (1995: 291). Naming her first collection of journalism *Nothing Sacred* (1982d), she also uses the phrase to describe the irreverent appropriation of styles in the 1960s in 'Notes For a Theory of Sixties Style': 'in the pursuit of magnificence, nothing is sacred. Hitherto sacrosanct imagery is desecrated' (1997: 108). But, as Michel Wood argues in his review of *Nothing Sacred*, 'Carter is not an iconoclast. She is something more subtle: a libertarian':

> 'Is nothing sacred?' is what frightened people mutter when they see the safe strongholds of accepted behaviour crumbling into carnival, and Angela Carter's cheerful answer is no.
> Nothing is holy in this sense, nothing is immune to jokes or irreverence or questions. (1982: 267)

If Carter is a committed materialist, she is also a committed atheist. Responding to Sage's interview question, 'you feel one needs still to be anti-God?' Carter rejoins: 'Oh yes! It's like being a feminist, you have to keep the flag flying. Atheism is a very rigorous system of disbelief, and one should keep proclaiming it. One ought not to be furtive about it' (Sage, 1977: 51–7). Demonstrating this committed atheism, Carmen Callil claims that Carter refused to be godmother to her children, offering to be a 'Marxmother' instead (Callil and Sage, 1993). Carter's atheism,

then, is clearly imbricated in her feminist politics and her demythologising strategy of writing. Indeed, in 'Notes From the Front Line' Carter
states:

> It seems obvious to an impartial observer, that Western European
> civilisation as we know it has just about run its course and the emergence
> of the Women's Movement, and all that implies, is both symptom and
> product of the unravelling of the culture based on Judaeo-Christianity.
> (1983d: 72–3)

Carter's irreverent treatment of Christian art in *The Holy Family Album*
is both a product of her atheism and her committed materialism. Indeed,
Carter's choice of *The Holly Family Album* as a title is possibly a direct
reference to Marx and Engels', *The Holy Family*, a polemic diatribe against
the followers of Hegelian idealism. 'The holy family' was an ironic
nickname for Bruno Bauer and other Young Hegelians whom Marx and
Engels attack, using a religious framework and vocabulary to offer a
profane version of Hegel's history of 'Absolute Criticism' (Marx and
Engels, [1884] 1980: 154). This is precisely what Carter does in her profane
history of Christ. But while Marx and Engels use the sacred to attack the
secular, Carter uses a secular framework to examine an ostensibly religious theme. Ostensibly religious, because while seeming to deal directly
with the life of Christ, the programme's main concern is in fact the ways
in which Christ has been represented within the Western art historical
tradition.[3] Viewed in the context of *The Holy Family*, the programme
becomes as much about the death of 'Absolute Criticism', as to use Sage's
phrase, the death of the 'Almighty Author' (1994: 59).

Carter's statement of intent about the programme was designed to
grate: 'my intention was not to blaspheme because I do not believe you
can blaspheme against something that does not exist' (Januszczak, 1991).
A *Daily Telegraph* review: 'undeniably offensive, not to say blasphemous',
is typical of the response from the establishment press (Stanbrook, 1991:
16). But Carter's polemical programme not only offended moral and
aesthetic sensibilities, but could have proved legally controversial. As
producer John Ellis explains in a letter to Max Ernst's wife, Dorothea
Tunning: 'blasphemy is still, here, a crime for which one can be jailed. So
we are hoping that we will not have Christmas in jail!' (Ellis, 1991). As
John Gray argues, in response to Jack Straw's proposal to extend the law
on blasphemy to include other religions:

> there has only been one prosecution for blasphemy during the last 70
> years. In a modern, plural society, having an established religion is itself
> an anomaly. But it cannot be remedied by legislating to confer on other
> religious communities the privileges wrongly retained by established

Christianity. There is a better way to give all religions equal treatment under the law. It is to abolish the offence of blasphemy altogether. (1997: 13)

It becomes clear that Carter's *The Holy Family Album* offers a political as well as cultural critique of religion, but what seems particularly problematic for the establishment is the medium in which it is presented. Where an editorial comment on blasphemy can go unnoticed in the *Guardian*, Carter chose to use the domestic medium of television. Given her take on the function of television in 'The Box Does Furnish a Room', this is a highly subversive tactic:

> The contemporary interpenetration of broadcasting and daily life can only be compared with that of yesteryear's religions ... I'm not saying that television *is* a religion, mind, only that it functions rather like a religion – as consolation, entertainment and a method of relating to the real world by proxy. (1997: 411)

Choosing to work in television Carter intentionally transgresses the boundary between the domestic and the political both in terms of her highly controversial subject matter and the way in which she uses television as a visual medium. The relationship between the viewer and the screen is different from that between the eye and the page, and this is perhaps why the question of censorship differs so greatly from one medium to another. The different reception of Kazanlzakis's book *The Last Temptation of Christ*, Martin Scorcese's film, and the controversy surrounding its broadcast and the video release testify to this point, emphasising in particular moral panics surrounding the different effects of viewing a film on television. Television, because it is transmitted straight into the heart of the home, is seen to have a different moral effect than cinema. There is something highly significant, therefore, about the fact that Carter chose the medium of television, one of the most domestic of media, to disseminate such highly subversive and controversial views.

In order to understand Carter's project it is helpful to turn to her writing about the surrealists. In 'Georges Bataille: *Story of the Eye*', Carter refers to a surrealist photograph of Benjamin Peret insulting a priest. For Carter, both this photograph, and Georges Bataille's *Story of the Eye*, illustrate the difference between French intellectuals and the British bourgeois intelligentsia: 'we think blasphemy is silly. They are exhilarated by it' (1992: 37). She refers to the 'fine European tradition of anti-clericalism', which she sees as underpinning Bataille's 'theory of active sexuality as the assertion of human freedom against the laws of church and state'(Carter, 1992: 37). She also, significantly, cites him as a 'grand old surrealist fellow-traveller and sexual philosophe', positioning herself alongside Bataille within that European anti-clerical tradition (Carter, 1992: 37).[4] Carter puts the difference between French and British attitudes towards both blasphemy and pornography down to differences between the Catholic and Protestant faiths. 'Bataille puts pornography squarely in the service of blasphemy', but blasphemy, Carter argues, is alien to the 'secular heritage of Protestant humanism' (1992: 37).[5] The article then goes on to sketch the historical and political background of *Story of the Eye* (Bataille, [1928] 1987):

> *Story of the Eye* was first published in France in 1928; two years later, French fascists smashed up the cinema in which Buñuel and Dali's *L'Age d'Or* was celebrating erotic blasphemy. Bataille was dicing with death and *Story of the Eye* is about fucking as existential affirmation against death, who is also God. (Carter, 1992: 38)

Carter summarises Bataille's practice of writing as: 'transgression, outrage, sacrilege, liberation of the senses through erotic frenzy, and the symbolic murder of God' (1992: 37) which might be a description of her own demythologising practice of writing and her specific project in *The Holy Family Album*. Indeed, a surrealist outlook underpins the entire programme. Significantly, Ellis explains that Carter had wanted to use an extract from Luis Buñuel's anti-establishment surrealist film, *L'Age d'Or*, the namesake of his production company, Large Door Productions Ltd, but they were unable to obtain permission (Ellis, 1995: 258).[6] In the script Carter requests: 'if possible although I suspect it is *not* possible ... but this would be the ideal place to insert the sequence from *L'Age d'Or* that is titled: *On the Hundred and Twenty First Day at Sodom*, and shows Jesus coming out of the Chateau at Silling, being momentarily arrested by the cry for help of a surviving prostitute, returning to the castle and ...' (Carter, 1991c: 20). Although they were unable to get permission for this clip, they were successful in getting permission for Buñuel's fellow surrealist Max Ernst's equally blasphemous painting, *The Virgin Mary Punishes the Infant Jesus in Front of Three Witnesses*, and the programme itself adopts various formal strategies to defamiliarise and disturb in the surrealist tradition, as I delineate below.

## Immaculate misconceptions

Because *The Holy Family Album* is not particularly well known or accessible, much of the rest of this chapter is spent outlining the programme's structure and content before moving on to a discussion of its critical reception. According to producer, John Ellis (1995), the programme had a long gestation from the original idea which was conceived in the mid-1980s to the programme being completed in 1991. As mentioned in Chapter 4, Carter had previously worked with Ellis in the early days of Channel 4, contributing to his cutting-edge cinema review, *Visions*. Ellis explains that the programme was born out of another series he produced called *Opening up the Family Album*. The director Nina Kellgren suggested to Carter that she might do something for the series:

> So, Angela said, just off the top of her head, 'well how about, you know, what really intrigues me is about religious painting and how about if you conceived it that God was a photographer and how weird religious painting would look if you took that point of view'. (Ellis, 1995: 250)

Large Door Productions Ltd was then commissioned to make the programme by Waldemar Januszczak, Channel 4's Commissioning Editor for Arts and Music at the time, who was looking for adventurous ideas for *Without Walls*, an eclectic arts series with an avant-garde brief. Already one might expect the programme to be 'unconventional' given the heady mix of Carter's committed materialist politics and Channel 4's alternative remit.[7] Carter was directly involved in the programme from the beginning, conceiving the idea and then putting it into effect in a vividly descriptive script (1991c). Kaplan maintains that, 'Angela was a real pleasure to work with, as a film-maker she was just like a dream script-writer to work with, particularly in this instance because she did actually write a very visual script in the sense of she had a very good notion of the pictures she wanted to work with' (1995: 260). This is illustrated by a detailed script which lists the paintings and suggests ideas for how they might be used (see Figures 13–16).

As Ellis concurs, 'it's an entirely visual script, you see, I mean it is, she typed it out in columns, just as one does, yeah, you see, you write words, pictures, and it's entirely a picture script' (1995: 254). As Kaplan argues, 'the choice of pictures for the most part were hers. I mean, if you look at the script, her script is a list of pictures ... she actually had chosen already a lot of the visuals, and they're a very eccentric collection of pictures' (1995: 260).

Halfway through preproduction Carter was diagnosed with a particularly virulent form of lung cancer. Ellis recounts, 'it was during the production that Angie discovered she was ill':

> So, it was very difficult from that point of view, but, we'd entered into this project ... it was commissioned, it was scripted, and we were doing the picture research, so it was all, it was in the middle ... so it was extremely difficult. (1995: 250–1)

13-14 First and penultimate pages of Carter's final draft script of *The Holy Family Album*

(89a)

FINAL DRAFT w/TEXT 15.4.91

(Subtitles images
(SEE STORY).1.

---

The Holy Family Album

SC.1 (ATRIUM/INTRO)

A/w + STOP-FRAME
PROMPTLINE
GJM

**Narrator**

A family album is a
bouquet of tender images
of parenting and the
happiness of children;
but father himself, the
cornerstone of the family,
is rarely in the picture
because he is usually the
one who is making the
picture - behind the camera,
calling the shots.

Why should the holy family
be any different?

---

Presented in the same way that "Rebecca"
and "Jamaica Inn" etc. are presented in their
credits, a large book - a Victorian family
album, the kind that looks like a family
bible, with an elaborate embossed cover and,
in Gothic script, the title:

THE HOLY FAMILY ALBUM.

The family album has a big clasp with a
lock at the right hand side; in the
lock is a little gold key.

The key turns in the lock. (Smoothly)

The book opens. (Smoothly)

---

(SC.20)

ROSTRUM

A/w

THE CRUCIFIXION: Stanley Spencer. Show
detail only, of man on left with mouthful
of nails, hammering nail into Christ's
hand.

PIERCING OF SIDE: Limoges enamel, on
album page.

Durer head, again.

ROSTRUM

+ LIVE-ACTION FX
WHITE STUDIO
(OBJ: TRAYING)

+ FX
(black
stocking:
plasters)

Cut to WINE CRUCIFIX: Armulf Rainer,
Tate Gallery. [filling frame]

CRUCIFIX: Eric Gill. Flood image with
red liquid.

Durer head, again.

CRUCIFIXION: Grunewald; hold on this
for a long time, exploiting this then move back,
taking in the full horror, until we see that it occupies a lugubriously
decorated frame on the album page.

(RADIO - FLORENCE)

ROSTRUM
SC.21 - PIETA

Cut to PIETA: MICHELANGELO. (photograph
of statue.) If there is a close-up of
Mary's face in a Michelangelo book, end up
on that.

A/w (ANGLES w/ BLACK BACKDROPS?)

+ TITLES in ALBUM PAGE

INTERCALATED

* possibly... concealing the
wounds with the same kind of
electronic dazzle they "imposed"
W.R. Mysteries by the Organism
for TV - i.e. if genitalia
are censored, why not censor
suppurating wounds? If wounds
taken, look at a white line or... colour registers.

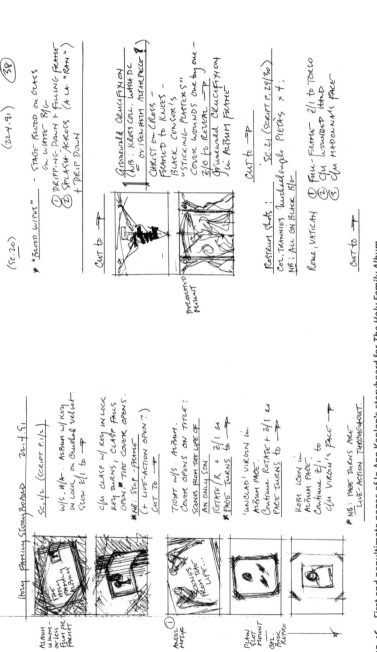

**15–16** First and penultimate pages of Jo Ann Kaplan's storyboard for *The Holy Family Album*

Bearing in mind that *The Holy Family Album* was one of her last sustained pieces of work, it seem particularly important that it should be examined.

The metaphor of the album is made concrete in the form of an adapted Victorian family bible: an ornate book lying on a background of red satin, on which the title of the programme is embossed in gold lettering. Historically, the photograph album itself evolved from the practice of keeping the family history in the back of the bible. George Eliot records this practice when Tom Tulliver writes down his father's curse against John Wakem in the family bible in *The Mill on the Floss* (Chapter 9, 'An item added to the family register'). As photographs became part of family history, the function of the bible gradually developed into that of a photograph album. Significantly, photographs have always been important archives of working-class history. During the slum clearances of the 1970s, the one thing that was sacrosanct was the family album, often the only surviving record of a family history.[8] In this context, *The Holy Family Album* can be seen as being even more subversive, because Carter transposes the paintings and artifacts of high-culture into the arena of the working-class family album.

Carter's opening narration sets up the premise of the family photograph album in which 'Dad' is never in the frame because he is always taking the pictures:

> A family album is a collection of griefs and joys and precious moments between parents and children. It shows the way the generations interplay. But father himself, the cornerstone, is rarely in the picture because he is usually the one who's making the picture, the one behind the camera, the one calling the shots. (Carter, 1991b)

Carter takes the metaphor of the photograph album to its logical conclusion: 'why should the Holy Family be any different?' (Carter, 1991b). The attack on the father is immediately apparent from this opening paragraph. He is both absent and omnipresent, out of the frame, but 'calling the shots,' like God, and like patriarchy itself: invisible but all-powerful.

As Carter's narration begins, the camera zooms in on a gold lock and key on the right-hand side of the album. We see the key turn as if by magic and the album cover swings open. This is a deliberate reference to the opening film credits of *Jamaica Inn* and *Rebecca* (see Figure 13 which director Kaplan worked into a storyboard in Figure 15).

The use of animation here is trademark Carter. As we have seen, such magical transformations are a feature of Carter's work in visual media, most obviously in *The Company of Wolves* (1984b) and *The Magic Toyshop*

(1986a), as well forming as prominent theme in her literary output. Kaplan explains how she shared Carter's love of old-fashioned animation techniques:

> we're all totally into this kind of very home-made looking animation, or very simple kinds of animation which the film is full of, and that partly comes from Angela and it partly comes from me. So it allowed me to do certain kinds of things I love doing ... which appear to be very old-fashioned kind of film animation, in actual fact a lot of them were effected by tape effects. (1995: 261)

The book opens magically, all by itself. With no intermediary turning the pages, the use of animation here creates an unmediated visual relationship between the album and viewer which works in tandem with Carter's narration. Significantly, Carter remains hidden as a narrator, choosing not to appear on camera. Ellis maintains that this was 'a deliberate choice',

> because you don't want people cluttering up the screen, unnecessarily! And this is very much to do with creating a world of the album, and then moving out from that space and the idea of the pages turning and so on, now had we had Angela in shot doing the narration, she would have had to have been turning the pages, and it would have made the thing literal, because actually it's a virtual object if you like, it doesn't actually exist. (1995: 251–2)

Having visually established the conceit of the album and set the tone for the discursive narration in the opening sequence, the programme is divided into nine sections, each examining the various representations of stages of the Christ story: 'Scenes From the Life of an Only Son'; 'The Ante-natal Period'; 'The Birth-day'; 'Childhood, Boyhood, Youth'; 'With his Cousin John'; 'Merry Pranks'; 'Best Friends'; 'Heart Trouble and High Anxiety'; and 'The Events Leading Up to his Death'. Each of these sections is introduced with a decorative caption card adorned with angels with the subtitle in illuminated gold script. These caption cards, masquerading as pages of the photograph album, serve to reinforce both the conceit of the album itself and the experience of watching a documentary, distancing the viewer from the images being presented.

The album opens on the first of these caption cards, 'Scenes From the Life of an Only Son'. The accompanying narration continues to uphold the conceit of God as photographer: 'he picked out the boy's mother as a child, he used to snap her as a school girl', introducing an unsavoury suggestion of child pornography. Carter casts the Holy Father as a keen photographer, 'he photographed him obsessively, the most assiduous photographer of all time and the most variously talented'. The first 'photograph', affixed by the corners in the album, is a naive representation of Mary in which only the face and hands have survived in gold, the rest of the image has faded: 'Oops, that one's underdeveloped!' The analogy of the photograph album is reinforced throughout the narration, acting as a frame for the whole programme: it is the first and last thing we see; the programme begins and ends with the key magically turning in the lock. We are invited, both visually and through the narration, to view the images as if we are looking at 'photographs' in Christ's family album, not paintings. By asking us to believe in the images as photographic artifacts, and repeatedly imposing the metaphor of the album throughout the narrative, Carter foregrounds the act of visual interpretation. This sets up an interesting process in which the act of suspending disbelief, believing in the conceit of the album, serves paradoxically to highlight the fact that these are not family photographs taken by God, but representations which are filtered through the sensibility of particular artists; the product of the culture and era in which they were created. The frame-metaphor of the album, the caption cards and Carter's self-conscious voice-over, create a distancing effect, drawing attention to the programme as text. The use of montage editing reinforces this slippage between text and anterior reality.[9]

The next section, 'The Ante-natal Period', cuts straight from the caption card to the image of an arched door opening suddenly and the Angel Gabriel poking out, 'like a cuckoo out of a cuckoo-clock – it occurs to me it would be lovely if we could animate just this movement, the angel popping out into the room' (Carter, 1991c: 3). This sudden movement reinforces the narration: 'then came her enlightenment and it seems to have come as something of a shock.' The camera then draws back to reveal Mary kneeling in Giotto's *Annunciation*. While there have already been elements of animation in the programme, for example the key turning in the lock and the album's pages turning, this is the first time that a work of art is animated. This could be seen as an example of a surrealist attack on classical art, or as a postmodern playfulness with cultural icons. Either way, the act of animating the painting crosses a boundary between the original medium of the painting and that of television, again drawing attention to the text.

There then follows a series of images of the annunciation framed on the album page by gold, gothic arches: *The Annunciation* by Simone Martini, Dante Gabriel Rossetti's *Ecce Ancilla Domini!*, and annunciations by Lowinsky and Arthur Hughes, all of which position the young Mary below the angel, looking rather perturbed. These images flow in sequence, one after the other, into a long held shot of a series of diagrams of the womb illustrating each stage of the gestation period, with the camera slowly panning right as if 'reading' the page, accompanied by a background of gently lapping waves. The camera holds on the last month, where 'the head of the baby in the picture engages' (Carter, 1991c: 4), accompanied by the splash of waters breaking and a sudden jump-cut to the next caption card, 'The Birth-day'.

There follows a rapid series of images. A sudden cut from the caption card to a pair of red velvet curtains, accompanied by a loud ripping noise, opening on the bulging seam in a pregnant woman's dress. The camera pans out to reveal the rest of the painting, Piero della Francesca's *Madonna del Parto* (1460), in which the pregnant Mary is framed by another set of curtains held open by a pair of angels within the painting; a brief glimpse of 'one of Corinna [Sargood]'s pop-up cards' popping open, followed by a sudden cut to graphic colour footage of actual childbirth, ending with a black and white still from *The Family of Man* exhibition, Wayne Miller (Carter, 1991c: 5). The use of sudden cutting and montage to create violent visual juxtapositions between unexpected images acts here to reinforce the narration. Like montage cinema, the effect is one of formal repetition. The rhythm of the editing propels the meaning. The violently jarring images, the cutting between the diagrams of the gestation in the womb, to the real curtains opening on a renaissance painting and the most disturbing cut from the pop-up Christmas card to a baby's head emerging from a vagina, together with the sound effects of splashing and ripping, all converge to highlight the fact that the birth of Christ is rarely, if ever, portrayed as a real physical birth. In an article on the publication of fashion photographs of pregnant models in *Frank* magazine, Jojo Moyes comments on how rarely images of pregnant women are seen in the media:

> The stomach, swollen with child, is a rare sight in even 'enlightened' 20th-century culture. The actress Demi Moore caused a controversy when, heavily pregnant, she appeared nude on the cover of *Vanity Fair* magazine. Piero della Francesca's *Madonna del Parto* unusually shows a Madonna heavily with Child rather than Madonna and Child. But these are rare examples; the National Gallery in London, for example, could not come up with a single artistic representation of pregnancy yesterday ... The pregnant form, it seems, still provokes equivocal feelings. (1997: 3)

But live footage of childbirth is even more rarely seen. Carter comments on this irony in the script, asking 'if genitalia are censored, why not censor suppurating wounds?' (Carter, 1991c: 29a) (see Figure 14). By using footage of actual childbirth Carter foregrounds not only the lack of representation of the birth of Christ, but the cultural taboo surrounding pregnancy and labour itself. In flippantly dismissing the radical implications of this visceral portrayal of childbirth, Hugh Hebert's *Guardian* review implicitly acknowledges it as taboo:

Angela Carter's film has invited all these predictable publicity-pushing responses by inserting a documentary, full colour close-up of a baby emerging messily from the womb in the Nativity sequence of a modest little survey of Christian iconography. (1991: 34)[10]

The programme moves on to a series of images of the nativity, beginning with a 'Peruvian folk-art box-shrine', the doors of which 'fly open like the doors of a cuckoo-clock, revealing a nativity scene inside ... a tin Mexican shooting star flies into place above the shrine' (Carter, 1991c: 6) The intercutting of these examples of 'primitive' art with the classical paintings is clearly political. The Christ story is, of course, culturally resonant beyond the arena of Western iconography, and by including examples of three-dimensional folk art Carter challenges the monopoly of Western religious painting in the art historical canon. This is part of her ongoing engagement with art and art criticism, as evidenced by numerous reviews collected in the 'Making Art' section in *Shaking a Leg* (1997), her Preface to *Images of Frida Kahlo* (Carter (ed.), 1989: 420–38), and the cultural critique of the work of Richard Dadd in her radio play, *Come Unto These Yellow Sands* ([1979] 1992a) which is discussed in detail in Chapter 3.[11] By situating classical paintings of Christ in the family photo album along side traditional art forms, Carter causes us to look anew at the ways in which Christ has been represented in art throughout history.

This cut from the opening doors of the shrine visually links the actual birth with the traditional nativity and signals a change of rhythm in the editing: 'the next sequence of images follows in a fluent manner, dissolving into one another at an even pace, not too fast, not too slow' (Carter, 1991c: 6). Carter's grasp of the medium is apparent in her concern with varying the pace of the editing, revealing an awareness of the potential danger of the studio-bound rostrum camera work becoming stilted. The images of the nativity that follow are accompanied by Carter's disquieting narration:

The Father did not forget to take his camera to the birth. He took his camera to the birth of course, but he had to be circumspect about it because he was the natural father, remember, not the legal father. Sometimes he puts the legal father in the picture, sometimes he leaves him out. Either way, the family album keeps its secrets, all you see is the pictures, what you can't know is what went on behind them. (Carter, 1991b)

According to Ellis (1995) this part of Carter's narrative was deeply offensive to some viewers. The narration continues: 'there isn't any privacy in the family album either, the images may be intimate, but they are set up for everyone to enjoy', accompanying a series of images of the virgin and child, particularly Jean Fouquet's painting in which Mary's rotund breast is revealed for all to see and culminating with Jan Gossaert's *The Adoration of the Kings* in which the mother and child are the focal point of a courtly scene: 'Everybody in the whole world is invited to come and look at his majesty the baby, trailing his clouds of glory, etc., etc., etc.' The voice fades away over a series of successive images, the ironic use of 'etc.' suggesting that the images shown are only a few of the thousands of possible representations of the nativity.

The tension between Carter's ironic narration and the images she describes is worth further analysis. By formally juxtaposing familiar images of the nativity with this defamiliarising voice-over, Carter self-consciously draws attention to the fact that we are watching a television programme. While documentary is perhaps already one of the most 'self-conscious' of genres because it explicitly addresses an audience, not all documentaries use this self-conscious technique. 'Fly-on-the-wall' documentaries, for example, attempt to hide their textuality by presenting themselves as actuality. Dai Vaughan (1976: 16) takes the view that good documentary must disguise itself in order to claim authenticity to 'anterior truth'. Criticising the 'reign of Mannerism' in the documentary of the early seventies, Vaughan examines the 'linguistic modes adopted by television':

> the function of a presenter introducing a documentary – or interpolated within it – is to diminish the authority of the people filmed and to posit the film itself, in contrast to the pro-filmic reality, as the object of scrutiny: so that what we are aware of watching is not the filmed event but the televised film (of the event). A similar result – an emphasis upon the double media-tion between ourselves and the reality – is achieved by the use of fades and dissolves and by the superimposition of lettering – traditionally titles and credits but, increasingly, all manner of miscellaneous information – upon the image. (1976; 16)

What Vaughan posits as negative qualities, Carter utilises. In fact, she consciously and constantly foregrounds this 'double mediation between ourselves and the reality' in the way the programme is narrated, how it is edited and with the use of what Vaughan calls the 'superimposition of lettering' (1976: 16).

Carter's self-conscious narration acts to diminish the authority of religious paintings and of religious representation itself, drawing attention to documentary as a fiction. However, according to Ellis 'Carter's original idea was that there should be no commentary. It was the producer who insisted that it would only work with some kind of voice'.[12] Nevertheless, as Kaplan suggests, Carter's voice-over is 'exceptional because she sounds like a normal person', rather than an authority figure (1995: 265).

However, for David Wheatley, director of *The Magic Toyshop*, Carter's voice-over misfires: 'from a technical point of view I don't think, dramatically, it's not very engaging ... Angela's voice I found too distant.' He goes on to argue:

> part of her text was ironical, and that kind of irony I think you need to observe on someone's face. It's tricky to get, and I know Angela, therefore I know the kind of ironical way she would say things with one eyebrow raised, and to see that, simply to see images and then this kind of one column of *The Daily Telegraph* read out over them, it didn't quite gel. (Wheatley, 1996: 246–7)

Wheatley's observation on the dangers of ironic strategies is telling in the light of my earlier discussion of the impossibility of guaranteeing 'right' readings in the Introduction and Chapter 2. But this alienation effect was clearly intentional. As we have already seen in Chapter 7, Carter enjoyed television's 'built-in alienation effect', arguing that adverts operate as 'constant reminders that the medium itself is artificial' (1997: 401, 403). She argues that 'television may be implicitly radical all the time, in spite of itself' because it shows up 'the disjunction between different kinds of reality' (Carter, 1997: 410). This is obviously her project in this programme. But subverting the generic conventions of the medium makes uncomfortable viewing. Wheatley suggests 'the images by themselves were interesting and fascinating, but I felt something was functionally wrong in the structure of the way that programme was made' (1996: 247). Remarking on the animated elements, he claims: 'the danger is, there are so few of those things in the programme, in the part of the programme that I watched, that they start becoming rather self-conscious' (Wheatley, 1996: 247–8). But, as we have seen, Carter's use of a variety of alienation techniques is deliberately 'self-conscious': the ironic disparity between narrative voice-over and the image, the use of old-fashioned trick photography and intertitles, deliberately foreground the fact that we are watching a documentary, subverting the usual practice of effacing the medium. This subversion of genre is similar to that undertaken in Carter's 'artificial' biographies of Dadd and Firbank discussed in Chapter 3. Carter's willingness to experiment with the medium was written into the script right from the very beginning (see Figures 13 and 14). As Kaplan attests, 'that's also why I valued it, it gave me a chance to make something unusual which explored televisual language more than you'd get a chance to because most television is precisely very formulaic both in the content and its realisation. So rather than do an archetypal "documentary", it gave me freedom to experiment' (1995: 265).

   I will now briefly continue to outline the rest of the programme, before turning to its critical reception. The next section, 'Childhood, Boyhood, Youth,' reinforces the conceit of the photograph album. The caption card magically turns over to the sound of a wind-up music box, leading into a series of images of the baby Christ. These culminate in a close up of the Christ child lying across Mary's lap in *The Virgin Mary Punishes the Infant Jesus in Front of Three Witnesses*, by Max Ernst. 'Watch out, here come the social workers!':

> The image is crudely animated so that the halo – which initially has been replaced in its rightful position by the art department – falls off and hits the ground with a tinny tinkle as Mary's arm goes up and down whacking his bottom. (Carter, 1991c: 10)

The camera moves up to and closes in on the three men 'looking censoriously through the window' (Carter, 1991c: 10). The voice-over adds, 'I think it's the anti-God squad, Eluard, Aragon and André Breton, they'd like to take that baby away to a place of safety, but the father won't let them into the house'.[13] In the following section, 'With his Cousin John', the understated narration is undercut by the images and music. The camera pans up the body of a kneeling figure to the haloed head, it then cuts to a man with a sword poised to strike, the camera then zooms out to the whole painting, *The Beheading of John the Baptist* by Puvis de Cavannes, revealing that the sword is aimed at John's head. Ominous, thundering piano chords accompany a series of violent images of the severed head:[14] *Beheading of John the Baptist* by Dürer; *The Dancer's Reward* by Aubrey Beardsley; *Head of a Martyr* by Odilon Redon; *Salome Receives the Head of St John the Baptist* by Caravaggio: 'He seems to have got angry with cousin John. He even took some pictures of the terrible thing that happened to cousin John, some rather gloating pictures.'

The least successful element of the programme, for me, is the section entitled 'Merry Pranks' in which Christ is figured as a magician in top hat and tails (performed by Micha Bergese who also, incidentally, stars as the Werewolf in *The Company of Wolves*). Largely composed of mime sequences shot against a white studio background, this section illustrates both Kaplan's and Carter's penchant for cinema magic: miracles become conjuring tricks using all the techniques of photographic illusion. However, once we 'get' the initial idea, the joke wears thin. But perhaps that is the very aim – in overemphasising the point Carter completely demystifies miracles, even subjecting Christ to a little pop psychology: 'He did it to attract attention I suppose, perhaps he did it to attract his father's attention?' which prefigures her re-evaluation of the Oedipal conflict at the end of the programme. The album proceeds on a whistle-stop tour through Christ's life: 'Best Friends' examines the representation of his relationship with Mary Magdalene,[15] and 'Heart Trouble and High Anxiety' consists of montage of images of bleeding heart iconography, intercut with footage of 'real' hearts (they used sheep hearts, rather appropriately in the context of Christ as the 'Lamb of God').

The final section, 'The Events Leading Up to his Death,' begins with a crescendo of images of the crucifixion. These are overlaid with Carter's acerbic voice-over: 'Shelley said no decent man could ever get to heaven because the more he reverenced the son who endured the pain, the more he must execrate the father who caused it, whom it gratified.' She makes a similar point in an interview with John Haffenden (1985: 80), 'the theory of the Fortunate Fall has it that it was fortunate because it incurred the Crucifixion, an idea which I think only an unpleasant mind could have dreamt up', referring to her allusion to the 'fortunate fall' at the end of *The Magic Toyshop*. In *The Holy Family Album* she takes this argument further, asserting: 'he was a cruel God. He was a cruel father. Remember he planned all this.'

The programme culminates with two images in which the crucifixion is desecrated. The first of these is a 'blood wipe' over Arnulf Rainer's *Wine Crucifix*. As indicated on Kaplan's storyboard this involved dripping stage blood down a plate of glass over the image (Kaplan, 1991: 38) (Figure 16). Next, there is a sudden cut to an image of Grünewald's *Crucifixion*, which is then censored: black sticking tape is placed over the wounds in Christ's wrists, sides and feet. Carter's narration continues: 'if this were not a picture of the son of God, this grisly, sadomasochistic icon would be banned. Every family holds a secret, this is the dreadful secret of the Holy Family Album.' This iconoclastic graffiti attacks both the religious image and the art-historical tradition. Furthermore, if we return to her note on the script – 'if genitalia are censored, why not censor suppurating wounds?' (Figure 14) – it becomes clear that Carter is implying that something is drastically wrong in a society which censors sex, but worships sadomasochistic images of the bleeding Christ. Indeed, marking the image draws attention to its existence as image, as cruci-fiction, challenging its value as a symbol, as an icon. As if to highlight this Carter consistently spells crucifixion as crucifiction in the script (see Figure 14).

For Carter, then, the family album offers the ideal metaphor through which to explore two main elements linked by the concept of the Father: established religion and the patriarchal institution of Western criticism and the art historical tradition. The programme ends with images of the *pietà*, which accompany Carter's most controversial statement in the narrative:

> Perhaps we read Oedipal conflict the wrong way. Perhaps men don't want to kill their fathers. Surely not, or how could Christianity have lasted all

this time. But deep down they want to kill their sons. Just like God did. To get rid of the rival.[16]

Ellis states that quite late on in the production:

> she did some retakes on the voice and it was actually quite difficult to match because her voice was, although we did it in the same place, her voice had changed quite a lot ... and I think that Angela took the opportunity to put in certain things, particularly the final line about the [Oedipal] relationship. That seems like a kind of message left behind. (1995: 251–2)

## Vitriolic response

Both Ellis and Kaplan recount how Channel 4 got cold feet and attempted to downplay the blasphemous content of the programme. Kaplan explains:

> I think they got frightened, if you ask me, at exactly how blasphemous the thing was and so they very much billed it as an art history programme ... on the surface of it it's about imagery, representations of Christ, of the Christian story, of 'The Greatest Story Ever Told' ... but Angela being Angela it always has a critically social dimension. (1995: 264)

Initially, in an attempt to get some media interest Ellis got in touch with a press contact at the *Observer* who informed the Catholic lobby who, Ellis claims, went 'really overboard' and lashed out in a *Times* editorial, 'Liberal treasons':

> Tonight's much-publicised Channel 4 programme, *The Holy Family Album*, may be watched but should be disdained. It is so offensive to Christians that, hardly surprisingly, some have called for it to be banned ... Channel 4 is fast becoming the British shrine of 'political correctness' – holding that certain groups deserve establishment protection and favour while declaring open war upon the rest. Christians clearly now fall into the latter group. *The Holy Family Album*, had it been made about the Jewish or Hindu faiths, would never have been commissioned. It was made by the novelist Angela Carter, who would doubtless call herself a liberal. But liberal implies 'live and let live', which surely includes not insulting the religious beliefs of others. The programme depicts female genitalia merging into an image of the Christian nativity, calls the crucifix a 'grisly sadomasochistic icon' and lampoons Holy Communion. ... The icons and images held sacred by certain citizens should not be gratuitously insulted by others of different persuasions or none. (Ellis, 1991)

Kaplan comments on the irony that Channel 4 balked at the public response and sidelined Carter, whereas it was they who had 'pointed it up' (1995: 264) in the first place by transmitting the programme in the run-up to Christmas 1991. It is important to remember that Channel 4 does not make its own programmes but acts as a 'publisher broadcaster', commissioning programmes from independent television production companies (Laws (ed.), 1994: 3). This is what enabled the company to abnegate responsibility for Carter's controversial views, while at the same time maintaining editorial control over them. Ellis maintains that 'by the time we got to the level of an editorial in *The Times*, Channel 4 were distancing themselves from the programme' and they 'then put an embargo on any publicity whatsoever' (1995: 254), so there was none of the usual pre-publicity, no tapes went out to the reviewers.

There were mixed television reviews.[17] 'Novelist Angela Carter takes a dubious view of Christianity and its art' reads the *Evening Standard* (1991).The *Daily Telegraph* reported:

> Making extensive use of the old masters as if they were snaps from God's Box Brownie, it depicts the Incarnation as illegitimacy; the miracles as straight conjuring tricks; the Crucifixion as 'a grisly sadomasochistic icon' that would be banned if it were not an image of the Son of God. (Stanbrook, 1991: 16)

The less conservative *Time Out* listings dub it an 'irreverent programme':

> Devout Christians will probably be horrified by the flippant tone and blasphemous nature of Carter's commentary. For the rest of us it's a mildly amusing romp through Christian imagery from high tack to the classics. (*Time Out*, 1991)

*City Limits* is slightly more forgiving, emphasising Carter's irony:

> Angela Carter's *The Holy Family Album* is in the lapsed catholic vein of Biblical analysis and for the most part functions as a rostrum camera-man's dream. Long loving scans of annunciations, nativities to the highlights of God's boy's life in iconic form are accompanied by Angela Carter's acerbic narrative which ultimately reaches the conclusion that our interpretation of the Oedipal myth is the wrong way round. (*City Limits*, 1991)

Channel 4 released a statement distancing themselves from the programme, responding directly to *The Times* editorial :

> You assert that Channel 4 is selective in its commitment to freedom of expression, that some sort of political correctness regime is in operation and we 'call down damnation and the law on those whose views [we] dislike'. No evidence is advanced, not a name, not a date, not a programme title to support this nonsense. I flatly deny your assertion, and refer you to a stream of programmes on Channel 4 that clearly slaughter the sacred cows which, you allege, graze around Charlotte Street ... I defy you to find

a broader spread of opinion and belief anywhere in British broadcasting. Angela Carter's film is a highly personal and imaginative rumination upon religious art by one of Britain's most respected novelists. Her work has consistently interested itself in a the way that belief, myth, symbolism and magic overlap and fertilise each other; critics have used the phrase 'magic realism' to describe such writing. *The Holy Family Album* certainly belongs to this rich and international tradition. Since there is no actual description of Jesus Christ in the Bible, Western artists have always had to find an image of Christ in their imaginations. As the film makes clear, the results have been varied; Angela Carter continues this process. (Forgan, 1991)[18]

Ellis comments on the initial reception and ongoing impact of the programme, 'it really affected people who watched it and it does, having shown this to groups of students and so on, it is a very powerful piece of work'.[19] On the night of the broadcast there was a rush of complaints to Channel 4.[20] Many of these callers particularly resented Christ being portrayed as a conjurer. Another main strand is of the 'if you'd portrayed other minority faiths in the same way you wouldn't get away with it' kind: one viewer claims, 'Islam wouldn't stand for it'. Interestingly, Ellis claims Carter originally hoped to narrate the programme in the form of a dialogue with Salman Rushdie, but prudently perhaps, in the light of the programme's reception and his own experience of religious intolerance, Rushdie declined. 'This will be raised in parliament' declares a Mr McCann. Mrs Gray suggests 'someone needs shooting'. 'That vile woman Angela Carter' opines Mrs Sheldon Jenkins. An anonymous male caller asserts: 'it was no different than a school boy writing graffiti on a church wall or Joe Orton scribbling in his library books.'[21]

The programme also generated a great deal of letters, mainly from offended Christian sensibilities, especially because the programme finishes before the resurrection, so fails to tell the 'whole story'.[22] Many letters also mention the conjuring tricks as deeply offensive. Kaplan states, 'it didn't surprise me, though I suppose it surprised me the extent of it':

> but then I wasn't brought up a devout Christian and so, though I was brought up in a Christian culture, the prevalent culture was Christian and you were looking at it, so even if you have a Jewish background like I do, the prevalent culture is Christian and in fact my mother was Christian. So, I can sit on both sides of the fence as it were, but I'm in no way offended by any of it and I very much subscribe to Angela's point of view about Christianity, I don't think I'm personally quite so vehement, but then she was brought up as a Christian and I wasn't, so that accounts for a difference. So the letters from the public didn't surprise me but then me being a very liberal person I can never understand the extent of other people's offence in their belief. (1995: 263–4)

## There should be more of Angela Carter

However, there was also a limited positive response. As Ellis argues, 'it wasn't just Christian blasphemy, blah' there was also a 'Low Church, as it were, religious public saying good, you know, this is a good thing to have done'. One caller, the Reverend Kenneth Fraser, found it 'whimsical and thought provoking' and Carl Gardner (who signs himself a 'TV critic, lapsed') writes,

> Absolutely loved the *Without Walls* with Angela Carter – provocative, unpredictable, iconoclastic, under-stated, full of ideas, visually arresting (despite video's supposed limitations). Everything we ever thought television should (or could) be. Well done to you and the director, Jo Ann Kaplan (and of course Angela – no auteurism here!) – Great telly. P.S. Any chance of a VHS copy?

Ellis explains that Januszczak defended the programme on Channel 4's *Right to Reply*, but failed to keep Large Door Productions informed of what was going on (1995: 254):

> he didn't consult Angela, he didn't consult me about it, which was wrong, he should have done. And Angela was really furious at being sidelined in this because she liked a good fight, actually, she wanted a good fight ...we knew nothing about this going on, since, you know, *Guardian* readers, we didn't know about this *Times* editorial! There was a real failure of communication between Channel 4 and us, which was very bad, and Angela felt very harshly about it, because ... being, well basically a sort of atheist and surrealist, that side of her is what was coming to the fore in this particular programme.

Following the *Right to Reply* complaint, there was more positive feedback in support of the programme.[23] Lawrence Marden, states: 'I find it amazing that what was essentially a non-controversial programme was ganged up upon by the hysterical Christians. If anything the programme didn't go far enough.' Mr Yardley suggests, 'someone should say that the programme was good and I think it was excellent, there should be more of Angela Carter'. Another viewer writes, 'congratulations on your programme *The Holy Family Album*. I intended writing immediately – but of course didn't – but last evening seeing *Right to Reply* – I want to add my support hoping to encourage more programmes showing the opposite view to the brain-washed certainty of the truth of the God story – which I reject true or myth.'

A complaint to the Broadcasting Standards Council on behalf of Mrs Lander of Devon and nine other viewers who complained of bad taste in *Without Walls*, was not upheld:

The council is aware of the offence which is caused by the unthinking use of religious images and symbols. On this occasion, however, their use was the result of careful selection made after much reflection. The theme which was explored by the programme is one of great importance within Western religious and cultural traditions to both believers and non-believers. The Council felt that the two warnings which had been supplied in advance alert the audience to what they might expect to see and hear. While recognising the genuine nature of the distress which was caused to those who had complained about the programme, the Council did not uphold the complaints.

## Uncomfortable viewing

Ellis claims that although Carter was 'a TV figure' (she had been involved in various arts programming, including his own *Visions* series), she had 'a very, very idiosyncratic way of presenting herself on TV, which was actually kind of just to speak how she normally did! With kind of random pauses where she was thinking of things, and a lot of people in television didn't like that' (1995: 256). Kaplan similarly notes Carter's uncomfortable screen presence: 'she's difficult and television likes things that are comfortable to a certain extent ... Angela was not comfortable to people in power and she made people uncomfortable' (1995: 282).

Just before Christmas 1991, director Kim Evans was beginning to negotiate with Carter about the possibility of making an *Omnibus* programme about her, which became *Angela Carter's Curious Room* (Evans, 1992).[24] Unlike *Without Walls*, the *Omnibus* series does not set itself a brief to be challenging or experimental, as the contrast between the ideas encoded in their two names testifies. 'Omnibus' invokes 'the man on the Clapham Omnibus', the man or woman in the street, in the most literal sense: public transport, a vehicle plying on a fixed route – all suggesting an accessible arts programme which aims to address the average punter using safe, comfortable and reliable means. This is taking the connotations of the word to an extreme, but it is to make the point that the BBC, already symbolic of the media-establishment, is attempting to address a broad public spectrum and in so doing, perhaps tends to use more conventional means. This contrasts with the context of *The Holy Family Album* which was made by an independent production company for Channel 4's supposedly avant-garde art series, *Without Walls*. And let's not forget Channel 4's brief to cater for tastes not covered by the other terrestrial channels, which further reinforces the expectation of an 'alternative' output.

Within this establishment context it is inevitable, perhaps, that *Angela Carter's Curious Room* upholds, to a certain extent, the very documentary conventions that Carter was attempting to subvert in *The Holy Family Album*. Kim Evans comments on her sense of achievement in this regard: 'in terms of the construction, I do like the fact that it did feel like a coherent film, inhabiting a world' (1996: 299). My project here is patently not to denigrate the programme, which fulfils an important function in acknowledging Carter's importance as a writer. Furthermore, given the context of the programme's production in lead up to and aftermath of Carter's death in February 1992, Evans' sensitivity in handling the material is clear. However, it is interesting to compare the straightforward biographical treatment of Carter in this programme with her own experiments with 'artificial' biography as discussed in Chapter 3. The *Omnibus* programme's most successful achievement is in letting Carter's interview speak for itself. Evans maintains: 'that's the thing I feel proudest of, it just makes you courageous to listen to her talking' (1996: 299). Although Kaplan also regards Carter's interview as the most important element of the programme, she is critical of the what she sees as the unimaginative realisation of the animation. Kaplan also suggests that Carter became a less problematic figure for the media establishment after her death:

> it was far easier to deal with Angela once she was not going to then be on the scene, like at that time, than she was in close work and that's very apparent in the way she's been taken up since she, you know, died, and all these sort of people say 'I agree with her'. She's been taken up and been paid attention to in a way she wasn't being paid attention to when she was alive. (1995: 282–3)[25]

Ironically Kim Evans says much the same thing, but from a different perspective, when she suggests:

> it would have been very interesting to see how she would have stood in relation to herself, if she'd been involved, if she'd come down to the sets, I suppose it would have been pretty daunting in some ways having to turn somebody's work into images before their very eyes and in a curious way it was much more helpful having her there as a spiritual guide for it, perhaps, and that was very positive, rather than actually having her standing there on set, which could have been very daunting in some ways. (1996: 298)

This is indicative of Carter's marginal and sometimes marginalised relationship with the establishment and the mainstream. However it was important that the BBC establishment finally took her on board, and in the circumstances of Carter's illness and death it was, perhaps, not the moment for avant-garde televisual experimentation. Indeed, Carter's decision to go ahead with the *Omnibus* programme may have been influenced by the reception of *The Holy Family Album*, and her feelings of being sidelined by the establishment – because it enabled her to have the last word on herself.

It seems likely that Carter would have gone on to write more for television. An adaptation of the radio play, *Come Unto These Yellow Sands*, was already under discussion with Large Door Productions Ltd, but Carter died before the project got underway. Kaplan went on to do a treatment but, sadly, they were unable to find a willing outlet, 'nobody would buy it, it was just too eccentric' (1995: 281). It appears that after *The Holy Family Album*, Carter remained an uncomfortable figure for the media establishment. However, as Kaplan suggests, 'given time people in film and television, the powers that be, might have discovered that instead of taking a literary text of hers they could've put their money behind developing an original script with her, or having her actually working on the script of her own material and developing it in some other kind of way' (1995: 288). Kaplan agrees with the project of this book, that Carter's work in media is not a digression, 'it's a major aspect of her work, it's not just an aspect, I think it's core' (1995: 289).

In a letter to Januszczak, Ellis states that Carter offered the screenplay 'as one of Chatto's *Counterblasts*, which would be a novel form of publicity as well as a novel item for that series' (1990). A series of short polemics, Chatto & Windus' *Counterblasts*, seems a highly suitable vehicle for *The Holy Family Album*, but the suggestion was not taken up, and as I have already observed, the script is yet to be published. In her Introduction to *The Curious Room* (Carter, 1996: x), Susannah Clapp claims, 'it lost too much without pictures and colour and animation to include here'. As I argue in my review of the latter, 'the same could be said of many plays and most screenplays' (Crofts, 1996: 34). It seems more likely that the script has been neglected because it remains an uncomfortable presence in Carter's oeuvre. This is indicative of the way in which Carter has been canonised and packaged as a 'fairy-tale figure' since her death, as Merja Makinen (1992) was one of the first to note. Lorna Sage notes the 'change in tone enjoined on us all by the fact of her premature death. If she'd stayed around, her canonization would almost certainly have been postponed' (1994: 58–9). As Makinen warns, 'this concurrence of white witch/fairy godmother mythologizing needs watching; it is always the dangerously problematic that are mythologized in order to make them less dangerous' (1992: 2). The effectual censorship of *The Holy Family Album* by the literary establishment is, in part, an extension of this mythologising process. As Sage laments, 'now that her voice is silenced, we're left with the orphaned words on the page, which line up and behave' (1994: 59).

The programme's lack of recognition within the academy is also indicative of the greater critical neglect of Carter's work in media. As Ellis asserts, 'so far as I know, in the Angela Carter canon this is a bit of a lost work, because it exists in the wrong medium, you know, a medium in which she shouldn't have been working, etc., etc., etc.' (1995: 256). Kaplan suggests that the programme is one of the most successful realisations of Carter's work in visual media 'because it's not an adaptation of a literary work of hers, that's one of the key things, she wrote it specifically for television, so it came straight out of her and there was no intermediary' (1995: 280). Kaplan feels that it is an 'exceptional programme, both at the level of writing and at the level of visual realisation' – 'it's unique, I mean I haven't seen anything else like it on television' (1995: 265). However disturbing, however uncomfortable and however incongruous the pro- gramme is within the Carter canon, it deserves critical attention because it reminds us of the dangerous edge of Carter's feminist strategy.

## Notes

1 Makinen cites obituaries by Margaret Atwood, Lorna Sage, J. G. Ballard and Salman Rushdie. It is interesting to examine the BBC's *Omnibus* programme as an example of the television establishment's construction of Carter as an author in the light of this myth-making (Evans (dir.), 1992).

2 Despite my own involvement as a researcher for the book, and my suggestion of its inclusion, the script was not included in *Shaking a Leg* (1997), neither does it appear in Carter's collected dramatic writings, *The Curious Room* (1996).

3 This clearly corresponds with Carter's deconstruction of both art history and biography in *Come Unto These Yellow Sands* ([1979] 1992a). In *The Holy Family Album* she similarly deconstructs the hagiographical representation of Christ in Western art.

4 In 'The Alchemy of the Word', however, Carter maintains that 'the surrealists were not good with women. That is why, although I thought they were wonderful. I had to give them up in the end. They were, with a few patronised exceptions, all men, and they told me that I was the source of all mystery, beauty and otherness, because I was a woman – and I knew that was not true' (1992: 512).

5 This is an obvious echo of Carter's argument that Sade puts pornography in the service of women in *The Sadeian Woman* ([1979] 1992b).

6 Large Door Productions Ltd is a rendition of *L'Age d'Or*.

7 Channel 4's remit under the Broadcasting Act 1980 was 'to provide programmes that calculated to appeal to tastes not generally catered for by ITV, and to encourage innovation and experimentation in the form and content of programmes ... in particular programmes for ethnic, cultural and occupational minority groups. It also has to ensure that a suitable proportion of programmes are of an educational nature or of a recognizably religious aim' (MacDonald, 1988: 24, 79).

8 I am indebted to Stella Halkyard at the John Rylands University Library of Manchester for this information.

9  Significantly, montage cinema was historically the propaganda tool of post-Revolution Russia in which the organisation of shots is of central importance.

10  Joan Smith (1989: 65) uses a similarly blasphemous approach in her discussion of abortion in, 'Immaculate Misconceptions'.

11  It is worth noting the multi-media presentation of the first publication of the script which was printed alongside reproductions of Dadd's paintings (Carter, 1985). Kaplan comments on Carter's knowledge of art history, negotiating her way quickly to favourite paintings during a research trip to the National Gallery (1995: 269).

12  John Ellis in personal correspondence.

13  Carter's reference to the anti-God squad clearly evolves from her engagement with surrealism discussed earlier.

14  According to the transmission information compiled for Channel 4, 'Jazz improvisation master Keith Tippet composed a score using a "prepared piano"'(Large Door Productions Ltd archive). Commenting on this chapter Ellis stresses Carter's contribution to the music (in personal correspondence).

15  Michèle Roberts rewrites the Christ story from the point of view of Mary Magdalene in *The Wild Girl* (1984).

16  As Aidan Day (1998: 27–8) points out, the figure of Uncle Philip in *The Magic Toyshop* prefigures Carter's reversal of the Oedipal conflict here. Philip represents a 'picture of a patriarch harbouring vengeful, murderous feelings towards a younger man', just as she suggests God does towards Jesus.

17  See Brooks and Beaumont (1991: 3); *Daily Mail* (1991: 23); *Daily Telegraph* (1991); *Guardian* (1991: 36); Hebert (1991: 34); *The Times* (1991b: 19).

18  Liz Forgan was then director of programmes at Channel 4.

19  John Ellis in personal correspondence. Ellis refers to his experience lecturing film, television studies, media studies students at Bournemouth University.

20  See the Duty Report, Channel 4, 3 December 1991, in response to *The Holy Family Album*, Large Door Productions Ltd archive.

21  Bearing in mind Carter's enthusiasm for the photograph of Peret insulting a priest, this was presumably the desired effect of the programme. This caller also illustrates the cultural as well as the religious profanity of Carter's desecration of canonic art.

22  All letters referred to are in Large Door Productions Ltd archive.

23  See the Duty Report, Channel 4, 7 December 1991, in response to *Right to Reply*.

24  Evans became director of Music and Arts at the BBC on the strength of her documentary on Carter and went on to become executive director of the Arts Council of Great Britain.

25  However, Kaplan acknowledges the importance of Evans' contribution: 'I think Kim is a wonderful commissioning editor, I think she really has a nose for the right subjects, particularly women's subjects' (1995: 282).

# 'Envoi'

I side with Linden Peach when he suggests that Angela Carter did not approve of conclusions and so ends his book with a 'Postscript' (1998: 159).[1] But an academic text requires a conclusion, so I borrow Carter's term, 'envoi', from the end of *Nights at the Circus*, as a suitable subtitle with which to qualify the conclusiveness of a conclusion. As Lorna Sage suggests (1994: 59), 'nothing stays, endings are final, which is why they are also beginnings', echoing Carter's own words, 'we start from our conclusions', at the end of *The Passion of New Eve* ([1977] 1990: 191). In this brief final stanza, then, I do not offer an overview of Carter's work, nor do I recapitulate on material already discussed in detail in the book: the chapters should speak for themselves. I do offer an envoy, a message in a bottle, to those who are busy recouping Carter's transgressive writing into the literary canon.

Carter's work in media has been sidelined by the academy because it does not fit neatly into generic or canonic categories. But in editing out her mediated texts, contemporary critical responses offer an incomplete picture of her work. As the texts discussed here reveal, Carter's writing for radio, film and television is not an aberration from her real vocation as a writer of fiction, but 'an extension and an amplification of writing for the printed page' (Carter, 1985: 12–13).[2] Radio allowed her to recreate the 'atavistic lure, the atavistic power, of voices in the dark' (1985: 13), and she describes with glee: 'the quite unhealthy sense of power with which you feel that you're actually beaming the figments of your imagination across the city, across the country, across the world', on the release of her first feature film, *The Company of Wolves* (Mars-Jones, 1984b). As the controversial and still unpublished *The Holy Family Album* attests, Carter remains an uncomfortable figure for the establishment, despite the enthusiasm with which it has embraced her literary work since her death.

Furthermore, as indicated in the Introduction, Carter wrote a number of other texts for stage and screen which are not discussed in this book, primarily because they were never realised and consequently do not constitute 'mediated' texts. These include two original film scripts which demonstrate her ongoing commitment to the cinema. When working on the script for *The Magic Toyshop* with director David Wheatley, Carter suggested scrapping the novel entirely and starting on something completely fresh (1996: 233). Fortunately, Wheatley persuaded her to continue with *The Magic Toyshop* project, but they went on to develop a screenplay together called 'Gun for the Devil' (Carter, 1996).[3] As Mark Bell explains, she was 'inspired to write a revenge tragedy set in the Wild West by Carl von Weber's opera, *Der Freischütz*, based on the German folk-tale of a forester ridiculed for poor marksmanship' (Carter, 1996: 509). He sells his soul to the Devil for a magic gun which will never miss its target, save for the final bullet which belongs to the Devil himself.[4] Sergio Leone meets Jan Svankmayer – the screenplay combines the *mise-en-scène* of the spaghetti western (recreating the traditional flyblown border town) with supernatural elements reminiscent of Svankmayer's *Faust* (with its animated devils and disturbing transformations). Visually arresting, even on the page, the directions include precise camera angles and point-of-view shots, revealing a growing competence in writing directly for the medium. Carter delivered the script in 1987, but according to Bell, the project was 'written off' in 1989 (Carter, 1996: 509).

Less satisfying is 'The Christchurch Murder', which depicts the true story of a bizarre matricide in New Zealand in the 1950s. It returns to the theme of violence towards parents which Carter explored in her two short stories about the parent-killer Lizzie Borden, 'The Fall River Axe Murders' ([1985] 1986) and 'Lizzie's Tiger' (1993), and in her radio documentary-drama about the Victorian parricide, Richard Dadd, *Come Unto These Yellow Sands* ([1979] 1992a and 1985).[5] Euston Films commissioned the screenplay in 1987 but failed to find a production company and the project was abandoned in 1988 (Carter, 1996: 509). Carter developed the screenplay from newspaper cuttings, the girls' police statements and transcripts of the trial, but the script reached only its second draft.[6] What is there is well written, with detailed visual cues, but there are few of the imaginative transformation sequences we might normally expect from a Carter screenplay.[7] Although they do not fall within the brief of this book, these screenplays deserve further scrutiny. The fact that Carter chose to write directly for the medium as well as adapting her own work for film suggests an increasing confidence in her skills as a screenwriter, and a continuing fascination with cinema as a medium.

She also wrote for the stage. But, while she found theatricality a useful metaphor for the construction of femininity in her fiction, as we have seen, she had little time for 'live' theatre, 'that dreadful spectacle of painted loons in the middle distance making fools of themselves' (Carter, 1982d: 124). She was commissioned to write the libretto for an opera based on Woolf's *Orlando* in 1979 for the Glyndebourne Opera House, but the project never reached fruition. According to Mark Bell, 'partly for reasons of copyright costs, and partly because of Glyndebourne's current caution about new operas, the proposed production went no further than the second draft' (Carter, 1996: 506). The unfinished libretto, 'Orlando: or, the Enigma of the Sexes', reveals an imaginative engagement with Woolf's parodic biography which illuminates Carter's own artificial bio-graphies, *Come Unto These Yellow Sands* and *The Self-Made Man*, discussed in Chapter 3. Finding the physical limitations of the stage frustrating after the freedom of radio, Carter was forced to replace Shelmerdine's original entrance in a biplane with a logistically pragmatic parachute.

Uncomfortable on the stage, Carter was more at home manipulating the distinctive possibilities of a range of electronic media, as her stilted reworking of Frank Wedekind's two 'Lulu' plays also confirms. Commis-sioned by Richard Eyre, director of the National Theatre, in 1987, the project 'presented problems', as Mark Bell attests, because of 'tensions between the demands of "translation" and the desire to create a new work … and differences of conception between Carter and the prospective director, Howard Davies' (Carter, 1996: 510). It was eventually dropped in 1988. Ultimately, Carter was more in love with Pabst's film adaptation, *Pandora's Box*, and its star, the silent movie icon Louise Brooks, than Wedekind's original play. Frustrated with Wedekind's characterisation of Lulu she writes, 'it was left to one exceptional actress and one exceptional film-maker to flesh out that life and show that it is in absolute contradiction to the text' (1982d: 119).[8] Without Brooks' transgressive sexual force the play falls flat, and Carter can only partially resuscitate it.

Commenting on the gap in Carter's fictional production between the publication of *Nights at the Circus* ([1984] 1985) and *Wise Children* (1991a), Sarah Gamble suggests 'it is not surprising that Carter's output of fiction slowed down quite dramatically' (1997: 146), listing her stints as Visiting Professor of Creative Writing at various universities at home and abroad and the birth of her son in 1983, as supporting evidence. But far from being a fallow period, Carter was busy working on the script for *A Self-Made Man* (1984a), collaborating with Neil Jordan and David Wheatley on her two film adaptations, *The Company of Wolves* (1984b) and *The Magic Toyshop* (1986a) and continuing to publish a range of journalism. Furthermore, as these unrealised texts demonstrate, Carter was putting considerable creative energy into a number of projects which, for one reason or another, did not come to fruition between 1987 and 1989. The irreverent treatment of traditional theatre in *Wise Children* may stem from her unfruitful collaborations with the Glyndebourne Opera House and the National Theatre, the highest echelons of 'high art'. The balancing act between her critique and celebration of the Hollywood production of *The Dream* might also be read in the light of the successes and the failures of her various film projects. The novel is steeped with allusion to cinema, television, video and digital technology, demonstrating the cross-fertilisation between her work in media and her writing for the printed page. Within the limits of this study these can remain only interesting speculations. Although it has not been my central project here, there clearly remains a need for these unrealised dramatic writings to be addressed.

Considering the extent of her engagement with radio, film and television, both the realised texts and those dramatic writings which never came to fruition, it seems likely that Carter would have continued to work with media, in addition to her literary output. As Jo Ann Kaplan suggests, 'if she was still alive, I would have been going to work with her on another original project, not adapting a book she'd already written, but another original project, whether it be fiction, cinema, or television' (1995: 283).

That Carter was interested in blurring the perceived boundary between popular culture and traditional art-forms is evident in her journalism and fiction, and is enacted in her mediated texts. An analysis of Carter's writing for media other than the printed page is central to an under-standing of her work as a whole. It can also illuminate the way in which we think about writing and reading literature, reflecting contemporary debates within the disciplines of feminist, literary, film and cultural theory. No Luddite, Carter actively embraced the possibilities of modern media. Her preoccupation with the oral tradition, and her writing for radio, screen and stage, are all testimony to her belief in the power and energy of story-telling and narrative pleasure, which she believed would outlive the ascendancy of the printed word: 'human beings told each other stories ... before there was such a thing even as writing and will doubtless continue to do so because the *really* important thing is narrative' (Carter, 1992: 2). Indeed Carter sees narrative as positively flourishing in the future: 'Now we have machines to do our dreaming for us. But within that "video gadgetry" might lie the source of a continuation, even a trans-formation of storytelling and story-performance' (Carter (ed.), 1990: xxi).

Carter's work in mass media is important because it speaks to us at a point at which the boundaries between high art and low culture are becoming increasingly eroded. Instead of viewing it as a threat Carter celebrated this diversity of media culture and tenaciously explored the uncomfortable interstices between literature and popular entertainment in her fiction, her journalism and in her writing for radio, film and television. The fact that one of our most prominent contemporary authors increasingly chose to write for electronic media suggests that we not only need to reevaluate the Carter canon, we also need to reassess the constitution of the literary canon itself. By ignoring her work in media, traditional English studies is in danger of missing the opportunity that her interdisciplinarity presents to challenge and expand the boundaries of the academy. Furthermore by failing to acknowledge Carter's productive engagement with the mainstream, there is also a danger that academic feminism may underestimate the wider impact of her subversive practice of writing.

## Notes

1 Sarah Gamble (1997) similarly ends her book with an 'Epilogue'; Elaine Jordan contributes an 'Afterword' to the collection of critical essays in *The Infernal Desires of Angela Carter* (Bristow and Broughton (eds), 1997), and Aidan Day (1998) decides against a conclusion at all in *Angela Carter: The Rational Glass*.

2 Although Carter is specifically referring to her writing for radio, here, I extend this to include her writing for other media.

3 A prose film treatment of the same name was published in *American Ghosts and Old World Wonders* (1993). The link between revenge tragedy and the Western is also explored in Carter's short story-cum-screenplay, 'John Ford's *'Tis Pity She's a Whore'*, also collected in *American Ghosts*.

4 This and the following material is adapted from my review of *The Curious Room: Angela Carter's Dramatic Writings* (Crofts, 1996: 34).

5 As argued in Chapter 3, Carter reads parricide in terms of a glitch in the Oedipal trajectory which defamiliarises and denaturalises the 'normal' process of subject formation in the process of patriarchal acculturation.

6 Mark Bell, editor of Carter's collected dramatic works (1996) has generously given me access to his archive of Carter's papers, which include an outline of the murder and trial by Sheryn Brandt and Dr R. W. Medlicott (psychiatrist for the defence) and an unsourced newspaper article, 'Two Adolescent Homicides'.

7 The same story inspired the Peter Jackson film, *Heavenly Creatures* (1994), which recreates the fantasy world of the two girls using the sophisticated make-up and animation techniques we might have expected from Carter.

8 'Femmes Fatales' demonstrates Carter's fascination with the film star as icon of femininity, and her particular love of Louise Brooks' portrayal of the Lulu role in Pabst's adaptation. See also, 'Brooksie and Faust' (1997; 387–92), a review of Barry Paris' biography, *Louise Brooks*.

# Bibliography

## Primary texts: works by Angela Carter

Works are arranged in chronological order by date of first publication: where this is different from the date of the edition used, I have used square brackets.

## Fiction

Carter, Angela (1966a), *Shadow Dance*, London: Heinemann.
—— (1966b), *Unicorn*, Leeds: Location Press (first published in *Vision Magazine*, Bristol).
—— [1967] (1981), *The Magic Toyshop*, London: Virago.
—— (1968), *Several Perceptions*, London: Heinemann.
—— [1969] (1981), *Heroes and Villains*, Harmondsworth: Penguin.
—— [1971] (1987), *Love*, London: Pan (revised edition).
—— [1972] (1982), *The Infernal Desire Machines of Doctor Hoffman*, Harmondsworth: Penguin.
—— [1974] (1987), *Fireworks: Nine Profane Pieces*, London: Virago (revised edition).
—— [1977] (1990), *The Passion of New Eve*, London: Virago.
—— [1979] (1981), *The Bloody Chamber*, Harmondsworth: Penguin.
—— (1980a), 'Cousins', *Granta 3: The End of the English Novel*, Cambridge: Cambridge University Library.
—— [1984] (1985), *Nights at the Circus*, London: Pan.
—— [1985] (1986), *Black Venus*, London: Pan.
—— [1987] (1990), 'Ashputtle: or The Mother's Ghost', in Richard Dalby (ed.), *The Virago Book of Ghost Stories*, London: Virago, 324–5.
—— (1991a), *Wise Children*, London: Chatto & Windus.
—— (1993), *American Ghosts and Old World Wonders*, London: Chatto & Windus.
—— (1995), *Burning Your Boats*, London: Chatto & Windus.
Carter, Angela and Justin Todd (1982), *Moon Shadow*, London: Gollancz.

### DRAMATIC WRITINGS

Carter, Angela (1985), *Come unto these Yellow Sands: Four Radio Plays*, Newcastle upon Tyne: Bloodaxe Books.
—— (1996), *The Curious Room: Collected Dramatic Works*, Mark Bell (ed.), London: Chatto & Windus.

### RADIO PLAYS IN PERFORMANCE

Carter, Angela [1976] (1992), *Vampirella*, Glyn Dearman (dir.), BBC Radio 4, 15 November.
—— [1979] (1992a), *Come Unto These Yellow Sands*, Glyn Dearman (dir.), BBC Radio 3, 7 April.

—— [1980] (1992), *The Company of Wolves*, Glyn Dearman (dir.), BBC Radio 4, 19 November.

—— [1982] (1992), *Puss in Boots*, Glyn Dearman (dir.), BBC Radio 4, 16 November.

—— (1984a), *A Self-Made Man*, Glyn Dearman (dir.), BBC Radio 3, 4 May.

FILMS

Carter, Angela (1984b), *The Company of Wolves*, Neil Jordan (dir.), Palace/ITC Entertainment.

—— (1986a), *The Magic Toyshop*, David Wheatley (dir.), Granada TV/Palace Pictures.

TELEVISION

Carter, Angela (1982a), 'Review of *The Draughtsman's Contract*', *Visions*, Large Door Productions Ltd for Channel 4, 10 November, collected as 'The Draughtsman's Contract' in Carter (1997), 372–7.

—— (1983a), 'Godard: History: Passion', *Visions*, Large Door Productions Ltd for Channel 4, 11 May, collected as 'Jean-Luc Godard' in Carter (1997), 380–1.

—— (1984c), 'Review of *The Company of Wolves*', *Visions*, Large Door Productions Ltd for Channel 4, 17 October.

—— (1991b), *The Holy Family Album*, *Without Walls*, Jo Ann Kaplan (dir.) and John Ellis (prod.), Large Door Productions Ltd for Channel 4, 3 December.

—— (1991c), *The Holy Family Album*, final draft script, Large Door Productions Ltd archive (annotated by Jo Ann Kaplan).

## Non-fiction

Carter, Angela (1974), 'Afterword', *Fireworks: Nine Profane Pieces*, London: Quartet (not in 1987 revised edition).

—— (1976), 'The Better to Eat You With', *New Society*, 22 July, 188–9.

—— (1977), 'The Power of Porn', *Observer*, 10 April, 9.

—— [1979] (1992b), *The Sadeian Woman: An Exercise in Cultural History*, London: Virago.

—— (1980b), 'The Language of Sisterhood', in Leonard Michaels and Christopher Ricks (eds), *The State of The Language*, Berkeley: University of California Press, 226–34.

—— (1982b), '"Fools Are My Theme, Let Satire Be My Song"', *Vector*, 109, 26–36.

—— (1982c), Introduction, Walter de la Mare's *Memoirs of a Midget*, Oxford: Oxford University Press.

—— (1982d), *Nothing Sacred: Selected Writings*, London: Virago.

—— (1983b), 'Alison's Giggle', in Eileen Phillips (ed.), *The Left and the Erotic*, London: Lawrence & Wishart, 53–68.

—— (1983c), 'Anger in a Black Landscape', in Dorothy Thompson (ed.), *Over our Dead Bodies: Women against the Bomb*, London: Virago.

—— (1983d), 'Notes From the Front Line', in Michelene Wandor (ed.), *On Gender and Writing*, London: Pandora, 69–77.

—— (1983e), 'Shoot the Wolf', *New Society*, 8 September, 367–8.

—— (1986b), 'Occidentalism', *Guardian*, 3 April, 9.

—— (1988), 'Truly, It Felt Like Year One', in Sarah Maitland (ed.) (1988), *Very Heaven: Looking Back at the 1960s*, London: Virago, 209–16.

—— (1992), *Expletives Deleted: Selected Writings*, London: Chatto & Windus.

—— (1997), *Shaking a Leg: Collected Journalism and Writings*, Jenny Uglow (ed.), London: Chatto & Windus.

Carter, Angela (ed. and trans.) (1977), *The Fairy Tales of Charles Perrault*, London: Gollancz.

—— (1982), *Sleeping Beauty and Other Favourite Fairy Tales*, London: Gollancz.

Carter (ed.) [1986] (1992), *Wayward Girls and Wicked Women*, London: Virago.

—— (1989), *Images of Frida Kahlo*, London: Redstone Press.

—— (1990), *The Virago Book of Fairy Tales*, London: Virago.

—— [1992] (1993), *The Second Virago Book of Fairy Tales*, London: Virago.


## Secondary texts

Ackroyd, Peter (1984), 'The Dark Forest', *Spectator*, 29 September, 33–4.

Alexander, Flora (1989), *Contemporary Women Novelists*, London: Edward Arnold, 61–75.

Alexander, Marguerite (1990), *Flights from Realism: Themes and Strategies in Postmodernist British and American Fiction*, London: Edward Arnold.

Allderidge, Patricia (1974), *The Late Richard Dadd 1817–1886*, London: Academy Editions.

Allport , G. W. and H. Cantrill, (1972), 'Judging Personality from Voice', in J. Laver and S. Hutcheson (eds), *Communication in Face to Face Interaction*, Harmondsworth: Penguin.

Almansi, Guido (1994), 'In the Alchemist's Cave: Radio Plays', in Sage (ed.), 216–29.

Altevers, Nanette (1994), 'Gender Matters in *The Sadeian Woman*', *The Review of Contemporary Fiction*, 14:3, Autumn, 18–23.

Anwell, Maggie (1988), 'Lolita Meets the Werewolf: *The Company of Wolves*', in Gamman and Marshment (eds), 76–85.

Atwood, Margaret (1992), 'Magic Token Through the Dark Forest', *Observer*, 23 February, 61.

—— (1994), 'Running with the Tigers', in Sage (ed.), 117–35.

Bacchilega, Cristina (1988), 'Cracking the Mirror: Three Revisions of Snow White', *Boundary*, 2, 15:16, Spring/Autumn, 1–25.

Bailey, Paul (1992), Interview with Angela Carter, *Third Ear*, Radio 3, 7 April.

Baker, Simon and Olwen Terris (eds) (1994), *A–Z: The TV Holdings of the National Film and Television Archive 1936–1979*, London: British Film Institute.

Baron, Saskia (1987), 'Toying with Fantasies', *Independent*, 31 July, 26.

Barthes, Roland [1957] (1993), *Mythologies*, London: Vintage.

—— (1977), 'The Death of the Author', *Image, Music, Text*, London: Flamingo, 142–8.

—— (1993), *Camera Lucida*, Richard Howard (trans.), London: Vintage.

Bataille, Georges [1928] (1987), *Story of the Eye*, San Francisco: City Lights Books.

Batchelor, John (1995), *The Art of Literary Biography*, Oxford: Oxford University Press.

Bayley, John (1992), 'Fighting for the Crown', *The New York Review of Books*, 23 April, 9–11.

Bell, Michael (1992), 'Narration as Action: Goethe's "Bekenntnisse Einer Schonen Seele" and Angela Carter's *Nights at the Circus*', *German Life and Letters*, 45, January, 16–32.

Benkovitz, Miriam (1969), *Ronald Firbank: A Biography*, New York: Knopf.

Bennett, Catherine (1995), 'Hype and Heritage', *Guardian*, 22 September, 2-4.

Berry, Philippa (1994), 'The Burning Glass: Paradoxes of Feminist Revelation in *Speculum*', in Burke, Schor and Whitford (eds), 229–46.

Bettelheim, Bruno (1979), *The Uses of Enchantment: The Meaning and Importance of Fairy Tale*, New York: Alfred A. Knopf.

Bradfield, Scot (1994), 'Remembering Angela Carter', *The Review of Contemporary Fiction*, 14:3, Autumn, 90–3.

Branston, Gill and Roy Stafford (1996), *The Media Student's Handbook*, London: Routledge.

Bristow, Joseph and Trev Lynn Broughton (eds) (1997), *The Infernal Desires of Angela Carter: Fiction, Femininity, Feminism*, Essex: Longman.

Britzolakis, Christina (1995), 'Angela Carter's Fetishism', *Textual Practice*, 9:3, 459–76.

Brooks, Richard and Peter Beaumont (1991), *Observer on Sunday*, 1 December, 3.

Brophy, Brigid (1973), *The Prancing Novelist*, London: Macmillan.

Brophy, Philip (1986), 'Horrality – the Textuality of Contemporary Horror Films', *Screen*, 27:1, January–February, 2–13.

Browder, Clifford (1967), *André Breton: Arbiter of Surrealism*, Geneva: Librairie Droz.

Bryant, Sylvia (1990), 'Re-Constructing Oedipus Through "Beauty and the Beast"', *Criticisms: A Quarterly for Literature and the Arts*, 31:4, Autumn, 439–53.

Buckingham, David (1991), 'Teaching About the Media', in Lusted (ed.).

Bulgakov, Sergei (1979), *Karl Marx as a Religious Type*, Luba Barna (trans.), Belmont, Massachusetts: Norland Publishing Company.

Bunbury, Stephanie (1987), 'The Write Stuff', *Cinema Papers*, September, 37–8.

Burgin, Victor, James Donald and Cora Kaplan (eds) (1986), *Formations of Fantasy*, London: Methuen.

Burke, Carolyn, Naomi Schor and Margaret Whitford (eds) (1994), *Engaging with Irigaray: Feminist Philosophy and Modern European Thought*, New York: Columbia University Press.

Butler, Judith (1990), *Gender Trouble: Feminism and the Subversion of Identity*, London and New York: Routledge.

—— (1993), *Bodies that Matter: On the Discursive Limits of 'Sex'*, London and New York: Routledge.

Callil, Carmen (1992), 'Flying Jewellery', *Sunday Times*, Section 7, 23 February, 6.

Callil, Carmen and Lorna Sage (1993), 'In Praise of Angela Carter', talk at Cheltenham Festival, 16 October.

Cameron, Deborah (ed.) (1990), *The Feminist Critique of Language: A Reader*, London and New York: Routledge.

Campbell-Dixon, Anne (1987), 'Mae West Would Have Approved', *Daily Telegraph*, 31 July.

Carroll, Noël (1982), 'The Future of Allusion: Hollywood in the Seventies (and Beyond)', *October*, 20, Spring.

Cartmell, Deborah, I. Q. Hunter, Heidi Kaye and Imelda Whelehan (eds) (1996), *Pulping Fictions: Consuming Culture Across the Literature/Media Divide*, London and Chicago: Pluto Press.

—— (1997), *Trash Aesthetics: Popular Culture and its Audience*, London and Chicago: Pluto Press.

—— (1998), *Sisterhoods: Across the Literature/Media Divide*, London and Sterling, Virginia: Pluto Press.

Castell, David (1984), Review of *The Company of Wolves*, *Daily Telegraph*, November, quoted in Anwell (1988).

Caws, Mary Ann (1985), *The Poetry of Dada and Surrealism: Aragon, Breton, Tzara, Eluard and Desnos*, Princeton, New Jersey: Princeton University Press.

Cholodenko, Alan (ed.) (1991), *The Illusion of Life: Essays on Animation*, Sydney: Power Publications.

Cixous, Hélène [1976] (1980), 'The Laugh of the Medusa', Keith Cohen and Paula Cohen (trans.), *Signs*, 1, Summer, 875–99, in Marks and de Courtivron (eds), 245–64.

Clapp, Susannah (1991), 'On Madness, Men and Fairy-tales', *Independent on Sunday Review Supplement*, 9 June, 26.

Clark, Robert (1987), 'Angela Carter's Desire Machine', *Women's Studies: An Interdisciplinary Journal*, 14:2, 147–61.

Clover, Carol J. (1993), *Men, Women and Chainsaws: Gender in The Modern Horror Film*, London: British Film Institute.

Cohen, Margaret (1993), *Profane Illumination: Walter Benjamin and the Paris of Surrealist Revolution*, Berkeley and Los Angeles, California: University of California Press.

Collick, John (1991), 'Wolves Through the Window: Writing Dreams/Dreaming Films/Filming Dreams', *Critical Survey*, 3:3, 283–9.

Comolli, Jean-Louis (1980), 'Machines of the Visible', in de Lauretis and Heath (eds), 121–42.

Connor, Rachel and Charlotte Crofts (1999), 'Assuming White Identities: Racial and Gendered Looking across the Literature/Media Divide', in *White?Women: Critical Perspectives on Race and Gender*, York: Raw Nerve Books.

Coover, Robert (1994), 'A Passionate Remembrance', *The Review of Contemporary Fiction*, 14: 3, Autumn, 9.

Cox, Steve (1995), 'Shots, Scenes and Stories: A History of Film Style', lecture series at Cornerhouse: Visual Arts Centre, Manchester, 5 October–7 December.

Cranny-Francis, Anne (1990), *Feminist Fiction: Feminist Uses of Generic Fiction*, Cambridge: Polity Press.

Creed, Barbara (1993), *The Monstrous-Feminine: Film, Feminism, Psychoanalysis*, London and New York: Routledge.

Crofts, Charlotte (1996), 'Mirage Bombardment', *Times Literary Supplement*, 8 November, 34.

—— (1998a), 'Curiously Downbeat Hybrid or Radical Retelling?: Neil Jordan's and Angela Carter's *The Company of Wolves*', in Cartmell, Hunter, Kaye and Whelehan (eds) (1998), 48–63.

—— (1998b), 'Mediated Texts: Angela Carter's Writing for Radio, Film and Television', PhD thesis, University of Manchester.

—— (1999a), Entries on Angela Carter's *The Bloody Chamber*, *Nights at the Circus* and Edna O'Brien's *The Country Girls*, in Lorna Sage (ed.), *The Cambridge Guide to Women's Writing in English*, Cambridge: Cambridge University Press, 69, 155, 469.

—— (1999b), '"The Other of the Other": Angela Carter's "New-Fangled" Orientalism', unpublished paper, White?Women Conference, University of York, 17 April.

—— (2001), 'From the "Hegemony of the Eye" to the "Hierarchy of Perception": The Reconfiguration of Sound and Image in Terrence Malick's *Days of Heaven*', *Journal of Media Practice*, 2:1, 19–29.

Cunningham, Valentine (1995), 'Roll Up for the Necrophiliacs' Party', *Observer Review*, 19 February, 17.

Day, Aidan (1998), *Angela Carter: The Rational Glass*, Manchester and New York: Manchester University Press.

Dearman, Glyn (1992), Angela Carter Obituary, *The Times*, 20 February.

de Lauretis, Teresa (1984), *Alice Doesn't: Feminism, Semiotics, Cinema*, London: Macmillan.

—— (1989), *Technologies of Gender: Essays on Theory, Film and Fiction*, London: Macmillan.

de Lauretis, Teresa and Stephen Heath (eds) (1980), *The Cinematic Apparatus*, London: Macmillan.

Doane, Mary Ann [1978] (1980), 'Ideology and the Practice of Sound Editing and Mixing', in de Lauretis and Heath (eds), 47–60.

—— [1980] (1986), 'The Voice in Cinema: The Articulation of Body and Space', in Rosen (ed.), 335–48.

—— (1984), '"The Woman's Film": Possession and Address', in Doane, Mellencamp and Williams (eds), 67–82.

—— (1987), *The Desire to Desire: The Woman's Film of the 1940s*, London: Macmillan.

—— (1991), *Femmes Fatales: Feminism, Film Theory and Psychoanalysis*, New York and London: Routledge.

Doane, Mary Ann, Patricia Mellencamp and Linda Williams (eds) (1984), *Re-Vision: Essays in Feminist Film and Criticism*, Los Angeles: American Film Institute.

Donelly, Frances (1987), 'Edinburgh by Carter and Son', *Observer*, 15–21 August, 85.

Drakakis, John (ed.) (1981), *Introduction to British Radio Drama*, Cambridge: Cambridge University Press.

Duncker, Patricia (1984), 'Re-Imagining the Fairy Tales: Angela Carter's Bloody Chambers', *Literature and History*, 10:1, Spring, 3–14.

Dworkin, Andrea (1974), *Woman Hating*, New York: Dutton

—— (1982), *Pornography: Men Possessing Women*, London: Women's Press.

Dyer, Richard (1992), *Only Entertainment*, London: Routledge.

Easthope, Antony (ed.) (1993), *Contemporary Film Theory*, London and New York: Longman.

Ecker, Gisela (ed.) (1985), *Feminist Aesthetics*, London: Women's Press.

Ellis, John (1982), *Visible Fictions: Cinema, Television, Video*, London: Routledge & Kegan Paul.

—— (1985), Publicity Brochure for *Visions*, Large Door Productions Ltd archive.

—— (1990), Letter to Waldemar Januszczak, Large Door Productions Ltd archive, 14 May.

—— (1991), Letter to Dorothea Tunning, Large Door Productions Ltd archive, 14 November.

—— (1995), Interview, London, 23 November, transcribed in Crofts (1998b).

—— (2000), *Seeing Things: Television in the Age of Uncertainty*, London: I. B. Tauris.

Engstrom, John (1988), 'Bewitching Wit', *Boston Globe*, 28 October, 51–62.

Enzenberger, Magnus (1974), *The Consciousness Industry: On Literature, Politics and the Media*, Michael Roloff (ed. and trans.), New York: Seabury Press.

Erens, Patricia (ed.) (1990), *Issues in Feminist Film Criticism*, Bloomington and Indianapolis: Indiana University Press.

Esslin, Martin (1980), *Mediations: Essays on Brecht, Beckett and the Media*, London: Abacus.

Evans, Kim (dir.) (1992), *Angela Carter's Curious Room*, Omnibus, BBC1, 15 September.

—— (1996), Interview, London, 16 January, transcribed in Crofts (1998b).

Evans, Kim and Angela Carter (1992), Post-production script of *Angela Carter's Curious Room*, *Omnibus*, BBC Music and Arts Department archive, part published as 'The Granada, Tooting', in Carter (1997), 400.

Fernihough, Anne (1997), '"Is She Fact or Is She Fiction?": Angela Carter and the Enigma of Woman', *Textual Practice*, 11:1, 89–107.

Ferrell, Robyn (1991), 'Life-Threatening Life: Angela Carter and the Uncanny', in Cholodenko (ed.), 131–44.

Firbank, Ronald [1915] (1934), *The Artificial Princess*, London: Duckworth.

Fletcher, I. K. (1930), *Ronald Firbank: A Memoir*, London: Duckworth.

Forgan, Liz (1991), 'Sacred Cows on C4', *The Times*, 5 December.

French, Philip (1984), 'Rosaleen and the Wolves', *Observer*, 23 September, 9.

Freud, Sigmund (1955), 'The Uncanny', *Standard Edition of the Complete Psychological Works*, 17, London: Hogarth.

Gallop, Jane (1982), *Feminism and Psychoanalysis: The Daughter's Seduction*, London: Macmillan, 58.

Gamble, Sarah (1997), *Angela Carter: Writing From the Front Line*, Edinburgh: Edinburgh University Press.

Gamman, Lorraine and Margaret Marshment (eds) (1988), *The Female Gaze: Women as Viewers of Popular Culture*, London: Women's Press.

Garber, Marjorie (1992), *Vested Interests*, London: Routledge.

Gerrard, Nicci (1989), *Into the Mainstream: How Feminism Has Changed Women's Writing*, London: Pandora.

Gibbs, Jeanne K. (1992), 'Wise Children', *The Review of Contemporary Fiction*, 12, Summer, 195–6.

Gibson, Pamela Church and Roma Gibson (eds) (1993), *Dirty Looks: Women, Pornography, Power*, London: British Film Institute.

Gledhill, Christine (ed.) (1991), *Stardom: The Industry of Desire*, London: Routledge.

Goldsworthy, Kerryn (1985), 'Angela Carter', *Meanjin*, 44:1, 4–13.

Gorra, Michael (1987), 'Saints and Strangers', *The Hudson Review*, 40, Spring, 136–48.

Gray, John (1997), 'Time to Get Rid of the Crime of Blasphemy', *Daily Telegraph*, 12 August.

Grimshaw, Jean (1992), 'Review of Margaret Whitford, *Luce Irigaray: Philosophy in the Feminine*', *Feminist Review*, 42, Autumn, 111–14.

Grossman, Michele (1988), '"Born to Bleed": Myth, Pornography and Romance in Angela Carter's "The Bloody Chamber"', *The Minnesota Review*, 30/31, Spring, 148–60.

Haase, Donald P. (1990), 'Is Seeing Believing?: Proverbs and the Film Adaptation of a Fairy Tale', *Proverbium*, 7, 89–104.

Haffenden, John (1985), *Novelists in Interview*, London: Methuen, 76–96.

Hanson, Clare (1988), 'Each Other: Images of Otherness in the Short Fiction of Doris Lessing, Jean Rhys and Angela Carter', *Journal of the Short Story in English*, 10, Spring, 67–82.

—— (ed.) (1989), *Re-Reading the Short Story*, London: Macmillan.

Hayward, Susan (1996), *Key Concepts in Cinema Studies*, London and New York: Routledge.

Heath, Stephen (1978), 'Sexual Difference and Representation', *Screen*, Autumn, 19, 51–112.

—— (1986), 'Joan Riviere and the Masquerade', in Burgin, Donald and Kaplan (eds), 45–61.

Hebert, Huge (1991), 'A Slice of the Action that Was Pie in the Sky', *Guardian*, 4 December, 34.

Hill, Joanne (1987), 'Dream Machines', *City Life*, 9–23 October, 12.

Holden, Kate (1985), 'Women's Writing and the Carnivalesque', *Literature Teaching Politics*, 4, 5–15.

hooks, bell (1992), 'The Oppositional Gaze', *Black Looks: Race and Representation*, Boston: Southend Press, 115–31.

—— (1996), *Reel to Real: Race, Sex and Class at the Movies*, London: Routledge.

Hutcheon, Linda (1988), *A Poetics of Postmodernism: History, Theory, Fiction*, London: Routledge.

—— (1989), *The Politics of Postmodernism*, London: Routledge.

Hutchings, Peter (1991), 'The Work-Shop of Filthy Animation', in Cholodenko (ed.), 161–81.

—— (1993), *Hammer and Beyond: The British Horror Film*, Manchester: Manchester University Press.

Irigaray, Luce (1985), *This Sex Which is Not One*, Catherine Porter (trans.), Ithaca, New York: Cornell University Press.

Jackson, Rosemary (1981), *Fantasy: The Literature of Subversion*, London: Routledge.

Jameson, Frederic (1984), 'Postmodernism, or the Cultural Logic of Late Capitalism', *New Left Review*, 146, 53–93.

Jancovich, Mark (1992), *Horror*, London: Batsford.

Januszczak, Waldemar (1991), Letter to John Ellis, Large Door Productions Ltd archive, 28 November.

Jeffrey, Richard (1987), 'An Artistic Pilferer', *Daily Yomiuri*, Japan, found in David Wheatley's archive.

Johnstone, Iain (1984), 'Old Wolves' Tales', *Sunday Times*, 23 September, 55.

Jordan, Elaine (1990), 'Enthralment: Angela Carter's Speculative Fictions', in Linda Anderson (ed.), *Plotting Change: Contemporary Women's Fiction*, London: Edward Arnold, 19–40.

—— (1992), 'The Dangers of Angela Carter', in Isobel Armstrong (ed.), *New Feminist Discourses*, London: Routledge, 119–31.

—— (1994), 'The Dangerous Edge', in Sage (ed.), 189-215.

Kaplan, E. Ann [1983] (1993), *Women + Film: Both Sides of the Camera*, London and New York: Routledge

Kaplan, Jo Ann (dir.) (1991), Story Board of *The Holy Family Album*, Large Door Productions Ltd archive.

—— (1995), Interview, Bristol, 22 December, transcribed in Crofts (1998b).

Kappeler, Susanne (1986), *The Pornography of Representation*, Minneapolis: University of Minnesota Press.

Katsavos, Anna (1994), 'An Interview with Angela Carter', *The Review of Contemporary Fiction*, 14:3, Autumn, 11–17.

Kearns, George (1989), 'History and Games', *Hudson Review*, 42:2, Summer, 335–44.

Keenan, Sally (1997), 'Angela Carter's *The Sadeian Woman*: Feminism as Treason', in Bristow and Broughton (eds), 132–48.

Kellner, Douglas (1995), *Media Culture: Cultural Studies, Identity and the Politics Between the Modern and the Postmodern*, London and New York: Routledge.

Kelly, Mary (1984), *Post Partum Document*, London: Routledge.

Kemp, Peter (1991), 'Magical History Tour', *Sunday Times*, Section 6, 9 June, 6–7.

Kenyon, Olga (1988), *Women Novelists Today: A Survey of English Writing in the Seventies and Eighties*, Brighton: Harvester.

Kristeva, Julia [1977] (1986), 'A New Type of Intellectual: the Dissident', *Tel Quel*, 74, Winter, 3–8, in Kristeva (1986), 294-301.

—— [1979] (1986), 'Ellipsis on Dread and the Specular Seduction', *Wide Angle*, 3:3, 42–7, in Rosen (ed.), 236–43.

—— (1982), *The Powers of Horror*, New York: Columbia University Press.

—— (1984), *Desire in Language*, London: Basil Blackwell.

—— (1986), *The Kristeva Reader*, Toril Moi (ed.), Oxford: Basil Blackwell.

Landon, Brooks (1986), 'Eve at the End of the World: Sexuality and the Reversal of Expectations in Novels by Joanna Russ, Angela Carter and Thomas Berger', in Donald Palumbo (ed.), *Erotic Universe: Sexuality and Fantastic Literature*, Connecticut: Greenwood Press, 61–74.

Lang, Andrew (1888), *Perrault's Popular Tales*, London: Clarendon Press.

Laws, Sarah (ed.) (1994), *The Blue Book of British Broadcasting*, London: Tellex Monitors Ltd.

Lawson, Mark (1995), 'How Television Has Saved Classic Literature', paper given at Literature on Radio and Television conference, University of Oxford, April.

Laye, Mike (1986), 'Flights of Fancy in Balham', *Observer*, 9 November.

Lee, Hermione (1992), 'Angela Carter's Profane Pleasures', *Times Literary Supplement*, 19 June, 5–6.

—— (1994), '"A Room of One's Own" or a Bloody Chamber?: Angela Carter and Political Correctness', in Sage (ed.), 308–20.

Lewallen, Avis (1988), 'Wayward Girls But Wicked Women?: Female Sexuality in Angela Carter's *The Bloody Chamber*', in Gary Day and Clive Bloom (eds), *Perspectives on Pornography: Sexuality in Film and Literature*, New York: St Martin's Press, 144–58.

Lewis, Percy Wyndham (1937), *Blasting and Bombardiering*, London: Eyre & Spottiswoode.

Lieberman, Marcia K. (1986), '"Some Day My Prince Will Come": Female Acculturation Through the Fairy Tale', in Zipes (ed.), 185–200.

Ling, Trevor (1980), *Karl Marx and Religion in Europe and India*, London: Macmillan.

Lokke, Kari E. (1988), 'Bluebeard and *The Bloody Chamber*: The Grotesque of Self-Parody and Self-Assertion', *Frontiers: A Journal of Women's Studies*, 10:1, 7–12.

Lusted, David (ed.) (1991), *The Media Studies Book: A Guide for Teachers*, London and New York: Routledge.

MacDonald, Barrie (1988), *Broadcasting in the United Kingdom: A Guide to Information Sources*, London and New York: Mansell.

Macintyre, Alasdair (1968), *Marxism and Christianity*, London: Gerald Duckworth.

Magrs, Paul (1997), 'Boys Keep Swinging: Angela Carter and the Subject of Men', in Bristow and Broughton (eds), 184–97.

Makinen, Merja (1992), 'Angela Carter's *The Bloody Chamber* and the Decolonization of Feminine Sexuality', *Feminist Review*, 42, Autumn, 2–15.

Malcolm, Derek (1984), 'A Furry Tale for Grown-Ups', *Guardian*, 20 September, 11.

Mansfield, Paul (1990), 'Tell-Tale Sisters', *Guardian*, 25 October, 32.

Marks, Elaine and Isabelle de Courtivron (eds) (1980), *New French Feminisms*, Brighton: Harvester.

Mars-Jones, Adam (1984a), 'Nights at the Circus', *Times Literary Supplement*, 28 September, 1083.

—— (1984b), *Writers in Conversation*, London: ICA Video.

Marx, Karl and Frederick Engels [1884] (1980), *The Holy Family, or Critique of Critical Criticism: Against Bruno Bauer and Company*, Richard Dixon and Clemens Dutt (trans.), Moscow: Progress Publishers, 154.

Matus, Jill (1991), 'Blonde, Black and Hottentot Venus: Context and Critique in Angela Carter's *Black Venus*', *Studies in Short Fiction*, 28, Autumn, 467–76.

Mayer, David (1969), *Harlequin in His Element: The English Pantomime, 1806–1836*, Cambridge, Massachusetts: Harvard University Press.

Mayne, Judith (1984), 'The Woman at the Keyhole: Women's Cinema and Feminist Criticism', in Doane, Mellencamp and Williams (eds), 49–66.

McAsh, Iain F. (1984), 'Wolves at the Palace', *Films*, 4:9, September, 5.

McDowell, Margaret B. (1986), 'Angela Carter', in *Contemporary Novelists*, London: St James Press, 173–5.

McEwan, Ian (1984), 'Sweet Smell of Excess', *Sunday Times Magazine*, 9 September, 42–4.

McHale, Brian (1987), *Postmodernist Fiction*, New York: Methuen.

McKee Charnas, Suzy (1990), 'Boobs', in Tuttle (ed.), 18–38.

McLellan, David T. (1985), *Was Marx a Religious Thinker?*, Canterbury: University of Kent Centre for the Study of Religion and Society.

McNair, Brian (1996), *Mediated Sex: Pornography and Postmodern Culture*, London and New York: Arnold.

Metz, Christian [1975] (1986), 'The Imaginary Signifier', in Rosen (ed.), 244–78.

Michael, Magali Cornier (1994), 'Angela Carter's *Nights at the Circus*: An Engaged Feminism Via Subversive Postmodern Strategies', *Contemporary Literature*, 35, Autumn, 492–521.

Mills, Sara, Lynne Pearce, Sue Spaull and Elaine Millard (1989), *Feminist Readings/ Feminists Reading*, Hemel Hempsted: Harvester Wheatsheaf.

Moers, Ellen (1977), *Literary Women*, London: Women's Press.

Moi, Toril (1989), *Sexual/Textual Politics: Feminist Literary Theory*, London: Routledge.

Monteith, Moria (ed.) (1986), *Women's Writing: A Challenge to Theory*, Brighton: Harvester.

Morgan-Griffiths, Lauris (1990), 'Well Wicked Times by Word of Mouth', *Observer*, 21 October.

Mortimer, John (1982), 'The Stylish Prime of Miss Carter', *Sunday Times*, 24 January, 36.

Moyes, Jojo (1997), 'Pregnant With Meaning – Or a Slight on Motherhood?', *Independent*, 11 September, 3.

Müller, Anja (1997), *Angela Carter: Identity Constructed/Deconstructed*, Heidelburg: Universitäts-verlag C. Winter.

Mulvey, Laura [1975] (1989), 'Visual Pleasure and Narrative Cinema', *Screen*, 16:3, Autumn, 6–18, in Mulvey, 14–26.

—— [1981] (1989), 'Afterthoughts on "Visual Pleasure and Narrative Cinema" Inspired by King Vidor's *Duel in the Sun* (1946)', *Framework*, 15/16/17, 12–15, in Mulvey, 29–37.

—— (1989), *Visual and Other Pleasures*, London and Basingstoke: Macmillan.

—— (1994), 'Cinema Magic and the Old Monsters: Angela Carter's Cinema', in Sage (ed.), 230–42.

—— (1996), *Fetishism and Curiosity*, London: British Film Institute.

Mulvey, Laura and Wollen, Peter (1979), 'An Interview with Laura Mulvey and Peter Wollen', *Millennium Film Journal*, No. 4/5, 24.

National Touring Exhibition Catalogue (1997), 'The Quick and the Dead: Artists and Anatomy', London: Haywood Gallery, South Bank Centre.

Neale, Catherine (1996), 'Pleasure and Interpretation: Film Adaptations of Angela Carter's Fiction', in Cartmell, Hunter, Kaye and Whelehan (eds), 99–109.

O'Brien, Geraldine (1987), 'Putting Pen to Celluloid', *Sydney Morning Herald*, 29 September.

O'Brien, John (ed.) (1994), *The Review of Contemporary Fiction*, 14:3, Autumn.

O'Day, Marc (1994), 'Mutability is Having a Field Day: The Sixties Aura of Angela Carter's Bristol Trilogy', in Sage (ed.), 24–59.

Ong, Walter J. (1962), *The Barbarian Within: And Other Fugitive Essays and Studies*, London and New York: Macmillan.

—— (1967), *The Human Grain:Further Exploration of Contemporary Culture*, London and New York: Macmillan.

—— (1971), *Rhetoric, Romance and Technology: Studies in the Interaction of Expression and Culture*, New York: Cornell University Press.

Opie, Iona and Peter (1974), *The Classic Fairy Tales*, Oxford: Oxford University Press.

Oreglia, Giacomo (1968), *The Commedia Dell'Arte*, London: Methuen.

Orodenker, Richard (1983), '*Fireworks*: Nine Story-Tellers', *The North American Review*, 268:1, March, 68–72.

Pagan, Nicholas (1993), *Rethinking Literary Biography: A Postmodern Approach to Tennessee Williams*, Cranbury, New Jersey: Associated University Press.

Palmer, Paulina (1987), 'From "Coded Mannequin" to Bird Woman: Angela Carter's Magic Flight', in Roe (ed.), 177–205.

—— (1989), *Contemporary Women's Fiction: Narrative Practice and Feminist Theory*, Jackson: University of Mississippi.

—— (1997), 'Gender as Performance in the Fiction of Angela Carter and Margaret Atwood', in Bristow and Broughton (eds), 24–42.

Parente, William (1984), 'Haunting Tales from the Forest', *The Scotsman*, 22 September, 6.

Paterson, Moira (1986), 'Flights of Fancy in Balham: Filming *The Magic Toyshop*', *Observer Magazine*, 9 November, 42–3, 45.

Peach, Linden (1998), *Angela Carter*, Basingstoke: Macmillan.

Perino, Joy (dir.) (1990), 'The Kitchen Child', *Short and Curlies*, Channel 4, 30 June.

Petrie, Duncan (ed.) (1993), *Cinema and the Realms of Enchantment*, London, British Film Institute.

Plath, Sylvia (1965), *Ariel*, London: Faber & Faber

Punter, David (1980), *The Literature of Terror: A History of Gothic Fictions from 1764 to the Present Day*, London: Longman.

—— (1984), 'Angela Carter: Supersessions of the Masculine', *Critique: Studies in Modern Fiction*, 25:4, 209–22.

Pym, John (1984), 'If You Go Down to the Woods Today', *Financial Times*, 21 September, 23.

Riviere, Joan [1929] (1986), 'Womanliness as a Masquerade' in Burgin, Donald and Kaplan (eds), 35–44.

Roberts, Michèle (1984), *The Wild Girl*, London: Minerva.

Rodowick, D. N. (1991), *The Difficulty of Difference*, London: Routledge.

Roe, Sue (ed.) (1987), *Women Reading Women's Writing*, Brighton: Harvester.

Romney, Jonathan (1985), 'Mother of Invention', *New Musical Express*, 9 November, 31.

Rose, Ellen Cronan (1983), 'Through the Looking Glass: When Women Tell Fairy Tales', in Elizabeth Abel, Marianne Hirsch and Elizabeth Langland (eds), *The Voyage In: Fictions of Female Development*, Hanover: University Press of New England, 209–43.

Rose, Jacqueline (1986), *Sexuality in the Field of Vision: Women in Literature and Moving Pictures*, London: Verso.

Rosen, Philip (ed.) (1986), *Narrative, Apparatus, Ideology*, New York and Chichester: Columbia University Press.

Rosinsky, Natalie M. (1984), *Feminist Futures: Contemporary Women's Speculative Fiction*, Michigan: UMI Research, 10–19.

Rowe, Karen E. (1986), 'Feminism and Fairy Tales', in Zipes (ed.), 209–26.

Rushdie, Salman (1992), *The Wizard of Oz*, London: British Film Institute.

Sage, Lorna (1973), 'Angela Carter', in Jay L. Halio (ed.), *Dictionary of Literary Biography, Volume. 14: British Novelists Since 1960*, Detroit, Michigan: Bruccoli Clark, 205–12.

—— (1977), 'The Savage Sideshow', *New Review*, 39/40, 51–7.

—— (1992), *Women in The House of Fiction*, London: Macmillan.

—— (1994), *Angela Carter: Writers and Their Work*, Plymouth: Northcote House.

Sage, Lorna (ed.) (1994), *Flesh and the Mirror: Essays on the Art of Angela Carter*, London: Virago.

Said, Edward (1978), *Orientalism*, London and Henley: Routledge & Kegan Paul.

—— (1993), *Culture and Imperialism*, London: Chatto & Windus.

—— (1995), 'East Isn't East: The Impending End of the Age of Orientalism', *Times Literary Supplement*, 3 February.

Salerno, Henry F. (trans.) (1967), *Scenarios of the Commedia Dell'Arte: Flaminio Scala's Il Teatro Delle Favole Rappresentative*, New York: New York University Press.

Sanders, Claire (1994), 'Quota Plan May Save Pre-modern Literature', *Times Higher Education Supplement*, 8 April, 6.

Sceats, Sarah (1997), 'The Infernal Appetites of Angela Carter', in Bristow and Broughton (eds), 100–15.

Schmidt, Ricarda (1989), 'The Journey of the Subject in Angela Carter's Fiction', *Textual Practice*, 3:1, Spring, 56–75.

Schwarts, I. A. (1933), *The Commedia Dell'Arte and Its Influence on French Comedy in the Seventeenth Century*, Paris: Librairie H. Samuel.

Schlesinger, Philip R., Emerson Dobash, Russell P. Dobash and C. Kay Weaver (eds) (1992), *Women Viewing Violence*, London: British Film Institute.

Schor, Naomi (1994), 'This Essentialism Which is Not One', in Burke, Schor and Whitford (eds).

Sebastyen, Amanda (1987), 'The Mannerist Marketplace', *New Socialist*, March, 34–9.

Shaughnessy, Nicola (1996), 'Is s/he or isn't s/he: Screening *Orlando*', in Cartmell, Hunter, Kaye and Whelehan (eds), 43–55.

Sheets, Robin Ann (1991), 'Pornography, Fairy Tales, and Feminism: Angela Carter's "The Bloody Chamber"', in Tucker (ed.) (1998), 96–118.

Shelston, Alan (1977), *Biography*, London: Methuen.

Silverman, Kaja (1990), 'Dis-Embodying the Female Voice', in Erens (ed.), 309–27.

Sitwell, Osbert (1949), *Nobel Essences or Courteous Revelations*, London: Macmillan.

Smith, Anne (1985), 'Myths and the Erotic', *Women's Review*, 1, November, 28–9.

Smith, Barbara (1985), 'From Classical Archetypes to Modern Stereotypes', *Spare Rib*, November, 36–9.

Smith, Joan (1989), *Misogynies*, London: Faber & Faber.

—— (1997), Introduction to Carter (1997), xii–iv.

Snitow, Ann (1989), 'Angela Carter: Wild Thing', *The Village Voice Literary Supplement*, June, 14–17.

Stam, Robert (1989), *Subversive Pleasures: Bakhtin, Cultural Criticism and Film*, Baltimore: Johns Hopkins University Press.

Stanbrook, Alan (1991), 'Snapshots on the Road to Blasphemy', *Daily Telegraph*, 4 December, 16.

Stanley, Liz (1992), *The Auto/Biographical I*, Manchester: Manchester University Press.

Storey, Robert (1985), *Pierrots on the Stage of Desire: Nineteenth Century French Artists and the Comic Pantomime*, Princeton, New Jersey: Princeton University Press.

Styan, J. L. (1960), *The Elements of Drama*, Cambridge: Cambridge University Press.

Suleiman, Susan Rubin (ed.) (1986), *The Female Body in Western Culture: Contemporary Perspectives*, Cambridge, Massachusetts: Harvard University Press.

—— (1990), *Subversive Intent: Gender, Politics, and the Avant-Garde*, Cambridge, Massachusetts: Harvard University Press.

Sutton, Paul and Anne White (1997), 'Framing the Text: in *The Company of Wolves*', *ManuScript*, 2:1, Summer, 27–38.

Tasker, Yvonne (1993), *Spectacular Bodies: Gender, Genre and the Action Cinema*, London: Routledge.

Thompson, John O. (1996), '"Vanishing" Worlds: Film Adaptation and the Mystery of the Original', in Cartmell, Hunter, Kaye and Whelehan (eds), 11–28.

Thornham, Sue (1997), *Passionate Detachments: An Introduction to Feminist Film Theory*, London and New York: Arnold.

Tolley, Michael J. (1986), 'Angela Carter', in Curtis Smith (ed.), *Twentieth-Century Science-Fiction Writers*, 2nd edition, London: St James Press, 122–3.

Trahair, Lisa (1991), 'For the Noise of a Fly', in Cholodenko (ed.), 183–208.

Tucker, Lindsey (ed.) (1998), *Critical Essays on Angela Carter*, New York: G. K. Hall & Co.

Tudor, Andrew (1989), *Monsters and Mad Scientists: A Cultural History of the Horror Movie*, London: Basil Blackwell.

Turner, Rory P. B. (1987), 'Subjects and Symbols: Transformations of Identity in *Nights at the Circus*', *Folklore Forum*, 20:1/2, 39–60.

Tuttle, Lisa (ed.) (1990), *Skin of the Soul: New Horror Stories by Women*, London: Women's Press.

Twitchell, James B. (1985), *Dreadful Pleasures: An Anatomy of Modern Horror*, Oxford and New York: Oxford University Press.

Vaughan, Dai (1976), *Television Documentary Usage*, London: British Film Institute.

Vice, Sue (ed.) (1996), *Psychoanalytic Criticism: A Reader*, Cambridge: Polity Press.

Wade, David (1981), 'British Radio Drama Since 1960', in Drakakis (ed.), 218–32.

Warner, Marina (1993a), 'Through a Child's Eyes', in Petrie (ed.), 36–50.

—— (1993b), 'The Uses of Enchantment', in Petrie (ed.), 13–35.

—— (1993c), 'Women Against Women in the Old Wives' Tale', in Petrie (ed.), 63–78.

—— (1994), *From the Beast to the Blonde: On Fairy Tales and Their Tellers*, London: Chatto & Windus.

Waugh, Patricia (1986), 'Winged Women and Werewolves: How Do We Read Angela Carter?', *Ideas and Production: A Journal in the History of Ideas*, 4, 87–98.

—— (1989), *Feminine Fictions: Revisiting the Postmodern*, London: Routledge.

Weigel, Sigrid (1985), 'Double Focus: On the History of Women's Writing', in Ecker (ed.), 59–80.

Whatling, Clare (1997), *Screen Dreams: Fantasising Lesbians in Film*, Manchester: Manchester University Press.

Wheatley, David (1996), Interview, London, 5 April, transcribed in Crofts (1998b).

Wicke, Jennifer (1993), 'Through a Gaze Darkly: Pornography's Academic Market', in Gibson and Gibson (eds), 62–80.

Willemen, Paul (1994), *Looks and Frictions: Essays in Cultural Studies and Film Theory*, London: British Film Institute.

Williams, Linda (1984), 'When the Woman Looks', in Doane, Mellencamp and Williams (eds), 83–99.

—— (1990), *Hard Core: Power, Pleasure and the 'Frenzy of the Visible'*, London: Pandora.

Williams, Linda Ruth (1994), 'Visceral Pleasures: The Spectacular Bodies of David Cronenberg', conference paper at The Gothic Survival: Film, Fiction and Theory conference, Manchester Metropolitan University, 7 May.

Williamson, Judith (1993), *Deadline at Dawn: Film Criticism 1980–1990*, London: Marion Boyars.

Wilson, Robert Rawdon (1989), 'Slip Page: Angela Carter In/Out/In the Postmodern Nexus', *Ariel: A Review of International English Literature*, 20:4, October, 96–114.

Wisker, Gina (1984), 'Woman Writer, Woman Reader, Male Institution: The Experience of a Contemporary Women's Writing Seminar', *Literature Teaching Politics*, 3, 18–31.

—— (1997), 'The Revenge of the Living Doll: Angela Carter's Horror Writing', in Bristow and Broughton (eds), 116–31.

Wollen, Peter (1982), *Readings and Writings*, London: Verso.

Wood, Michael (1982), 'A Libertarian', *New Society*, 11 November, 267.

Woolf, Virginia [1928] (1993), *Orlando*, Harmondsworth: Penguin.

—— (1994), *Virginia Woolf: Collected Essays, Volume 4: 1925–1928*, Andrew McNeillie (ed.), London: Hogarth Press.

Zipes, Jack (1983), *The Trials and Tribulations of Little Red Riding Hood: Versions of the Tale in Sociocultural Context*, London: Heinemann.

—— (ed.) (1986), *Don't Bet On the Prince: Contemporary Feminist Fairy Tales in North America and England*, Aldershot: Gower.

—— (1995), *Creative Storytelling: Building Community, Changing Lives*, London and New York: Routledge.

## Anonymous newspaper articles, radio programmes and archive material

*City Limits* (1991), Listings, 28 November.

*Daily Mail* (1991), Editorial, 3 December, 23.

*Daily Star* (1988), 'Full Frontal Nude Scene in Front of a Mirror in this "Adult" Fairy Tale', 5 November.

*Daily Telegraph* (1991), 'Snapshots on the Road to Blasphemy', 4 December

*The Economist* (1984), 'Seeing is Believing', 22 September, 100.

*Evening Standard* (1991), 3 December.

Granada Television (1988), Press Release prior to the first television broadcast of *The Magic Toyshop*, 5 November, David Wheatley's archive.

*Guardian* (1991), TV listings, 3 December, 36.

*Marxism Today* (1985), 'The Company of Angela Carter', January, 20–2.

Minneapolis City Council, Government Operations Committee (1998), *Pornography and Sexual Violence: Evidence of the Links*, London: Everywoman.

Radio 4 (1989), *Britannia – The Film 7: Fantasy by Gaslight*, 12 August.

*Sun* (1988), 'Prancing Naked in Front of Mirrors', 9 November.

*The Times* (1991a), 'Liberal Treasons', 3 December, 15.

—— (1991b), TV Listings, 3 December, 19.

*Time Out* (1991), Listings, 27 November–4 December.

# Index